W9-BKW-509

# The Huguenots:
## A
## Biography
## of a Minority

**Paris in 1611**—At this time the city was still walled and moated. In the center of the picture is the Cathedral of Notre Dame. Just beyond it, the open space is the Place de Grève, site of many executions. Across the river on the far right is the fortress of the Bastille. The hill in the upper left (beneath the city's old Roman name, "Lutetia") is the Montmartre.

# The Huguenots:

# A
# Biography
# of a Minority

G. A. Rothrock

**Nelson-Hall** nh **Chicago**

All photos unless otherwise noted are from the Bibliothèque Nationale, Paris.

Library of Congress Cataloging in Publication Data

Rothrock, George A.
    The Huguenots.

    Bibliography: p.
    Includes index.
    1. Huguenots—History. 2. Church and state in France—History. 3. France—History—16th century. 4. France—History—17th century. I. Title.
BX9454.2.R67        272'.4          78-23476
ISBN 0-88229-277-3

Copyright © 1979 by George A. Rothrock

All rights reserved. No part of this book may be reproduced in any form without permission in writing from the publisher, except by a reviewer who wishes to quote brief passages in connection with a review written for broadcast or for inclusion in a magazine or newspaper. For information address Nelson-Hall Inc., Publishers, 111 North Canal Street, Chicago, Illinois 60606.

Manufactured in the United States of America

10    9    8    7    6    5    4    3    2    1

# Contents

# Preface

DEFINITIONS OF HISTORY have ranged all the way from Lord Acton's optimistic assertion that it is the record of the "progress of liberty" to Henry Ford's opinion that "history is bunk." And new works continue to appear in which historians argue vigorously among themselves concerning the nature and meaning of historical study. Clearly history is no dead record, for there is a dynamic element, a continuing transformation of the meaning of events in the past.

As a living tradition, history must be considered a collective memory, offering a sense of continuity to people in any age, and its focus must remain flexible, sensitive to the changing interests of different times. Those who like certainties and seek eternal verities find history an uncomfortable subject, for even its most basic assumptions of cause and effect are frequently unprovable, and its "conclusions" are constantly being challenged. Skeptics sometimes remark that every generation rewrites history, apparently suggesting that because its conclusions cannot be made immutable, it has little validity. But, in fact, the comment elucidates the vitality of historical study and points up its chief claim to validity. Each generation *must* rewrite history because it seeks new perspectives upon its own problems, which differ from those of its predecessors, and therefore it asks different questions about the past.

Few subjects have been more fundamental to the development of modern social patterns and attitudes than religion, and few developments have been interpreted so variously. Accounts range all the way from denunciations of religious dissent as inexcusable heresy to adulation of such dissent as the liberation of the Christian conscience. The Reformation of the sixteenth century can be viewed either as the affirmation of the renaissance spirit in religious affairs—individualism, free inquiry and anti-authoritarianism; or as the Christian, almost medieval, reaction against the humanism and secularism of the renaissance—a repudiation of reason and amelioration in favor of faith and salvation.

Among the many examples of religious enthusiasms that erupted in Europe during the late medieval and early modern periods, the growth of "Reformed" Christianity in sixteenth-century France holds a special attraction. On the one hand, it entailed a fusion of dynamic individuals and a colorful period with deep-seated emotionalism and dedication, capable of producing both heroism and startlingly dispassionate cruelty. On the other, it evoked a depth of commitment that refutes beyond argument both the old Catholic contention that the chief appeal of the new faith was secular advantage and the hallowed Protestant myth that there was some sort of liberal sympathy for dissent and freedom of conscience among sixteenth- and seventeenth-century religious radicals.

In a word, the rise and fall of the *Huguenots*—a French word with both the meaning and the connotations of "the Covenanters"—offers a microcosmic view of the human experience: a mixture of wisdom and folly, of altruism and self-interest. In such a welter of biases and cross-currents, no one can claim a total objectivity, but the following account at least attempts to avoid advocacy of sectarian positions.

Obviously a subject with so many facets has evoked previous studies, and one might ask why yet another. The answer is both simple and complex. Most simply, a generation has passed since anyone has attempted to review and evaluate the Huguenot experience in the English language, and not much less in the French; and some aspects of our heritage are of sufficient importance to merit review from time to time. While studies of various aspects of Huguenot history abound, and short treatments as part of general histories of the Reformation are relatively plentiful, there have been few efforts to consider the Huguenots broadly, as a social and political phenomenon of early modern France. Finally, modern scholarship has so greatly revised our views of renaissance monarchies and so thoroughly challenged our understandings of early absolutism, nascent nationalism, and the development of the governmental apparatus of the modern state that any group or institution caught up in the web of evolving royal authority has to be reappraised.

A book such as this necessarily involves a number of decisions regarding forms and usages. Titles of French figures have been rendered as they were used by their possessors, duc de Mayenne, not Duke of Mayenne, for instance. This usage has long been common in professional journals and monographs, since English forms are not always the exact equivalents, and there seemed no compelling reason not to extend the practice to this more general work. Throughout the book, regnal dates are given for popes and French kings. Dates for other persons of significance indicate birth and death.

Names of people and places always pose problems—especially for the period under consideration, when language was still very much in flux. In the case of famous people, whose names are well established in the English language (often in adaptations from the Latin forms that they signed themselves), I have followed accepted usage—writing John Calvin, not Jean Cauvin, and Theodore de Beza, not Théodore de Bèze. On the other hand, I have left the names of less established figures as they signed them. Inevitably this produces some inconsistencies: William Farel but Guillaume Budé, King Francis I but François de Guise. Where there are variants, often the result of foreign origins, I have followed the form the person used in France: thus Marie, not Maria, and Médicis, not Medici. When in doubt, I have generally followed the usages of *Encyclopaedia Britannica*.

A work of synthesis necessarily is indebted to the patient researches of literally dozens of scholars, and beyond listing their many studies in the bibliography, it is impossible to pay tribute to them all. Comparably, no historian could hope to complete a work of this scope without the assistance of innumerable librarians and institutions. A full list is impossible, but my special appreciation is due to the Bibliothèque Nationale, the Société de l'Histoire du Protestantisme Français, the Newberry Library, and most of all my home institution, the University of Alberta. Special thanks are due to *History Today* for allowing the reprinting of substantial sections of the author's article "The Siege of La Rochelle," which appeared in the November and December 1969 issues of the magazine.

It is customary at this point to thank one's wife for her tolerance and loving patience. In this case such an observation would be a grossly inadequate recognition of endless hours of serving as sounding board for ideas, days of critical reading and weeks of final typing. I should also like to thank my good friend and colleague, Professor C. S. Mackinnon, who suffered through the entire labor, read the whole work and offered invaluable criticism. My thanks go also to Mr. R. S. Love for his assistance in the preparation of the map. Needless to say, surviving mistakes are entirely my own responsibility. *Errare humanum est.*

# Introduction:
# Church and State
# in Medieval France

PEOPLE IN THE English-speaking world often seem to find the French rather contradictory and more than a little confusing. Nowhere is this more true than in the role of religion in French life. Catholic but anticlerical, Roman but fervently nationalist, the French seem to embrace mutual incompatibles quite happily. They can claim the first European king to accept Catholicism; another king who gave refuge to a fleeing pope, half-blinded and in fear for his life; and another who was canonized for his piety. But another French king sent a gang of toughs to Rome to resolve a quarrel by brutally kidnapping a pope; a French republican government made mockery of the mass by setting up altars to the goddess Reason, served by actresses; and a French emperor summoned a pope like a lackey to watch him crown himself.

Often it is pointed out that though eighty per cent of Frenchmen designate themselves Catholic, this only means that they are baptized into and buried out of the Church and that many rarely see the inside of one otherwise. Certainly France, though a Catholic nation, has produced her share of dissenters—Protestants, deists, atheists—in various gradations of piety, irreligiosity and anti-religiosity.

Yet there is a subtle relationship between religion and society in France. Catholicism, and especially the organized Church, has occupied a special position in the life of France's people and the policy of her governments from the earliest days of the nation's existence. It might be embraced or repudiated, supported or opposed; it might be considered a civilizing influence or a repressive force, the cradle of the nation or a divisive issue that set Frenchmen against one another. But it could not be ignored. To understand the innumerable ramifications of religious dissent in early modern France, it is necessary first to consider briefly the birth of the French Church and its place in the development of medieval French society.

FROM THE EARLIEST days of the Frankish monarchy Christianity played an extraordinarily important role. Vigorous Christian communities had grown up in the towns of Gaul under the Roman Empire, especially after the reign of Constantine in the early fourth century, when the government began to encourage them. With the deterioration of Roman authority in the face of Germanic invasions, the Christian Church became even more important. In fact, the growth of a unified and reasonably secure Frankish monarchy was interwoven inextricably with the growth of the French Church.

By the late fifth century Roman authority in Gaul had disappeared, and in its place stood a number of Germanic kingdoms: those of the Ostrogoths and the Visigoths in the south, of the Franks in the north, and of smaller groups—most notably the Burgundians and Alemans—in the east. Most of these Germans were utterly unacceptable to the older Gallo-Roman population on which they had imposed themselves, however, because of a religious issue. In the early fourth century a Greek theologian, Arius, had preached a form of Christianity, to which missionaries of his persuasion had converted many of the Germanic tribes. Subsequently, a council of churchmen had condemned Arius' views as heretical. Their judgment was accepted by the clergy of the Roman Empire. Beyond the borders of the empire, however, the German tribes held to the Arian faith of their original conversion; so when they invaded and settled Roman lands, the religious dissension between them and the local clergy and populace was irresoluble.

The Franks constituted an exception to this general pattern of explosive religious tension. Their homelands lay in the lower reaches of the Rhine Valley, far removed from Roman cultural influences, and most of them had never been converted to any form of Christianity. Consequently, when their raids became migrations and they drifted southward to settle across most of northern Gaul, they arrived as pagans, not heretics. The difference was significant. Whereas a heretic was a foul perverter of religious truth, the pagan was an innocent, a soul ripe for instruction and salvation. Thus, from the outset the Franks tended to get on rather better with their Gallo-Roman subjects than did most of their Germanic neighbors, and the situation improved even further when the Franks accepted Catholic Christianity. This conversion of the Franks was a momentous event with surprisingly direct effects upon the later history of the Huguenots.

At end of the fifth century a capable Frankish king, Clovis (481–511), of a family called the Merovingians, crushed the last Roman military power in northern Gaul and then defeated neighboring Frankish chieftains. Subsequently he overcame both the Burgundian and Visigothic tribal states to the south and southwest, creating an enormous single kingdom. Finally, consolidating his achievements, he had himself and many of his warriors baptized as Catholic Christians in A.D. 496. Records from that period are too scanty to allow any certainty of his motives. He had married a Catholic girl; he knew the power and influence of the Catholic clergy; and he claimed that an appeal to the Christian god had brought him victory in a battle with the Alemans. Whatever his motives, this conversion, which made Clovis' rule acceptable to the older peoples of Gaul, was enormously important. It made Catholic Christianity an element of the foundations of the French monarchy and made the Frankish high king the Sword of God, the defender of orthodoxy against the competing influences of heresy.

These early years of the nascent French monarchy also witnessed the establishment of another tradition that was to have considerable impact upon French history and especially upon the history of the Huguenots, the Salic Law. Germanic law, unlike that of the Romans, was based upon tribal customs and traditions rather than upon statutes and legislation; but the influence of the Romans, whom the Germans greatly admired, caused some of the tribes to have their laws written down in the pattern of the great Roman codifications. Fragments of these compilations have survived. Amongst others, the Frankish customs were recorded, probably between the late fifth and middle sixth centuries, including the inheritance rules of the Salian Franks. Though it may have been mere legend, a legal fiction, later Frenchmen firmly believed that these rules provided that only males could inherit or transmit claims of inheritance. Once hallowed by time, this custom became an integral part of French thought concerning the monarchy. The two principles of Catholicism and inheritance by male blood lines became the twin bases of the French crown, with something of the authority of constitutional limits. A thousand years later the rise of the Huguenots and the accidents of royal lineage brought these two principles into conflict and embittered an already bloody civil war.

In the history of French society after these fifth- and sixth-century beginnings, the Church grew ever wealthier through private and royal endowments of land and treasure. At the same time it became ever more important in French life and ever more closely linked to the monarchy. Though historians still dispute the extent and reasons for the decline of commerce and urban life under the Franks, there is no doubt that they did decline significantly, leaving monasteries and the administrative centers of bishops the most important population concentrations of early medieval France. Consequently, these became the focal points of the libraries and educational efforts through which some cultural activity survived. In the eighth century, though not altogether willingly, the Church provided lands to support a more effective military establishment. This enabled the Franks to defeat the Islamic invasions that threatened France through Spain. And a few years later it endorsed the transfer of the crown from an enfeebled Merovingian line to Pepin the Short, of the aggressive and vigorous Carolingian family, lending its authority and prestige to a governmental revival. The relationship was reciprocal, for Pepin proved to be a concerned and generous patron of the Church. To compensate for the income lost when much land had been transferred to the government's military purposes, Pepin established tithing, allowing the Church to collect a levy upon all produce grown in the kingdom. He also encouraged the spread of monasteries, imposing the highly successful Benedictine Rule upon them as the price of his patronage and endowment. This policy, which seeded the kingdom with communities of devout and hard-working monks, was one of the most important developments of the eighth century, for it was the vehicle which brought Christianity, hitherto confined largely to the towns and the royal courts, into the countryside. And following a policy inaugurated by his father, Pepin also lent enthusiastic support to the missionary efforts of St. Boniface amongst the German peoples beyond his eastern borders, giving Frankish Catholicism a special importance in the long-drawn process of Christianizing Europe. Thus, under the new Frankish ruling house the ties between throne and altar were strengthened.

The new Carolingian monarchy, in the persons of both Pepin and his son Charles—who came to be called "the Great," Charlemagne (768–814)—also developed a close connection with the increasingly important Roman papacy. Despite Scriptual texts advanced by early Roman "popes" (a title rather commonly used by prominent bishops) to support their claim to authority over other prelates, historically the growth of Roman supremacy was a very slow process which suffered many setbacks. It was only in the eighth century, with support from the Carolingians, that the medieval papacy began to take on its characteristic form.

In the ancient world the bishops and the congregations of several important cities had enjoyed special status and prestige, and sometimes they were asked to resolve disputes and to mediate quarrels arising in lesser communities. Naturally, Rome was one of these eminent centers as it was the original imperial capital and, in a more distinctively Christian context, the site of the martyrdom of the Apostles Peter and Paul. In the early Church the Bishop of

Rome, though greatly respected, shared honor with other prelates; however, as their dioceses were far off in the eastern Mediterranean, the western Church commonly looked to Rome for guidance. The explosive Muslim conquests of the seventh century further enhanced the position of the Roman pope as one after another of competing authorities fell before the march of Islam—Alexandria, Damascus, and even Jerusalem—until only Rome and Constantinople remained, a polarity that was to leave a permanent mark upon patterns of Christianity.

But though the Roman papacy had become, by the eighth century, an important institution in western Christendom, it remained far from secure as it was harassed by the Arian Lombards, an invading Germanic people who had occupied most of Italy. Moreover, the city of Rome itself was the scene of tumultuous and often violent political strife, in which the papacy sometimes was the pawn of factions. These circumstances favored the Carolingians, who appear to have grasped the potential advantages of a papal alliance; for though the pope's moral position was strong and growing stronger, his physical position was not. Clearly the pope needed armed help, and as the emperor in far-off Constantinople was unable to provide it, he cultivated eagerly the proximate power of the Franks. Thus, a close working alliance grew out of a community of interests.

Pepin once gave sanctuary to a pope fleeing for his life from the tumult in Rome; both Pepin and Charlemagne sent Frankish armies into Italy to curb and ultimately to crush the Lombards. And Pepin, probably believing that he was confirming an earlier arrangement made by Emperor Constantine, conferred upon the pope governmental authority in central Italy, thus founding the papal states. A side effect of these interventions was an effective end to Arianism. The Burgundians had long since submitted to the Catholicism of the Franks, and the Visigoths in Spain had accepted Catholic orthodoxy shortly before being overrun by the Muslims. With the defeat of the Lombards, Catholicism was everywhere triumphant. In return for these victories, achieved through Frankish arms, the papacy sanctioned Pepin's usurpation of the royal crown of the Merovingians; and in a famous ceremony on Christmas Day of the year 800 a pope set an imperial crown upon Charlemagne's head, reviving the title of emperor in the West.

Thus, for religious sanctions and moral authority the roots of the French monarchy were closely entwined not just with Christianity, nor even with Catholic orthodoxy; the association of throne and altar that developed was an alliance of kings and popes, grounded upon an institutionalized French Roman Catholic Church.

Ultimately many insoluble problems, especially fierce attacks by the Vikings, sapped the power of the Carolingians, and toward the end of the tenth century they gave way to another dynasty called the Capetians; but by then the close association of church and state was an integral part of the French crown. From the tenth through the twelfth centuries it was largely the moral and material support of the Church that enabled the Capetian monarchy to maintain itself against the challenge of great vassals whose resources often exceeded those of the kings. By the late twelfth century the French monarchy was again a power, very different in shape from the state of Pepin or Charlemagne but a force in the twelfth-century world. And the association of throne and altar was still intact.


By THE TWELFTH century the institutions of both state and church had become thoroughly feudalized, creating for most people relatively simple and easily grasped relationships. In the secular world the common man was obligated to his lord, who owed military and governmental service to an overlord, and he to yet a greater man in a vast pyramid, at the apex of which was the king. In matters of religion the layman recognized the authority of his priest, who was commanded by a bishop, who was subordinate to an archbishop, and he to the pope—who was God's lieutenant for the governance of His Church on this earth. These parallel structures of feudal character served admirably the needs of a mainly rural and preliterate subsistence society. They provided some organization and stability in a time when very poor transport and communications were complicated further by raiders and brigands. Thus, simple folk were free to devote themselves to the endless struggle to wrest a living from the land, leaving to one set of specialists the secular responsibilities of military and governmental problems and to another the religious responsibilities of church administration and doctrinal development.

In the late twelfth and thirteenth centuries these neat hierarchical patterns began to break down, chiefly as a consequence of growing social complexity involving a considerable revival of commerce, a consequent regrowth of towns and the rise of the universities. No area of French life was more dramatically affected by the subsequent tensions and dislocations than religion.

Already in the eleventh century a wave of reformist enthusiasm had swept through the Church, especially the monasteries, stimulating greater piety and a more personal religious commitment. In the twelfth century this movement began to spill over into the society at large, creating changed expectations of religious experience and growing criticism of the Church's administrative personnel, who appeared too deeply involved in worldly matters. This new spirit of Christianity is perhaps exemplified best by the emergence of the Gothic style, which swept France in the second half of the twelfth century and then spread over much of the rest of Europe. Though most often contrasted to the earlier romanesque style by its dramatic exaggerations in design, soaring vaults and sometimes florid decoration, more significant is the difference in the sculpted renditions of Christ. On the older Romanesque churches, He appears as an aloof and rather forbiddingly stern figure, a sort of divine emperor; while in Gothic portrayals He is humanized and appears as the compassionate Savior, radiating love and forgiveness. This shift of emphasis in the portrayal of Christ was accompanied by the rise of cults of female saints, especially the Virgin Mary, who previously had received little attention.

These developments reflected the increasing stress upon the humane and merciful rather than the authoritarian aspects of the Church. Such innovations can be taken to characterize a far-reaching reorientation of Latin Christianity: the conservative order-power relationships of a rigidly hierarchical society were being transformed into the love-experience relationships that could constitute the faith of humble people in a society where old patterns were blurring. This spiritual growth was intensified by urban expansion, for in burgeoning towns evangelical preachers could find the large audiences unavailable in rural districts, and they appeared in ever increasing numbers—often monks who emerged from their monasteries with a pious desire to exhort the faithful and ended as ranting fanatics damning the worldliness of bishops.

These conflicting views and goals concerning the role of religion in daily life were paralleled by an increasingly severe mood of confrontation on questions of doctrine. Through the seven hundred years from the early sixth to the late twelfth century the doctrinal development of the western Church had proceeded steadily and rather calmly. There had been some disagreements among rival theologians, of course, and popes or councils had declared some positions heretical; but no widely supported doctrinal quarrels affecting the masses of the people had arisen in western Christendom since the Arian issue had been laid to rest in the eighth century. Rather, Christian intellectuals, mostly monastic scholars, had fought their battles of interpretation in the rarefied atmosphere of letters to one another and marginal glosses upon old texts—all in Latin, naturally, and well removed from the experience of the common people. In the thirteenth century, however, such quarrels became not only more numerous and more intense, but also they began to involve more people. University theologians, who were beginning to experiment with Aristotelian logic, debated with one another before their students as well as colleagues. Both faculty and students moved from one university to another rather freely, and ever larger circles of people became involved.

The late twelfth- and early thirteenth-century Church also witnessed a third important development, a considerable increase in papal authority and the efficiency of papal administration. The foremost figure in this growth of the papacy was Innocent III (1198–1216), who held a clearly monarchical view of the pope's role in the Church and had far-reaching ambitions for the establishment of at least moral authority of popes over kings. Obviously these were highly political questions, which involved ranking churchmen in very serious quarrels with each other and with secular authorities.

THE ESOTERIC DISPUTES of university theologians, which often resulted in more legalistic definitions of the faith; the worldly involvement of bishops, an almost inevitable consequence of the growing complexity of re-urbanizing society; and the conflicts turning around an increasingly monarchical and authoritative papacy, as exemplified by Innocent III, ran counter to the populist spirit of thirteenth-century Christianity. These developments formed an explosive combination in which popular piety and doctrinal dissension began to interact. The result was that in the late twelfth and early thirteenth centuries popular heresy again became a serious problem.

It was in the south of France that the issue first grew to critical proportions. An early group, the Waldensians (who took their name from their founder, Valdes or Waldo, sometimes called Peter Waldo), enunciated many of the criticisms that were to be hurled at the Church for the next three centuries. They wanted frequent preaching, a return of churchmen to Apostolic poverty, Scriptures in the vernacular so that laymen could read them, greater attention to pastoral responsibilities and other similar populist reforms. When they insisted on preaching without the requisite episcopal licenses and even undertook unauthorized translations of parts of the Bible, they were condemned by the pope; but before any very effective action against them could be undertaken, all but a few in the wild hills of Provence were swallowed up by a far larger movement, the Albigensian heresy.

The *Cathari,* popularly called Albigensians because the town of Albi was their most important center, preached a faith that seems to have come to France through the Balkans. There are some grounds to believe that this faith was as old as Christianity, having constituted in the ancient world an alternative to it. So technically it may in fact have been a competing pagan religion rather than a Christian heresy, but after years of fertilization by Christian ideas the similarities were sufficient for thirteenth-century people to consider it a heresy.

To the criticisms of the Waldensians the Albigensians added a doctrinal challenge, arguing that Christianity as interpreted by the Church was altogether in error. They maintained that there was a dualism in the world between good and evil, that the crucifixion of

Jesus—who represented the force of goodness—had been a triumph for the forces of evil, that man was utterly corrupt and a pawn of evil, and that there could be no victory for goodness on this earth until the human race had perished.

Much remains unknown about the Albigensians. When the movement was crushed the victorious Christians deliberately undertook to wipe out all trace of it, and only very limited documentation has survived. However, it appears to have been more a community of religious practice than an organized church. Little was asked of simple believers, but the leaders of the movement—called the "perfect ones"—maintained an exemplary life of simplicity, frugality, chastity, and charity, almost a monastic discipline in the real world, preaching and counselling their followers. Comparably, the practice of the faith seems to have been very simple, including only a single sacrament, a sort of absolution normally taken only once, in anticipation of death. The piety and simplicity of the Albigensians stood in marked contrast to the worldliness and elaboration of the Roman Catholic Church of the thirteenth century, and they attracted a wide following among all classes.

Ultimately these heretical movements, which swept the south of France, succumbed to the alliance of the papacy and the monarchy and contributed to the strengthening of that alliance. The pope proclaimed a crusade against the heretics; the king granted his northern knights permission to participate in it; and soon a northern army launched a bloody campaign in the name of the pure faith. The heresy was crushed, and much of the local aristocracy died with it under the swords of the crusaders, to be replaced by new fiefholders more loyal to the king. Thus, Catholicism and the authority of the Church were restored. Likewise the governing authority of the king, which never had been very effective in the south, was strengthened considerably.

Once again the cooperation of king and pope had proved mutually advantageous. And as though to underscore the point, outside of France—where such collaboration was less common—the surge of popular piety continued. Sometimes this movement produced more heresies: the thirteenth through fifteenth centuries saw the Spiritual Franciscans in Italy, the Wycliffe Lollards in

England and the Hussites in Bohemia. But there also were many devout groups of enthusiasts who managed to maintain their orthodoxy, such as the bulk of the Franciscan Order, the Dominicans, the Rhineland-based "Friends of God" and the "Brothers of the Common Life". Thus, when cries for reform and personalization of the faith were enunciated explosively in the sixteenth century by Luther, Zwingli, Calvin, and others, they stood at the end of a long tradition.

THE RELATIONSHIPS CONNECTING the French Crown, the French Church, and the papacy underwent some radical changes between the early fourteenth and the early sixteenth centuries. This transformation was not unique to France but was, rather, part of a Europe-wide clash between papal and monarchical power. Though triggered by the aspirations of some very able and very ambitious popes, the conflicts might be viewed in a broader perspective as being the almost inevitable confrontation between the international or supranational interests of the papacy and the national interests of the ever stronger and ever more self-conscious monarchies.

Such clashes had not been unknown earlier, of course. In the late eleventh century the first major struggle had been launched by Pope Gregory VII, a quarrel with the Holy Roman Emperor concerning rights of appointment to overlapping clerical and secular offices in Germany and north Italy. Carried on by their successors for nearly half a century, this fight was a major factor in the failure of the emperors to be able to consolidate a strong monarchical authority in central Europe. Thus emboldened, papal ambitions grew, and as already noted, at the end of the twelfth and beginning of the thirteenth centuries Pope Innocent III asserted extensive claims to moral judgment of kings. In quarrels with the monarchs of both France and England, his will prevailed. It should be noted, however, that Innocent III had great political perspicacity, and he effectively exploited common interests with some rulers while undermining the positions of others.

The last of the great papal controversialists, and indeed a figure often considered the last of the medieval popes, was Boniface VIII

(1294–1303). A brilliant lawyer and diplomat before he was pope, he was ambitious, arrogant, and unshakably convinced of the justice of his cause. In the tradition of Gregory VII and Innocent III, he determined to uphold the superiority of papal authority, this time not only in questions of church appointments or moral issues but also in the politically sensitive area of taxation of the Church's property and personnel. There were vigorous responses from the kings of both England and France, and both monarchs found strong backing amongst their subjects. Clearly Boniface VIII had underestimated the strength of rising national consciousness. As the quarrel escalated, he soon paid a tragic price for his miscalculation.

The King of England contented himself with legal maneuvers that kept his clergy in check and effectively established a Church subject to the king's will in non-doctrinal matters. However, the King of France responded more forcefully to what he believed were exaggerated papal pretensions, dangerous to his authority: first he banned the export of precious metals from his kingdom, seriously crippling papal revenues; and then he sent a gang of strongmen to kidnap the pope and bring him onto French territory to be tried on various charges of malfeasance. Though the kidnapping attempt ultimately failed, the shock of it was too much for Boniface. He died a few days later, effectively ending the medieval papacy. Subsequently, the anarchy prevailing in Rome and the pressure of French influence effected the transfer of papal government to Avignon, a papal territory on the Rhône River in southern France. There it remained through seven pontificates, three quarters of a century, with popes regarded by most Europeans as prisoners or puppets of the French kings.

This waning of papal influence after Boniface VIII had widespread results, including a strong movement within the Church to establish the superiority of councils of bishops over popes, most strongly voiced in the general council held in Basel during the 1430s and 1440s. When anti-French influence succeeded in moving the papacy back to Rome in the early fifteenth century, the French monarchy began to support this conciliar movement, and in the Pragmatic Sanction of Bourges of 1438 King Charles VII clearly endorsed it. This Pragmatic Sanction also provided for French prelates to be elected by their clergy, which in practice usually meant election of the king's nominee, and denied any effective papal administrative power over French clerics.

Thus emerged what generally is called the Gallican Church—an institution run by its bishops under the king's authority, and free from any meaningful papal control over matters of taxation and discipline. In fact, this was part of a broader papal retreat paralleled in Germany and to a lesser extent in England. The old medieval collaboration of popes and kings had been eroded badly by the growing strength of national monarchy. Significantly, in France, and only in France, the collaboration was re-established by a compromise achieved early in the sixteenth century, just as Luther was about to unleash another tempest in western Christendom.

This new compact, signed in 1516, was called the Concordat of Bologna. In effect, the French king agreed to restore much of the pope's taxing power over the French clergy, especially the annates—the first year's revenues of new ecclesiastical appointees, in return for the pope's promise to accept the king's nominations for most high clerical positions in France. French churchmen protested vigorously that the Crown and the papacy had "divided between them the liberties of the Gallican Church," but both king and pope had cause to be well satisfied. The monarch's power of patronage was guaranteed and supported by the highest ecclesiastical authority, while papal finances were strengthened enormously by access to the monies of one of the wealthiest national churches in Europe. In addition, a dangerous friction had been resolved before it could escalate again.

In France, then, by the sixteenth century the social and political implications of religious dissent were enormous. Within the general pattern of Roman Catholic Christianity a Gallican Church had developed that was both self-conscious and aggressive. And not only was it a channel of cultural transmission from one generation to another, giving orientation and continuity to the French people; it also was a foundation and inspiration for French political life. The close alliance of church and state in France had not precluded some bitter church-state quarrels; but despite this the alliance of the French Crown and the Roman Catholic Church was one of the wellsprings of the national identity.

Such was the "establishment" that would-be religious reformers confronted in early modern France. From the fifth century to the sixteenth, with only occasional exceptions, the alliance of throne and altar had been very close. At their coronations French kings were blessed and annointed by the Church; throughout their reigns they drew both revenue and personnel into their service from the Church; generally their enemies were damned by churchmen, who threatened hell's fire for those who would harm a king or resist his legitimate authority; and the continuance of their lineage was guaranteed by the Church, which blessed their marriages and endorsed the legitimacy of their children. Nowhere in Europe had the highest civil authority greater cause to be well pleased with the existing religious settlement, or greater reason to be willing to defend it with all the awesome power of the state.

# Part One

## The Birth of the
## French Reformed
## Church

# Chapter One

# Humanists and Early Reformers in France

POPULAR CONCEPTIONS OF the Reformation of the sixteenth century often seem to envisage a separatist dissenting movement launched in Germany by Martin Luther which then spread to many parts of Europe and in the second generation developed several variants. In fact, the process was rather more complex than that. As already noted, ever since the thirteenth century Europe had been experiencing wave after wave of religious enthusiasm; and in the early sixteenth century, the concerns that Luther expressed in north Germany were strongly paralleled elsewhere. All over Europe it was widely recognized that the Church had suffered decay, and many laymen and churchmen alike called for reform.

In the late fifteenth and sixteenth centuries this spiritual restiveness was reinforced by the results of a new scholarship called humanism, linguistic and literary endeavors which had originated as an important aspect of the Italian Renaissance. In contrast to their medieval predecessors, who considered the natural world merely a "vale of tears" where the soul was tested and prepared for judgment, and who thought salvation the only proper goal of study, Renaissance humanists asserted the intrinsic value of human experience. In this they were influenced massively by the views of ancient writers, to read whose works they undertook serious study of ancient languages. At first, such study meant classical Latin and

Greek; then, as the ancient world became ever more fascinating for its own sake, Hebrew came to be included.

Moreover, the Christian enthusiasm of the late fifteenth and early sixteenth centuries quickly led to the use of the recently invented printing press to publish dozens and even hundreds of editions of the Bible, in whole or in part. These were in Latin, of course; but Latin was accessible to an ever-growing body of cultivated men, and the impact of this dissemination of the Scriptures is immeasurable. Christians were accustomed to a religion bound up in rituals, practices and formal observances; to a Church hierarchically organized around clergy, saints and the Virgin; and to a body of Holy Writ almost exclusively the possession of churchmen, who interpreted it to the laity. Then, literate Christians suddenly found in the *New Testament* a relatively simple, Christ-centered faith.

Obviously such developments had deep implications for religious studies—from fuller understanding of the ancient society in which Christianity had been born to critical appraisal of the often recopied, condensed, and sometimes distorted Scriptures on which understanding of early Christianity depended. Disconcertingly, the protagonists of the new scholarship were discovering everweightier evidence that the Church of their times bore little resemblance to the primitive Christianity of the Scriptures and that complex rites bore little relationship to Christ's message of love, faith, and salvation. In the consequent tide of criticism and challenge, Luther was simply one of the more dramatic and more persuasive voices.

By THE LATE fifteenth and early sixteenth centuries, the influence of the Italian Renaissance was being felt throughout Europe. Sometimes this was the result of traveling Italian scholars and artists, sometimes of foreigners who had gone to study with famous Italian masters and then had returned home. In France such influences were reinforced and greatly multiplied by a particular experience, a series of French invasions of Italy which began at the end of the fifteenth century.

In 1494 King Charles VIII (1483–1498), asserting claims to some Italian lands, led an army over the Alps, inaugurating a

half-century of French attempts to win domination of the penin-
sula. These efforts eventually proved politically unproductive, as
successive expeditions failed either to extend France's borders or to
win her a permanent bastion in Italy. Nationalist historians often
have regarded them as a profitless wastage of French resources.
However, these military efforts opened channels for a vast flow of
Renaissance influence into France.

Before the sparkling culture and glittering luxuries of the
Italians, the invading Frenchmen—from minor nobles to kings—
stood awed. And when they returned home, they carried away
masses of it: paintings and improved table manners, rich hangings
and new social graces, parade armor and books. Ultimately they
even lured producers of some of these wonders to France, a movement that reached its apex under Francis I (1515–1547), who
enticed both Leonardo da Vinci and Benvenuto Cellini to his
Court. Under the impact of so many and such varied Renaissance
influences, it is not surprising that humanist studies took root in
France.

Probably the greatest of the French humanists of this period
was Jacques Lefèvre d'Etaples (mid-1450s–1536). He visited Italy
twice at the end of the fifteenth century, immersed himself in
Greek studies, and emerged a classical and Biblical scholar strongly
influenced by neo-Platonic mysticism. He demonstrated an impressive scope of interest, writing student texts in the sciences and
translations of and commentaries upon Aristotle. His most important and influential work, believed to have had some impact upon
the development of Luther's thought, was in Biblical studies based
upon Hebrew and Greek originals. These latter included commentaries upon St. Paul's letters in 1512—already hinting at the concept of justification by faith alone, which Luther was to make
explicit five years later—a commentary upon the Gospels in 1522;
and translations into French of the New Testament in 1523, of the
Psalms in 1524 and of the Old Testament in 1528.

Lefèvre d'Etaples was more than a narrow scholar, however. In
the preface of his commentary on the Gospels he summoned all
Christians to restore the purity of the faith and to cling only to the
Word of God, observing that to know nothing but the Gospels was
to know everything. He added that the primitive Church had no

rule but the Gospels, knew no cult but that of Christ. No one has ever stated the basic tenets of Evangelical Christianity more succinctly. As a teacher and scholar in Paris in the first quarter of the sixteenth century, Lefèvre d'Etaples exercised a strong influence upon the humanist studies of younger men and upon the growing movement for reform of the Church.

A near contemporary of Lefèvre D'Etaples was Guillaume Budé (1467–1540). After a rather desultory youth, the middle-aged Budé became an enthusiastic scholar and acquired both an impressive erudition and connections at Court, where he became a royal secretary under Louis XII (1498–1515) and then under his successor Francis I. Guillaume Budé was an important figure in the development of the royal library and probably was the primary influence in Francis I's decision to found the *Collegium Trilinguae,* later renamed the *Collège de France,* a center of humanist studies free from the control of the very conservative University of Paris. He defended religious toleration; and his refusal of Catholic rites when he was dying suggests that he had privately broken faith with the established Church, though he never identified himself openly with any reform sect.

Considerably younger than these two was William Farel (1489–1565), a student of Lefèvre d'Etaples, who became first a professor and then Regent of the *Collège Cardinal LeMoine* in Paris. More an activist than a scholar, about 1520 he became a fervent advocate of the need for reformation of the Church. For the next decade and a half he was a chief figure in the growing movement of French reformed groups. He left his college to join a congregation at Meaux, a reform center just northeast of Paris. Then he traveled in the French provinces, where he developed contacts with remnants of the old Waldensian movement. Finally he went to Switzerland, where he settled in Geneva, just across the border from the province of his birth, the Dauphiné. In 1536 he managed to persuade John Calvin to join him in his religious work in Geneva. The remainder of Farel's life is rather overshadowed by the towering figure of his younger colleague. Farel exemplifies well the intellectual generation between Lefèvre d'Etaples and Calvin. Like his near-contemporary, Luther, who was just six years older, Farel was not a humanist himself; but humanist scholarship had combined with spiritual concerns to alienate him from the old Church, and he found refuge in a new Evangelical theology.

In fact, the religious life of France in the teens and twenties of the sixteenth century, when Luther's storm was just breaking over north Germany, showed considerable intellectual vigor. And, of course, French thought had not grown up in isolation. In addition to the humanists, other schools of thought with foreign roots influenced French religious development. A prominent figure in Paris at the end of the fifteenth century was the Netherlander Jean (or Jan) Standonck, Rector of the *Collège de Montaigu*. Educated by the Brothers of the Common Life, a Netherlandish and northwest German reformist movement of fourteenth century origins, Standonck was a fervent advocate of the Brothers' "modern devotion." This was a bit of a misnomer by Standonck's time, as it comprised a pious commitment to a Christ-centered and Paulist Christianity with frequent religious exercises, akin to the thirteenth-century pietist movements. Standonck is perhaps best remembered as one of the teachers of the great humanist and Church critic, Erasmus of Rotterdam, during the latter's period of study in Paris. He was a formidable figure, who, in contrast to the humanists, infused into French religious thought a strong element of the popular pietism of medieval protest.

In addition, Luther's views were known in Paris already in 1520, very shortly after their publication. In 1521 the Faculty of Theology of the University of Paris condemned them. Only a little later, in 1523, a would-be reformer named Jean Vallière was burned as a Lutheran heretic, shortly to be followed by others. Moreover, Guillaume Budé corresponded with two of the greatest humanist scholars of the day, Sir Thomas More and Erasmus. Temporary flights to the Imperial free city of Strasbourg, when Catholic reaction made Paris dangerous for critics, brought other French reformers, such as Farel, into contact with Martin Bucer, the chief spokesman of Swiss-Rhenish Evangelical thought.

Martin Bucer (1491–1551), an Alsatian by birth, had enormous though often indefinable influence on the growth of Evangelical Christianity. After some years in the Dominican Order, in the early 1520s he renounced Catholicism, married, and—under the influence of works of Erasmus and Luther—dedicated himself to

Christian reform. Strasbourg, where he settled, lay between two major reform movements: in the north German area reformist thought consisted chiefly of Luther's ideas, which were quickly becoming institutionalized. By contrast, the south German and Swiss areas were dominated by scholarly humanist influences mingled with the Evangelical teachings of Huldreich (or Ulrich) Zwingli of Zurich. From the mid-1520s to the mid-1540s Bucer was a primary figure in the efforts to work out compromises between the two groups of reformers. When his pragmatism finally destroyed his credibility with both sides, he accepted the invitation of Archbishop Cranmer to move to England, where he had significant influence upon the early course of the English Reformation during the last years of his life. Accepting the ideals of Christian humanism, Bucer sought a moral reformation of society and of all its institutions through dedication to the true Gospel, and he regarded any improvement as a step in the right direction. Hence, his was a rather tolerant and ameliorative voice in the extremist clamor of the Reformation debate.

Thus, though official condemnations tended to designate all dissenters as "Lutherans" in the 1520s, there actually was much more scope and variety to the reform movement in France than such terminology suggests. Not only were French critics no slavish followers of Luther, they were well acquainted with the theological disputes over the sacraments, and especially the Eucharist, which more and more came to divide Luther's followers from those called "Evangelical" or simply "Reformed."

In fact, the growing differences between the two groups of reformers were profound. Luther was a very conservative revolutionary, almost medieval in his mentality and in his opposition to the secularism of the Renaissance. He had been moved to an overt clash with the established Church primarily by his agony over the problem of salvation; and while his theology was Scripturally based, it seems to have derived its vigor from an almost mystical dedication of himself in personal faith. By contrast, the theological basis of the Swiss and Rhenish reformers was much more "modern," much more academic and rational, in the spirit of the new scholarship. Closer to Italian influences, and perhaps feeling the impact of urban growth and the ever-increasing movement of people and ideas, they reacted more strongly to the Italian urge to study sources—emphasizing the Scriptures, the Church Fathers and the primitive Church as models. All of these currents flowed through French intellectual circles in the 1520s. Given the strength of classicism in France, through the close French scholarly connection with Italy, the ideas of the Evangelicals seem to have met a particularly warm reception.

Naturally, the impact of these new ideas reached beyond narrow intellectual circles, for this was an era when thinkers and scholars, in fact almost all cultural producers, depended heavily upon patronage and protection. Thus, there were many people who, without being themselves religious reformers—at least not to the point of countenancing heresy—played an important role in the development of the reform movement. One must guard against the temptation to consider the religious situation of the early sixteenth century in the model of the late sixteenth and seventeenth centuries—when positions had clarified, divisions had widened and bitter fighting had hardened differences. In fact, "reform" in the early sixteenth century was not a concept that evoked visions of parties and of factional warfare. A great many Christians recognized that the Church had deep and serious problems and hoped for reform of some sort. Reform could be very controversial in that some varieties of it threatened discipline or challenged vested interests, but in principle it was widely desired. Hence, a great many people in both Church and state lent their support.

One of the most prominent figures of this sort in the early French reform movement was Guillaume Briçonnet (c. 1472–1534), Bishop of Meaux. His father, a counsellor of Charles VIII, had joined the clergy after his wife's death and eventually had become a cardinal. Young Briçonnet also became a cleric, and with such connections in both the Church and the Court he rose rapidly. King Francis I used him as a negotiator in matters concerning the Church, most notably as his representative in Rome in 1516 discussing details of the application of the Concordat of Bologna; and in that same year he was rewarded with the Bishopric of Meaux. Despite Briçonnet's governmental service and his advancement through royal patronage, he was a devout Christian and a dedicated bishop. He wrote and distributed many devotional tracts, and his

simple but moving sermons and his frequent visitations of his
congregations showed him to be a churchman who took his pastoral
duties seriously.

Briçonnet's reputation soon attracted many devout and re-
forming Christians to his diocese, where they formed a group called
"the Evangelicals of Meaux," a circle which at one time or another
included Lefèvre d'Etaples, Farel and many others whom growing
opposition forced to leave Paris. At Meaux Briçonnet protected
them, thus drawing suspicion upon himself. Though in 1523 he
formally condemned Lutheranism, and in fact was still a Catholic
when he died a decade later, he was twice summoned before the
Parlement of Paris, the kingdom's highest court, to defend himself
against accusations of heresy. Faced with this mounting pressure,
the group of Evangelicals broke up in the mid-1520s, but it had
served as an important incubator for the French reform, providing
for the cross-fertilization of ideas among many of the movement's
chief figures.

Another important patron and protector of the early
humanists was the sister of King Francis I. Marguerite of Angoulême, Queen of Navarre (1492–1549), was a person of some
literary importance herself for her poetry, letters, and a sort of
early novel. As a young woman she had been put under the spiritual
tutelage of Briçonnet, who was then at the height of his reputation
and enjoyed the king's favor. He inspired or awakened in her a
deep piety, which she maintained until her death. When a childless
first marriage ended in widowhood in the mid-1520s, she was
married again, this time to the King of Navarre, a tiny principality
in the Pyrenees. With money provided largely by her royal brother
of France, she undertook extensive patronage of scholars and
writers.

Not all of the recipients of Queen Marguerite's generosity
were religious enthusiasts (she also patronized François Rabelais),
but they included some of the most prominent—most notably
Lefèvre d'Etaples himself, who spent his last years under her protection. Despite this, and although her letters to her former men-
tor, Briçonnet, reveal pious commitment to a strongly Paulist faith,
like him she never left Catholicism. (Eventually this steadfast tra-
ditionalism was a cause of some estrangement from her daughter

and successor on the throne of Navarre, Jeanne d'Albret—herself a figure of considerable importance to the French reform movement.) Rather, Queen Marguerite remained a Catholic though a friend of the Evangelical critics. Abhorring the narrow pedantry of the university theologians and the mindless fanaticism of some anti-reform preachers, she attributed her tolerance to "compassion." Whatever her motives, she influenced Francis I to permit moderate criticism of the established Church. Her Courts at Nérac and Pau were important refuges for humanists and reformers, especially after the break-up of Briçonnet's group at Meaux.

Despite the recruitment of dedicated and energetic advocates and the attraction of highly placed patrons, however, the reform movement in Paris soon evoked powerful opposition. The twin pivots of this conservative resistance to religious innovation were the Sorbonne and the Parlement of Paris.

Originally an endowed residential college of the University of Paris, for impoverished scholars who wished to study theology, "the Sorbonne" more and more became coterminous with the Faculty of Theology. (This development was completed in the mid-sixteenth century when it was resolved that all general meetings of the theological faculty would be held there.) Long an important and recognized center of Catholic thought, the Sorbonne had grown in stature and importance with the emergence of the largely autonomous Gallican Church of the fifteenth century. Its professors had become accustomed to the role of arbitrators of the orthodoxy and propriety of religious opinions. Respectful of tradition, thoroughly Gallican, and cognizant of the storm that Luther had let loose in north Germany, the Sorbonne viewed with deep suspicion the Evangelical zeal of the early sixteenth century French reformers.

The Parlement of Paris was the most important organ of the king's several judicial roles. A complex institution whose various branches exercised many different jurisdictions—both original and appellate—it was, among other things, the highest court in the kingdom, and its judges were notably conservative. One of its many roles was the defense of religion and public morals, including censorship of books. Both on its own initiative and on application by the Sorbonne, it often enjoined publication of controversial works; and sometimes it banned the sale of those already published or even ordered them seized and burned.

In the early 1520s both of these institutions began to mount an attack upon the French reformers. Having already, in 1521, condemned the early writings of Luther, whose thought closely paralleled that of Lefèvre d'Etaples, in the summer of 1523 the Sorbonne obtained from the Parlement an order for the seizure of the latter's *Commentaries on the Gospels;* and it also summoned him to appear to defend certain of his propositions against charges of heresy. However, King Francis I intervened to suppress the proceedings and likewise forbade the seizure of the book. The Sorbonne complained bitterly about the king's interference, but with the foremost of the reformers clearly under royal protection, the theologians had to content themselves with harassing the lesser figures of the group at Meaux—some of whom had criticized popular belief in images and in the efficacy of prayers to special saints for medical cures.

At this point events quite unrelated to the religious quarrels intervened, to the disadvantage of the reformers. A deterioration of the French position in Italy, complicated by the treason of France's ranking military commander—the Constable de Bourbon (who went over to the Holy Roman Emperor), persuaded King Francis that he had to return to the wars. As was his habit on such occasions, he left his government largely in the hands of his middle-aged mother, Louise of Savoy, a very able woman but a cautious traditionalist in matters of religion. Desirous of the support of the Church, she gave the Sorbonne a sympathetic hearing of its complaints, and she supported a mission to combat "the Lutheran heresy," thus encouraging the opposition to the reformers. At the same time, fuel was added to the fires of controversy by the appearance late in 1523 of Lefèvre d'Etaples' French edition of the New Testament—provocative in itself by putting Scripture into the vernacular, and furnished with a fervently Evangelical preface. Thinking itself freer to act than before, the Parlement renewed its offensive and undertook preliminary moves toward condemning the new work. But the reaction was premature. King Francis was still only a few days from Paris, and once more he intervened, writing in the spring of 1524 to forbid further proceedings and to repeat that he esteemed Lefèvre d'Etaples highly. By this time it should have been obvious, however, that the reformers' position was extremely precarious. Having evoked the bitter enmity of the highest theological and judicial authorities, only the king's personal protection shielded them from vigorous persecution. And in 1525 that shield was to be lost.

Late in February 1525 the Italian wars reached one of their periodic crescendos. After a largely successful campaign in north Italy, Francis I faced an army of Emperor Charles V outside the city of Pavia, and a battle ensued. After promising preliminaries, through a combination of his own impulsiveness and the ineptitude of some of his younger commanders King Francis not only managed to lose the battle but finally found himself a captive. In the aftermath, the Emperor (who was also King of Spain) had Francis carried off to Madrid, where he remained a prisoner until March 1526, ultimately obtaining his release only by signing a humiliating treaty. During his captivity he declared his mother Regent of France, and thus all things—including the fortunes of the religious reformers—came to depend more heavily upon her.

The support that Louise of Savoy had found desirable during her son's absence on campaign became a necessity when the whole burden of government fell upon her for however long his captivity might last. Hence, the queen mother chose to remain aloof while the opponents of the reformers mounted an ever more intense campaign against the Meaux group, Lefèvre d'Etaples and others. She even obtained for the Parlement a papal brief delegating the judgment of heresy to two of its judges, thus avoiding any possibility of conflict of jurisdiction between secular and ecclesiastical courts.

Encouraged by these signs of governmental sympathy, an eager champion of conservative orthodoxy soon emerged, Noël Béda (or Beyde, or Bédier). Principal of the old *Collège de Montaigu* since 1502, he became Syndic of the university's Faculty of Theology in 1520, a post he held until 1533. A theological reactionary and an enthusiastic persecutor, he led the fight against the reformers in the 1520s, persuading the faculty to condemn many books and authors, including Erasmus. As clashes multiplied with the passing years, however, Béda became more and more intemperate.

He attempted to censure a book by the king's sister, Marguerite; launched a series of attacks upon the king's favored educational institute, the *Collège de France*; and finally, criticized the king himself for excessive tolerance of heresy.

By 1533 Béda had exhausted his credit, and the royal government ordered him dismissed from his posts and exiled him from Paris. After a few months the king relented, and he was permitted to return to the capital, without office; but again he proved to be an uncontrollable trouble-maker, and he was sent to prison, where he died in 1536. Despite ultimate personal disgrace, however, Béda directed a decade of far-reaching reaction.

The first victims of the new persecution were minor figures. In the spring of 1522 a frightened Briçonnet excommunicated those who had defaced some papal announcements at Meaux; and one of them, apprehended by agents of the Parlement, was branded and exiled. About the same time two men were publicly tortured and executed (one in January and one in July) at Metz for impiety. Late in August the Parlement, with the counsel of the Sorbonne, ordered the suppression of all French translations of both the Old and New Testaments, a sweeping condemnation of Lefèvre d'Etaples' work. And then, early in October, several members of the Meaux group were arrested, and prominent figures—including Lefèvre d'Etaples and Briçonnet—were ordered to appear to defend themselves before the Parlement's special commission on religion. At this point, judging discretion the better part of valor, Lefèvre d'Etaples fled to Strasbourg, where he could continue his work. However, Briçonnet crumbled, issuing public statements condemning Luther and affirming the existence of purgatory and the efficacy of the invocation of the Virgin—in a word, submitting totally to the conservative reaction.

One last crumb of royal support was thrown to the reformers. The king's sister, Marguerite, recently widowed, had gone to Madrid to console her captive brother. Largely because of her intercession, Francis I wrote in mid-November to say that he wished no more persecutions and that he particularly forbade harassment of Lefèvre d'Etaples. However, the Parlement, recognizing the impotence of a distant and captive king, simply replied to the Regent that in such matters it could not honestly, and without offense to

God, either change or suspend its activities. So the persecutions continued.

In the king's absence the fury of the reaction mounted. In October 1525 a young man recently returned from Scotland was burned for spreading "Lutheran" errors. In February of 1526 another, convicted of speaking critically of the Virgin and the saints, had his tongue slashed and then was strangled and burned. During these same months several of the simple communicants of Meaux, all of whom were under suspicion, were accused; and some of them were imprisoned. In August 1526 one of them who had made his submission to the Church and subsequently had repented it, reaffirming his Evangelical beliefs, was burned alive. Despite the king's return in the summer of 1526, the persecutions continued to multiply, and four more men were burned as heretics in 1527 and 1528.

As such incidents proliferated, the defenders of orthodoxy began to consolidate their position. In 1528, from February to October, French churchmen assembled for the Council of Sens (though the meetings actually were held in Paris) to consider the state of the Church and its critics. Foreshadowing the all-European Council of Trent a quarter of a century later, they denounced several Lutheran positions as heretical and impious. They affirmed sixteen points of doctrine and practise—including the seven sacraments, the validity of tradition, clerical celibacy, veneration of saints, the use of images, and the efficacy of both faith and works; and they called for some reform of clerical behavior in such matters as residency, preaching and general morals. In sum, they denounced minor human failings amongst the Church's servants but only as an afterthought to a solidly conservative affirmation of traditional Roman Catholic faith.

Only a few months after the closing of the council, in the spring of 1529, the great case of the time—that of Louis de Berquin—reached its climax. After Lefèvre d'Etaples, de Berquin probably was the prime target of Béda and the Sorbonne conservatives. A doctor of theology and a king's counsellor, he was also a correspondent of Erasmus, a translator of some of the German reformers and an author of Evangelically sympathetic works. Already in 1523 the Sorbonne and the Parlement of Paris had tried to move against him, but like Lefèvre d'Etaples he had been saved by royal protection. Once more, in 1526, he had been arrested and held for some months, but the newly returned king had eventually secured his release again.

Then, late in 1528 and early in 1529, amidst rising tensions, de Berquin's defenses of Erasmus made him once more a figure of controversy. He was arrested again, and this time the Parlement moved swiftly. On 16 April 1529 he was condemned to prison. His appeal was heard the next day, and not only was the conviction upheld but his punishment was changed to death. Sentence was pronounced that morning, and at noon he was executed. Francis I and his sister were at Blois, enjoying springtime in the Loire Valley, and de Berquin was dead before they heard of the new charges. The king was greatly angered by the judges' high-handed action, but faced with a *fait accompli* there was little that he could do. Perhaps as a sort of memorial to de Berquin, perhaps as a rebuff and a sort of counterpoise to the reactionaries, and certainly with the encouragement of Budé, in 1530 he founded the group of "royal lecturers" who eventually became the *Collegium Trilinguae* and then the *Collège de France*—to teach, free from the interference of the theological professors, the "heretical and Lutheran" languages of Greek and Hebrew in addition to the traditional Latin.

Thus, the first decade and a half of the French reform movement had witnessed the emergence of some fairly clear patterns. In France, as in much of the rest of Europe, there was widespread restlessness concerning the state of the Church as it then existed and a deeply felt desire for reform. In France reform proposals tended to follow a Swiss-south German Evangelical trend. And in France the foremost organs of both the ecclesiastical and the secular establishments had reacted with bitter hostility to the reform movement, restrained only by the personal sympathy of an urbane and sophisticated monarch and a few other highly placed persons.

In the face of considerable opposition, the achievements of the reformers had been impressive: translations of and commentaries upon Scripture; telling criticism of the mechanical and ritualistic practices of the established Church; generation of widespread popular support for reform; and the attraction of important protectors.

Despite persecutions, during these years the reformers—with their translations, their tracts, their preachers, and their martyrs—seemed to hold the initiative and to be making deep inroads into the established Church. And despite occasional dramatic outbreaks of violence, the quarrels had remained on the whole rather quiet. In the middle 1530s this began to change.

# Chapter Two
# Calvin and Geneva

DURING THE 1530s persecution of religious dissenters spread through the French provinces, with executions in Toulouse, Rouen, and Lyons, while harassment continued in Paris. The repression appears to have been sporadic and unorganized, but it suggests that all across France the religious establishment was consolidating to resist the challenge of the reformers. At the same time, the king's protection was becoming less certain. Francis I was still making treaties with German Protestant princes, and he exiled the fiercely intolerant Noël Béda from Paris; but on 10 December 1533 he wrote to the Parlement of Paris ordering it to press without exception for the extirpation of heresy. Moreover, early in 1534 Francis concluded negotiations which resulted in an alliance with the papacy against the Holy Roman Emperor and in an arrangement for the king's second son (and after 1536 his heir, the future Henry II) to marry the pope's young niece, Catherine de Médicis. Then in the winter of 1534–1535 new clashes definitely decided the wavering king in favor of repression.

The "Night of the Placards," 17–18 October 1534, proved pivotal to the religious history not just of France but of much of Europe and eventually of its colonial extensions. On that night enthusiastic critics launched a new attack upon the established Church in the form of harshly worded posters condemning the mass, the clergy, and Roman Catholic doctrine. The placards were

posted widely in Paris and in many of the cities and chateau-towns
of the Loire Valley, such as Orléans, Blois and Amboise. In the
chateau of Amboise one was even found attached to the king's own
door.

The audacity of the attack and the intemperate language of the
criticism evoked a Catholic reaction, a new wave of persecution
that sent many would-be reformers scurrying for cover until the
danger had passed. Amongst those who sought safety in exile was a
young Picard in his middle twenties, John Calvin. Wanting a place
where he could continue to study and to teach, Calvin sought
sanctuary in the relatively freer communities of the Rhineland and
the Swiss cantons. After residing awhile in Basel he reluctantly
agreed to join Farel in more active reform work in Geneva, never
suspecting that he would earn an immortal reputation there.

The man who was to inspire and guide the Evangelical reform
of the middle sixteenth century, and was to see his name attached
indelibly to a major branch of the reform movement, was born in
Noyon, in the northern French province of Picardy, on 10 July
1509. Modern industrial development and the regular passage of
armies through those border regions for more than four and a half
centuries have left little that is evocative of the land of Calvin's
boyhood except the wooded rolling hills, though a fine reproduc-
tion of the solid middle-class house in which he grew up stands in
Noyon, and market day on the nearby square cannot be very
different from what it was in his youth.

In the early sixteenth century Picardy was a province of both
geographical and economic significance, and of its several substantial towns Noyon deferred to none but the provincial capital of
Amiens. The social structure of provincial towns such as Noyon
generally was built around a handful of families which dominated
commercial and ecclesiastical affairs, and young Calvin grew up on
the fringes of these circles. His father, Gérard Cauvin, was a man of
low birth who had risen through education and ability to hold
secretarial and legal appointments under the bishop and the cathedral chapter (the association of the clergy of the cathedral) of Noyon.
Ultimately he had been accepted into the bourgeoisie of the
town—signifying his admission to the voting privileges and tax
obligations of full citizenship, which was the prerogative of rela-

tively well-to-do property owners. Gérard had married the daughter of an innkeeper, a bourgeois of the nearby town of Cambrai, and the future religious reformer was their fourth son. Young John (who Latinized the family name to Calvinus, whence Calvin) was intended originally for an ecclesiastical and then for a legal career. Educated at first with noble relatives of the Bishop of Noyon and then, with the support of "benefices" or fellowships from the diocese, in various colleges and universities in Paris, Orléans and Bourges, he eventually earned a doctorate in law.

A lack of autobiographical material or other documentation from this period makes it difficult to evaluate the influence of these early years upon young Calvin's intellectual development. Probably his understanding of bourgeois corporate town government and his later ability to cope with the political factions and social divisions of turbulent Geneva owed something to a youth spent in association with the governing elite of his smaller but comparable Picard home town. Theology was a major component of his education from the beginning. While he experienced some highly conservative and orthodox teachers—including Noël Béda himself—he was a student during the years when the French institutes of higher learning were being swept by enthusiasm for the new humanist studies, with the apparent encouragement of King Francis. There is no evidence to suggest that the young Calvin showed any particular sympathy for religious radicalism as a student. (Responsible scholars set his "conversion" as early as 1528 and as late as 1534.) But he did study under some of the best humanist scholars, and his associates included many men then or later famous as liberal and progressive religious thinkers.

Finally, there appears to have been a strong spirit of criticism and stubborn independence in Calvin's family. His father died in 1531 excommunicated and refusing the sacraments because of a bitter quarrel with the Noyon cathedral chapter. His older brother, carrying on the family fight though a chaplain of the cathedral, also died refusing the sacraments. In May of 1534 young John Calvin, by then closely identified with progressive theological circles in Paris, returned to Noyon—not to be ordained into the clergy as would have been normal for a man of his background and education but to resign his benefices, thus severing his ties with the diocese.

Whatever the timing of Calvin's intellectual development, events of the mid-1530s pushed him to act decisively. In 1533 a serious disturbance shook Parisian religious circles. A close friend of Calvin, Nicolas Cop, had been elected Rector of the University of Paris, and in his inaugural address he not only defended and praised humanism but quoted from a sermon of Luther. A royal proscription of the "Lutheran sect" was the high point of the reaction that ensued. Probably Calvin was not involved directly in the composition of the address, as sometimes has been alleged. However, he was closely enough identified with Cop and others considered "radical" that he thought it prudent to flee Paris for awhile. He spent most of the next several months in the provinces, continuing his studies privately as the guest of his friend Louis de Tillet, a cleric of Angoulême. On one occasion he visited the Nérac court of King Francis' sister Marguerite, where he met the aged Lefèvre d'Etaples. And, of course, it was at this time that he resigned his benefices at Noyon.

A brief return to Paris ended for Calvin in the tumult following the "Night of the Placards," and he fled again, this time out of the kingdom. For this second exile he went to Basel, where he spent the greater part of the next two years. There he undertook his first serious writing—a critique of some Anabaptist notions; a preface for a French translation of the Bible being prepared by his friend Olivétan; and, most significantly, the first edition of his *Institutes of the Christian Religion.*

The inspiration for the composition of the *Institutes* was the mounting persecution of religious reformers in Paris. As King Francis swung toward conformity and orthodoxy, he still sought to maintain his good relations with the Lutheran princes of Germany while encouraging the repression of reformers in France. Thus, he attempted to portray the latter as Anabaptists—supporters of a primitive Christianity as much abhorred by Lutherans as by Roman Catholics. It was to defend the Paris Evangelicals against this accusation that Calvin undertook the *Institutes,* a basic exposition of Evangelical reformed theology, which he dedicated hopefully to King Francis. Though the treatise quadrupled in size through successive editions over a quarter century, the first version of 1536, which was just over five hundred pages, swept comprehensively across Christian theology and contained all of Calvin's major themes, a remarkable achievement for a writer only in his middle twenties.

Calvin was convinced that he asserted no novelty but was only re-establishing the purity of Christianity which he thought had been distorted by papal pretensions and medieval scholasticism. In his own words, he had not knowingly "corrupted or twisted a single passage of the Scriptures." The inescapable basis of his theology, expounded most clearly in Book III of the last edition of the *Institutes,* is his predestinarian concept. Though foreshadowed by St. Augustine and Luther, never previously had it been stated so boldly.

As the basis of all truth Calvin affirmed the transcendent majesty of God. A corollary was the necessity and limitlessness of God's will for every occurrence in the world. From this he argued that God must have determined from the day of creation who would be saved and who would be damned through all eternity. Man, he asserted, was corrupted through original sin forever—not by association, through responsibility for Adam's sin, but as a personal curse in which each individual issued from the womb already containing the seeds of iniquity. Thus, it is impossible that any man could ever merit redemption. Nonetheless some are saved, the Elect, by God's inexplicable and gratuitous mercy through Christ.

The chief end of man, Calvin said, is to know and do the will of God, which is only possible through faith. He argued that faith really and effectively joins man to Christ and leads to repentance and finally to justification—again not earned, even by faith, but imputed through participation in Christ's righteousness. In this union with Christ the fortunate few, whom God for his own incomprehensible reasons has elected for salvation, find a confidence—though never absolute certainty—of redemption and forgiveness of sin. This gift of faith is nurtured and affirmed through the Holy Communion, which Calvin thought should be taken frequently, observing: "our souls are fed by the flesh and blood of Christ just as our corporeal life is preserved and sustained by bread and wine." Thus, in the matter of the sacrament he differed from both Roman Catholics and Lutherans, as well as from the more radical Protestants for whom it was merely a commemorative ceremony.

In Calvin's thought the Church then appears in two forms. God's true Church is all of the Elect of all time—but they are, of course, uncertain of themselves and unknown to each other. The visible Church at any given time is, therefore, all those who profess, to whom it offers the sacrament and moral guidance as support against human weakness. Theoretically, this Church could coexist with any government. Indeed, Calvin observed that forms of government change with historical circumstances; but he also asserted that rulers were legitimate only if they provided for "true" religion, of which presumably the ministers were the final arbiters. Thus, Calvin's doctrines were as fraught with political implications as those of any competing sect, especially as these theoretical positions were elucidated later by the development of his theocracy in Geneva.

The composition of the *Institutes* concluded Calvin's work in Basel. As the book went to press he left for a short journey to Italy, intending to settle thereafter to a scholarly life either in Basel or Strasbourg. Instead, on his return from Italy the exigencies of war caused him to detour through Geneva where his destiny awaited him.

The Geneva to which Calvin came in the summer of 1536 was dynamic and even tumultuous, its independence only recently established and none too secure. Situated at the west end of Lake Geneva, where the Rhône River debouches from the lake and begins its journey to the Mediterranean, the city held the strategic southern end of the route from the Rhône Valley to Basel in the Valley of the Rhine. It could trace its origins to Roman times, and in the Middle Ages it had been a commercial center of some importance.

The greatest danger to Geneva's corporate independence was the fact that the city was entangled in an ill-defined web of overlapping and often contradictory jurisdictions. On the other hand, this was also the city's salvation, for it often allowed the city council to play off ambitious rivals against one another. Geneva had emerged from the confusion of the early Middle Ages a prince-bishopric, like many central European towns. Then in the fourteenth century the propertied citizens had formed some semi-autonomous councils and had secured their recognition in charters. By about 1400 the town appeared to be developing into a sort of "free city" with mixed government, an amalgam of ecclesiastical and civil officials. However, about this time a serious threat to the city's aspirations emerged.

In 1401 the House of Savoy, a family from the mountainous regions to the south, bought the county of the Genevois, in which Geneva stood. Shortly thereafter, the Savoyards acquired the right of appointment to the Bishopric of Geneva. This was especially important in a prince-bishopric because of the legal authority of the bishop in civil matters. From the mid-fifteenth century until 1522 the bishops were, in fact, younger relatives of the Dukes of Savoy.

As a counterpoise to the Savoyards, the Genevans developed political connections with two neighboring Swiss cantons, Fribourg and Bern, with which they had close economic ties. These connections culminated in treaties establishing joint citizenship among the towns in the mid-1520s. This Swiss association was not entirely an unmixed blessing, however, for the cantons—especially Bern—were themselves ambitious; and often they tended to treat Geneva more as a dependent than as an ally.

Finally, on the basis of linguistic and cultural ties, a vague political connection running back to Caesar, and an ancient association of the French and Genevan churches, the King of France sometimes demonstrated a disturbing interest in Geneva's affairs. In the 1460s and 1470s this interest and a Franco-Savoyard alliance had damaged the Genevan economy badly when the French King had changed the dates of the famous Lyons fairs so as to compete with the trade fairs of Geneva. So something of a French threat also loomed over the city.

During the fifteenth and early sixteenth centuries Genevan city government had developed considerably despite this competition from other authorities. At its core was a medieval Grand Council comprising all male heads of families; around this had grown up smaller councils, a bit amorphous and often changed. In the mid-1520s a clearer pattern emerged. Probably in imitation of their Swiss allies in Bern and Fribourg, in 1526 the Genevans established firmly a Council of Two Hundred as a general assembly, which then chose a Council of Sixty for actual administrative control. Although property qualifications limited the franchise, they appear not to have been so severe as in the more patrician towns of north Italy or the Netherlands. Actually, a fairly wide spectrum of the population took part in the government of Geneva.

Amid so many political cross-currents, the issue of religious reform was potentially explosive. As a major commercial city at the intersection of important trade routes, Geneva naturally was exposed to the various reform movements—Zwinglian, Lutheran, Evangelical and Anabaptist. The fact that the Bishop of Geneva was an appointee of the Duke of Savoy reinforced an anticlerical sentiment in the citizenry. On the other hand, one of Geneva's two Swiss allies, Fribourg, remained Roman Catholic while Bern supported the Reformation. In Geneva anti-Romanism became strong enough to force the bishop to flee permanently in 1533 (he had been driven out temporarily on previous occasions). His authority promptly was claimed by the city government, which then consolidated its position in November of 1535 by proclaiming the abolition of the mass.

However, these gains in autonomy were not achieved without risk. Possibly as a result of the drift of Geneva's religious policy, Fribourg withdrew from the tri-city alliance in 1534. As Bern appeared unwilling to join in open warfare, in the face of a developing attack by the Duke of Savoy and the exiled bishop, the outlook for Geneva was grim. Late in 1535 the French offered help against Savoy, an offer so fraught with political implications that the Bernese, fearful of the establishment of French influence, finally committed themselves; in January of 1536 Bern intervened to assist Geneva, checkmating the Duke of Savoy and restabilizing the situation.

During these conflicts and dangers William Farel, a fiery and vigorous Evangelical preacher, had arrived in Geneva and had quickly become an important leader of the reform movement. His work enjoyed some success with the abolition of the mass in 1535 and more in May of 1536 when, by plebiscite, Geneva adopted the Evangelical faith. However, he felt incapable of organizing the new Church and an Evangelical state alone. When Calvin arrived only a few weeks after the plebiscite, Farel insisted that he remain—first begging his assistance and then threatening that God expected more of him than withdrawal into the scholarly life he desired so much. The result was that Calvin, who had intended to stay only one night in Geneva, agreed to make only a short trip to Basel to put his personal affairs in order, and in August he returned to assist Farel.

Calvin's reluctant mission in Geneva began undramatically with a series of unpaid lectures on St. Paul's Epistles delivered in the church of St. Pierre. However, such was the power of his intellect and the incisiveness of his criticism that he quickly acquired an ever-increasing influence in the life of the city. He was accepted as pastor of St. Pierre's, wrote a short *Instruction in Faith,* helped Farel to draft disciplinary rules for the new Church, and expounded Evangelical theology both within Geneva and as Geneva's spokesman in disputations with other towns such as Bern and Lucerne. Soon Calvin was involved in an incredible variety of activities—lecturing, preaching, teaching, writing, and organizing.

The Evangelical community that Farel and Calvin envisaged for Geneva was many-faceted and touched upon almost every aspect of life. Like their Roman Catholic and Lutheran contemporaries, they never doubted the common interest of the civil and ecclesiastical authorities in maintaining an orderly, decent and religiously homogeneous society. They took it as natural that the power of the state should enforce religious conformity and high moral standards. Thus, after public disputations in March 1537 the Council of Two Hundred ordered the expulsion of all Anabaptists. A few months later all citizens were required to swear an Evangelical confession of faith that Farel had written or face banishment.

The reformers' moral complaints suggest a rather low standard of public life in early sixteenth-century Genevan society, as they persuaded the city government to proscribe indecent dances, gambling, drunkenness, ostentation, obscene songs, and mixed public bathing. Arguing the need for frequent and worthy observation of the Lord's Supper, they inveighed against all immorality and advocated improved religious education. To this end they founded schools and Calvin wrote his *Instruction in Faith.* Clearly they aimed at a sober, dedicated community organized around Christian principles as the Evangelical clergy interpreted them from Scriptures. Not surprisingly, they evoked some opposition.

Given Calvin's ultimate success in Geneva, and a history subsequently seen through Calvinist eyes, his early opponents remain somewhat vague. Doubtless there were those who found his doctrinal positions too radical. They regretted the mass and thought that reform should have meant only the detachment of the old Church and its clergy from worldly involvements, or at most the simplifications of Luther. And as the disputations of 1537 indicate, there certainly were those who thought his theology too conservative, Anabaptists who believed that even the Evangelicals strayed too far from the truths of primitive Christianity. There were complaints that Farel and Calvin were establishing a new tyranny worse than that of the old prince-bishop. Given their desire to regulate moral behavior strictly, the reformers could hardly escape the enmity of tavern owners, brothel keepers and the whole population of the shadowy world of dubious entertainment, vagabondage, and petty crime that were part of every city.

The opposition to the Evangelicals eventually coalesced politically, but even then the issues were never altogether clear. The reformers' ambition to create in Geneva a truly godly state, as they understood it, without compromises, was implicitly rather isolationist. But with the ambitions of the House of Savoy still threatening, and religious wars looming in Germany, many believed that Geneva's security was dependent upon the connection with Bern and thought that the reformers ought to be restrained by the civil authority.

Even distinctly religious disputes took on political implications because of the question over authority to make decisions. Quarrels arose concerning the use of baptismal fonts and unleavened bread, which were maintained in the rites of the more traditional Bernese Church. Especially contentious was the question of exclusion from the communion, excommunication, the Evangelicals' only disciplinary weapon. More important than any of the particular issues was the question of who would decide them, for the reformers insisted that these were matters for the ministers and that the civil authorities should not meddle. Thus the whole problem of state-church relations came into contention. It became clear that Farel and Calvin envisaged a relationship in which the civil government would not interfere with, and perhaps even would be subordinate to, ecclesiastical authority in matters of morals and rites. It was this question of superiority of jurisdiction rather than any particular religious issue that eventually led to a clash.

The elections of February 1537 had produced a small majority favorable to the reformers in the Council of Two Hundred, hence the expulsion of the Anabaptists and the confession of faith required of the citizenry. However, elections in 1538 brought the opposition to power, men not opposed to the Reformation but rather more cautious about religious innovations, hesitant about the ministers' challenge to the council's power, and concerned about Geneva's relations with Bern.

This new council quickly forbade the ministers to exclude anyone from the communion and even formally adopted some of the Bernese rites without consulting the churchmen. This was open confrontation, of course. The ministers replied by refusing to administer the sacrament at all on Easter Sunday, alleging that they feared it might be profaned in the disturbances. They preached vigorously against the recent governmental decisions even though the council had forbidden them to do so. This defiance proved overbold, for the Council of Two Hundred then decreed the banishment of the leading ministers, including Farel and Calvin, and gave them three days to leave the city. Thus ended Calvin's first ministry in Geneva.

Upon their exile from Geneva, Farel took refuge in the Swiss town of Neuchâtel, where he had preached before, while Calvin continued on to Strasbourg, where he had long thought of settling. There he became pastor to a congregation of French refugees, whose community already numbered several hundred. He developed a close relationship with Martin Bucer, and also re-entered public life by representing Strasbourg at various religious conferences, in the course of which he met the famous German theologian Philipp Melanchthon. The three years that Calvin spent in Strasbourg were very satisfying to him. He married happily, and he rejoiced in the intellectual stimulation of Bucer and Melanchthon. He also wrote voluminously, including in 1541 a French translation of a revised edition of his *Institutes* (the original having been in Latin). Because of its lucidity and graceful exposition this latter work soon became a classic of the rapidly developing French language. During these years he maintained a regular correspondence with his supporters in Geneva, the most notable item of which was a letter written to oppose proposals to re-establish Roman Catholicism. This letter is generally considered one of the finest justifications of the Reformation ever written.

In 1541 political convulsions in Geneva brought the supporters of the Evangelicals to power again, and they invited Calvin to return. He was most reluctant, having found great happiness in his life at Strasbourg. After receiving several official letters and deputations he was overcome by his sense of duty, and on 3 September he re-entered the city.

The years of exile appear to have matured Calvin, perhaps tempering his fervor with greater patience, certainly refining his vision of the ecclesiastical polity which he wished to establish. He drafted a set of "Ecclesiastical Ordinances" which was adopted. These provided for minute regulation of daily life and established a consistory of pastors and elders, six ministers and twelve laymen, to act not only as the governing body of the Genevan Church but also as a court of morals. However, the only sanctions to be employed normally were remonstrances from the consistory and excommunication. Cases judged too serious for these punishments were to be referred to the councils, which could prescribe civil penalties. Nevertheless, while the conciliar form of Genevan government was not changed, and the consistory had a majority of laymen, the influence of the ministers often proved dominant within the consistory, and it in turn gradually assumed a great deal of initiative in all public affairs.

For a decade and a half stubborn opposition resisted the increasing authority of the churchmen, but Calvin was as determined as they. With the support of an ever more numerous flow of French refugees into Geneva, whose enfranchisement he achieved, he ultimately triumphed in creating the church-state that he so fervently desired. By sheer capacity, seemingly limitless energy, and involvement in an incredible variety of activities, he managed to dominate it until his death in 1564.

A slim pale man of middle height, sometimes described as

"pallid," Calvin's person was most notable for large eyes set in a thin, ascetic face. Certainly he did not appear to possess the prodigious energies which he expended regularly throughout his ministry in Geneva. He wrote and wrote, involved himself in the foundation of schools, participated in and often dominated conferences concerned with trade and diplomacy, was consulted on matters of law and police, and drafted sanitary regulations. All the while he maintained a full schedule of preaching and teaching, of course, and carrying on the continuing political struggles with the councils.

Probably Calvin's often professed humility was genuine, but in his dedication to his ministry he identified himself entirely with godliness and truth in the fight against iniquity and error. He made little distinction among personal, political and theological opposition. Against opponents he was implacable. In the late 1540s and early 1550s, as his power in the city grew, he showed from time to time what a terrible enemy he could be.

In 1546 Pierre Ameaux, a member of the Council of Sixty, incautiously criticized Calvin. As a manufacturer of toys and playing cards, he probably had reason to oppose the reformer. In any case, at a private dinner he observed that Calvin had become "more than a bishop" and possibly challenged some of the doctrines that he preached. When these remarks were repeated to Calvin, he demanded satisfaction from the councils. The Council of Sixty was very sympathetic, but when the question came before the Council of Two Hundred it ruled only that the offender should apologize to Calvin in a full council session. When Calvin protested, the Evangelical party was strong enough to obtain a second ruling that Ameaux should make public apology. Still unsatisfied, Calvin pressed the case and was able to secure yet another ruling utterly humiliating the councillor. Ameaux was required to make a round of the city—head bare, torch in hand and wearing a penitent's shirt—and then to kneel and publicly ask the Lord's mercy for having maligned "God, the Magistrate, and Master Calvin, the minister."

In 1546 began another controversy, the affair of Michael Servetus, that was to end tragically several years later. Servetus, a Spaniard by birth, was a former law student, a physician, and a self-taught theologian. As a critic of the worldliness of the Church, he probably thought of himself as a reformer. In fact, his obscure and often arrogant theological tracts scandalized Roman Catholics and Protestants about equally, as he attacked baptismal rites and some aspects of Trinitarian doctrines.

A highly controversial figure, Servetus had to change his residence frequently to escape the authorities. He lived at various times in Switzerland, the Rhineland cities, the southern Netherlands, and France. In the mid-1540s, after a decade and a half of public disputations and contentious publication, he was living incognito in Vienne in southeastern France, near Lyons. Outwardly a physician and a conforming Catholic, he was in fact still developing his own theological ideas. It was at this time that he began a correspondence with Calvin, sent him a manuscript of the book that he was writing and proposed that they meet. Over several years Servetus sent Calvin some thirty letters. After the first few the Genevan theologian refused to reply, refused to return the manuscript of the book, and remarked that if Servetus ever came to Geneva he would never leave alive.

In 1553 the affair reached its climax when Servetus secretly published his new book. In April a former Lyonnais living in Geneva, probably with Calvin's complicity, wrote to the Inquisitor General in Lyons revealing the author's real identity and residence and transmitting some of his letters to Calvin which would reinforce the case for charging him with heresy. In the aftermath, Servetus was arrested, managed to escape, fled, and was burned in effigy by the Roman Catholic authorities.

Despite this, shortly thereafter Servetus turned up in Geneva. Though he was incognito again, he was soon recognized and arrested. The trial, in which Calvin played a leading role, dragged on from mid-August to late October. In the course of it several Swiss Reformed Churches were asked for opinions. Nonetheless, the issues remained unclear. There was a consensus among Reformed theologians, as there had been among the Roman Catholics, that Servetus should be punished for heresy, but there were precedents for death, incarceration, or simple exile and banishment. Calvin demanded the death penalty. Though apparently he favored decapitation, in the end the secular authorities proved harsher than the minister. On 27 October 1553 Servetus was burned alive.

The execution triggered a controversy over the death penalty for heresy in which many prominent Protestant theologians participated. To this day Calvin's reputation suffers for his role in the affair. Certainly he showed neither mercy nor charity; and the endeavor to betray Servetus to the Roman Catholic authorities of Lyons, if he really had a part in it, was rather shabby. But in the end, all that can be said is that—contrary to the fond assumptions of the liberal conscience—in the sixteenth century there was little tolerance of dissent, especially in religious matters. Calvin was no different from most of his contemporaries in being willing to enforce his vision of truth with fire and sword if necessary.

In 1559 he established the Geneva Academy, one of his most far-reaching undertakings. Founded as a seminary to train Reformed clergy (and elevated to university status only late in the nineteenth century), its direction was entrusted to the forty-year old French refugee, Theodore de Beza (1519–1605), who already had worked with Calvin for a decade. Also a product of a humanist and legal education, Beza shared Calvin's enthusiasm for classical studies and his Evangelical faith. Over the years he became his closest collaborator, and from his post as Rector of the Academy, he carried on as effective director of the Genevan Church after Calvin's death.

Calvin's determined insistence that Geneva accept and grant rights to refugees—not just French but also English, German, and Italian—and the development of the Academy as the center of Evangelical Christianity rapidly transformed the city into one of the most cosmopolitan communities of Europe. In addition, it became the incubator of ideas that were to have a major impact as far away as Holland, Scotland, England, Bohemia, and Hungary, as well as the wider world opened up by European imperialism. As time passed, Calvin's ideas went through many modifications. These softened the inflexibility of his predestinarianism and accommodated the religious community to the princely form of government that was the more typical of sixteenth- and seventeenth-century Europe than was the Genevan republic. But Calvin's thought has remained fundamental to a vigorous and aggressive sect of Reformed Christianity to this day, and certainly it was Calvinism that gave shape to the Reform in France.

# Chapter Three
# The Organization of Repression

ACROSS MUCH OF western Europe significantly different religious patterns were emerging by the middle 1530s. In Germany the great Diet of Augsburg of 1529 had not resulted in agreement and reunification of the Churches but only in sharper definitions of Lutheran positions and in the formation of the Protestant Schmalkaldic League. The emperor's need for the support of the Lutheran princes against the Turks prevented him from launching a military effort against this league. So—except for sporadic operations against Anabaptists—Germany was still spared civil war; but contrary to the emperor's will and policy, Lutheran state Churches tightly controlled by their princes were developing rapidly all across north Germany.

At about the same time, in England Henry VIII's marital problems and his concern for the English succession were causing a crisis. Still without a son after twenty years of marriage, and keenly aware of the civil wars that the succession issue had caused in the latter half of the preceding century, the king desperately sought the Church's approval for annulment and remarriage. However, for a variety of reasons, some of them political, the papacy was reluctant to agree and instead adopted a delaying policy. The king's natural impatience was aggravated by the discovery that his mistress was pregnant, for only marriage could provide legitimacy to the expected child. In the face of continuing papal recalcitrance, the

English monarch found his own solution in the Act of Supremacy of 1534. This separated the English Church from Rome and subordinated it to the rule of the king. Even though no dramatic doctrinal changes were introduced during Henry VIII's reign, the unity of the western Church was further shattered as the Church of England was born.

In France the middle 1530s witnessed increasing religious enthusiasm, and the Evangelicals had no monopoly of this passion. In November 1533, on All Saints' Day, Nicolas Cop's Evangelical sermon raised the storm that resulted in Calvin's first flight from Paris. In that same city less than a year later, on 15 August 1534, Ignatius Loyola, Francis Xavier, and five others took the first vows of a special Roman Catholic dedication that eventually would mature into the Society of Jesus, the Jesuits. The most dramatic event of these years, however, was the "Night of the Placards," already referred to briefly.

Probably written by Antoine Marcourt, an enthusiastic religious controversialist who had fled the authorities of Lyons to find refuge in Switzerland in 1530 or 1531, the placards posted on 17–18 October 1534 bitterly attacked every aspect of Roman Catholicism. The use of placards, or broadsheets, was not new, for both sides of the reform quarrel had employed them several times before. But these were singularly intemperate. They condemned "this pompous and proud papal mass"; denounced "the pope and all his vermin of cardinals, bishops, priests, and monks" as liars and blasphemers; and asserted that it was "idolatry to believe the corporeal presence of Christ in the Eucharist." Widely displayed in Paris and the Loire Valley towns frequented by the Court, the placards caused a scandal and evoked a vicious backlash. Their influence upon the king, especially, appears to have been quite significant.

To understand the impact of the "Night of the Placards" upon Francis I, his religious policy must be set in a concise perspective of his other concerns. As with most rulers of his day, foreign policy—and especially war—was a major interest. After all, the fundamental justification of the whole feudal structure over which monarchs ruled, or tried to rule, was security; and historically the greatness of kings was judged largely by their military leadership. Hence, Francis I's primary concern was the great struggle with Emperor Charles V of the House of Habsburg. As Holy Roman Emperor, Charles dominated the German states, and through family connections he controlled Bohemia and Hungary. He was King of Spain, and through this crown also Lord of the Indies, where his *conquistadores* were carving out a whole new empire for him. He had extensive lordships in Italy, on the Rhine and in the Netherlands. Spanish Mediterranean shipping to Italy and Spanish Atlantic shipping to the Netherlands dominated the sea lanes in those regions. Under Charles V the House of Habsburg cast a gigantic shadow across Europe.

For the King of France it must have appeared a divine mercy that circumstances prevented Charles V from ever consolidating the resources of his far-flung holdings. The emperor faced the usual problems of local particularism that everywhere impeded the efficient collection and distribution of men and money. Moreover, he had to cope with the threat of the Turks in the east. He also was distracted by the internal upheaval consequent upon the spread of the Lutheran movement.

Francis I fought Charles V almost all of his adult life. Hence, when the German Protestants sought foreign aid against the emperor, he assisted them. The Lutheran princes became treasured allies of the Roman Catholic ruler of France. Open warfare also raged between Francis and Charles for domination of Italy, where both had historic interests. In the late 1520s shared concerns led to the renewal of the old Franco-papal alliance. Thus, in the early 1530s, while still cultivating his image as the Renaissance King, generous and tolerant patron of scholars and artists, Francis I was involved in a dangerous international struggle and was pursuing a hard-headed policy of exploiting religious divisions in Germany while seeking closer cooperation with the papacy in Italy.

Against this background the escalating religious clashes in France must be considered. Francis desperately wanted to strengthen his reputation as a good Roman Catholic in the eyes of the pope. He simply could not afford to abandon his heretical allies in Germany, but he could make some gestures in his own kingdom.

Withal, given his role in German affairs, Francis must have been as aware as anyone in Europe of the potential for political fragmentation implicit in religious pluralism. Thus, at the end of 1533, as he was beginning high level talks with the pope—which resulted in a new Franco-papal alliance and the Médicis marriage for his son, Henry—Francis I ordered his Parlement to press the campaign against heresy. Both the disturbing implications of the Protestant league in Germany and the exigencies of the papal alliance were pressing the king toward a more conservative religious policy in France.

Nonetheless, repression was not easy. There were some centers of learning which were sympathetic to reformers and, fortified by traditional charters and immunities, relatively secure from outside authority. The Universities of Orléans and Bourges, in north-central France, had highly respected reputations for humanist scholarship. Also notable was the University of Grenoble in the southeast, which had felt the impact of both the Renaissance in Italy and the Evangelical religious movements of the Swiss cantons and south Germany.

Significant, too, was the almost federal character of the monarchy, derived from its feudal origins. In Paris and the surrounding Ile-de-France the king, the Sorbonne and the Parlement could be fairly effective—at least so long as they concerted their efforts. In the provinces powerful figures such as Marguerite d'Angoulême, and after her aristocrats of the families of Montmorency and Bourbon, gave their protection to the reformers. There the central government was nearly impotent and the Church not much more effective. The sixteenth-century kingdom, despite some growth of royal bureaucracy, remained essentially a patchwork quilt of variegated feudal principalities and lordships loosely bound together by the king's authority. Little could be achieved without the cooperation of local authorities.

Finally, the sheer bulk of France and the slowness and fallibility of communications made hiding easy. For all practical purposes, a few miles from Paris a man disappeared from the eyes of the authorities. In his first flight from the capital Calvin lived with friends in the provinces, quietly continuing his studies, and he even dared to visit Noyon. Servetus lived securely under an incognito in the Rhone Valley, though sought by officers of the Church and state, and continued his writing. Such anonymity was even easier for figures of less prominence.

Despite these difficulties, when the "Night of the Placards" erupted, Francis I reacted forcefully. In January 1535 the "King of the Renaissance" forbade all publishing and ordered all bookstores closed. These prohibitions were relaxed only a month later when the Parlement established a panel of censors to which all manuscripts had to be submitted for licensing prior to publication. Also in January 1535, to dissociate himself publicly from any appearance of toleration of such extremist tactics as the violent placards, Francis ordered a massive Catholic procession, in which he joined. Such processions were very much a part of Catholic public life of the sixteenth century. They served both to demonstrate the devotional commitment of the authorities and to stir the piety and support of the masses of laity. They were colorful pageants, comprising large numbers of clergy and officials, processional crosses and banners, and many relics. The procession of January 1535 was received with enthusiasm by the Parisians, and it affirmed the king's essential orthodoxy.

The Parlement and the Sorbonne also reacted vigorously to the placards. After impassioned speeches there were new inquests and new arrests, then more burnings: a shoemaker, a mason and two merchants, a school-mistress, and a monk. In January thirty-five "Lutherans" were burned; and there were rumors of three hundred arrests in prospect. Many fled the city. In July the king tempered the reaction a little, despite the Sorbonne's severe dictum "one does not argue with heretics." He issued an edict of amnesty for all who would repudiate earlier errors and reconvert; but for recalcitrants the pace of persecution increased. It was the royal justifications of this policy that stimulated Calvin to publish the *Institutes* in Basel the next year.

Despite these mounting pressures, the reform movement continued to grow and to attract popular support. There are no reliable figures for numbers of adherents or even for numbers of congregations during the quarter of a century following the "Night of the Placards." Survival often depended upon secrecy, or at least discretion, and there was no unifying organization to give form to the movement. All that can be said with certainty is that there was considerable expansion. Reformed churches appeared all over France, independent congregations, ideally each with a minister and a consistory. Their existence is documented by scattered letters and diaries as well as by usually hostile official reports. They constituted, of course, a tiny minority in a population of fifteen or sixteen million people, but in the face of intensifying repression their simple survival was a considerable achievement.

Aside from growth of numbers, probably the most significant development of these years was Calvin's ever greater ascendancy over the French reform movement, especially after 1541 when his Genevan community began to take shape. Despite persecutions, France—like much of the rest of western Europe—experienced a veritable flood of popular preachers. Some were native Frenchmen, often former monks or priests won to the cause of reform. Others were foreigners, products of the Evangelical or Anabaptist communities and schools of Strasbourg, Geneva, Lausanne, and even distant north Germany. Naturally they preached in many different idioms and taught different doctrines. In consequence, there is a sort of incoherence about these years, though the enthusiasm of the popular response suggests a widespread spiritual hunger in France. Through it all emerges more and more the guiding role of Calvin.

There were many bases for the growth of Calvin's influence in the French reform movement. In the first place, he was French, even if he lived in exile, and a product of the new wave of humanist culture that was sweeping educated Frenchmen. He wrote and spoke in an idiom and from a perspective that had nothing foreign or imported about it. Moreover, he was brilliant; both the reasoning of his arguments and the lucidity of their exposition instantly made his *Institutes* one of Christianity's major theological works, and the whole body of his writings shows the same characteristics. But perhaps most important was his seemingly inexhaustible energy and careful attention to detail. He maintained an incredibly vast correspondence—answering a doctrinal question, describing the organization of the Genevan community, recommending someone for a pastoral appointment, encouraging a new congregation, chiding an unworthy minister, or pleading the Reform's interests to authorities. There seems to have been no problem, no issue, no cause related to Evangelical reform for which he could not make time.

Reinforcing the impact of this prodigious ministry was the growing maturity of the theocracy in Geneva. Whatever the disappointments and disasters in France—the executions, the confiscations, the backsliders—dedicated Evangelical Christians knew that just over the border was a community that lived by the True Word of God, that maintained a proper religious practice and a high moral standard. In their own struggles they drew hope and courage from that example.

Neither the secular nor the ecclesiastical authorities remained idle during the late 1530s and the 1540s, however. The reformers continued to hope for the king's favor. In fact, Calvin dedicated the first edition of his *Institutes* to Francis I in 1536, claiming that his primary purpose in their composition was to prepare the royal mind for a favorable consideration of the reformers' pleas. But they were to be disappointed. Though the king continued to patronize the arts and to protect the "modern" linguistic scholars of the *Collège de France* (to whom were added professors of medicine and mathematics about 1539), after the "Night of the Placards" he was ever conscious of the disruptive potential of religious dissent, and he sought to block it.

In 1538 Francis I found himself freer to attend to domestic problems than he had been for some time. In June of that year at Nice he, the pope, and the Holy Roman Emperor signed a truce. Almost immediately France experienced a renewed "Catholic policy." The king issued new edicts against "Lutherans." Their preamble noted how he had sought to drive out and exterminate evil errors and had thought his kingdom "purged and cleansed," only to find them slipping back. In 1540 he granted to all judicial officers the right of inquisition—examination of faith—over everyone including clerics, except those in Holy Orders. For the latter he guaranteed that the power of the state would support the prelates responsible for discipline. Occasionally the king intervened with a royal pardon when the sentences pronounced by his judges seemed excessive, but most often he encouraged their zeal. In 1542 and 1543 new measures were promulgated defining the jurisdictions of royal and ecclesiastical courts and further restricting publication.

And the executions continued, with burnings in both Paris and the provinces.

Probably the bloodiest event of the repression of the middle 1540s was the persecution of the surviving remnants of the old Waldensian movement in southern France, the Vaudois. Already in the 1520s Farel had preached the Evangelical Reform among them, and Vaudois leaders had entered into correspondence with other reformers. Then, in the 1530s, the Vaudois had formally adopted some changes in their old rites and had commissioned Olivétan to prepare a French Bible for them, from ancient sources. Hence, it appeared that they were aligning themselves with the Swiss Protestant Reform.

Naturally this reinvigoration of a dissenting movement was opposed by the establishment. The provincial high court—the Parlement of Aix—assumed the leadership of the repression. Minor expeditions were sent against the Vaudois in the late 1530s and early 1540s. At one point seventeen of them were burned alive and their families and servants banished. But the cult continued to grow, so in the spring of 1545 the president of the Parlement organized a campaign of extermination, using regular troops. Two or three towns and more than twenty villages were burned; hundreds of people were killed outright, including a number of women and children who were burned to death when the church in which they had taken refuge was fired; some two hundred and fifty were executed later; and six or seven hundred prisoners were sent to the rowers' benches of the king's galleys. A pitiful handful of survivors fled to Switzerland.

Even in an age that held life rather cheap, this bloody massacre evoked a revulsion, at least in the king. Francis I, whose health was deteriorating, charged his son with responsibility for investigating the excesses that had depopulated a prosperous area and turned it into a desert. Nothing much came of this belated compassion, however, for when Francis I died at the end of March of 1547, Henry II put the investigation into the hands of the judges of the Parlement of Paris, whose sympathies lay with their colleague in Aix. In 1550 they acquitted him of any wrongdoing, a vindication reinforced when the pope honored him with a papal knighthood. The only prosecution that came out of the whole effort was that of

the Advocate General of Provence, who was found guilty of pecula-
tion in disposing of confiscated property.

Another mass persecution occurred during the last years of
Francis I's reign, the affair of the Reformed Congregation of
Meaux. Early in September of 1546 sixty-one adherents of the
Reformed doctrine were arrested while meeting in a private home
in Meaux and were turned over to the Parlement of Paris, in whose
jurisdiction Meaux lay. Always thorough, the Parlement repri-
manded the Bishop of Meaux for allowing so large a secret congregation to develop. It called for extensive public preaching and
solemn processions, and ordered that the house in which the illegal
assembly had taken place should be razed and a Roman Catholic
chapel built in its place. Then the court turned its attention to the
prisoners. Fourteen men were ordered to be tortured and then
burned alive, a fifteenth to be hanged by his armpits during the
punishment of the others and then to be whipped and imprisoned.
Others of both sexes were ordered to observe the executions,
bare-headed and roped by the neck, to submit to a whipping and
then to make public confessions—after which some were released
and some were incarcerated.

A colorful individual also ran afoul of the authorities in 1546
and provided the occasion of yet another dramatic case. Etienne
Dolet, born in Orléans in 1509, studied in Paris and then in Italy
before settling in Toulouse as a university lecturer. Quarrelsome
and rather anti-clerical, his several minor disputes with authority
culminated in a grand clash in 1533 when he publicly denounced
edicts of the Parlement directed against student organizations.
Forced to flee Toulouse, he moved to Lyons, where he spent most
of the rest of his life as a printer of both secular and religious books
and writing. He wrote an important *Commentary on the Latin Language*, and he corresponded with such notable Renaissance figures as
Budé and Rabelais. But his life continued to be tumultuous.

In 1537 Dolet was convicted of murder, but he obtained a
royal pardon attesting that he had killed in self-defense. He was
imprisoned again in 1542 and 1544 because of various works he
had written or published, the latter including a French New Testament; but both times the king ordered him released. And some of
his works were burned by order of the Parlement of Paris in 1543.

In 1546 he was arrested once more, and in the late summer he was tortured, strangled, and burned.

Dolet remains a mystery. He was charged with atheism by the Parlement, and Calvin called him a blasphemer. However, he was a notable publisher of religious literature, and he often advocated regular reading of the Scriptures. He was not a great writer, but as a scholar and especially as a printer he was an important contributor to the progress of the French Renaissance. In sum, he appears to have been an intemperate and aggressive disputant, who would not compromise his convictions and whose violence of character alienated both Roman Catholics and Protestants. As such, he was perhaps less a martyr to the cause of religious freedom than an exponent of the assertive individualism of the Renaissance.


ON THE LAST day of March 1547, Francis I died. He was succeeded by his son Henry II (1547–1559), a morose and sullen prince whose chief characteristics, aside from a love of violent sport, appear to have been religious bigotry and a willingness to be dominated by stronger personalities. He also held the conviction that religious dissidence was dangerous to his authority. Hence, to the usual coronation oath to protect and defend the Church he added special personal vows to extirpate heresy. He soon intensified the repression that had characterized the last years of his father's reign.

Already in October 1547, just six months after Francis I's death, the new king established in the Parlement of Paris a special court for questions of heresy, which soon came to be called the *chambre ardente*—the "burning court." During the two and one half years of its existence, down to January 1550 when many of its functions were transferred to ecclesiastical tribunals, this court pronounced five hundred condemnations, sixty of them death by burning. If its victims promised not to try to address the crowd that always turned out to witness a public execution, they were strangled first; otherwise, they had their tongues cut out and were then burned alive. Clearly the king was taking his oath seriously.

A few years later Henry II tried to further coordinate a major campaign against the Reform movement with the Edict of

Châteaubriand, which he issued on 27 June 1551. In a lengthy preamble the king asserted that heresy had spread like a vile plague across much of the kingdom and through all social classes, and he exhorted all good Catholics to rally to God's cause in eliminating it. Then in forty-six articles that followed, he laid out a new plan of attack. He attempted better to differentiate the functions of secular and ecclesiastical courts so as to avoid jurisdictional quarrels. He commanded that no appeals for mercy be allowed in heresy convictions. He stiffened the censorship of publication and the laws governing the book trade. He denounced private Bible reading as a source of false interpretation. He enjoined all public officials to seek out and prosecute heresy wherever it might be found; and he demanded that anyone having knowledge of heretical activity give evidence, promising informers one third of all property confiscated in consequence of their action instead of one fourth as in the past. He commanded all good subjects to attend mass regularly and reverently. He announced that henceforth testimonials of good religious character would be required for all public appointments, especially in the judiciary and in educational posts. And he forbade all communication with refugees in Geneva, ordering their property confiscated.

These measures proved no more effective than earlier ones in halting the spread of heresy. In 1557 the king resolved to introduce the dreaded Inquisition into France, and he so informed his ambassador in Rome. The pope then sent Henry a consecrated sword to honor his decision. The opposition of the deeply entrenched French judicial bodies, which feared incursions upon their jurisdictions, blocked this project, and Henry had to settle for strengthening existing methods and institutions. Hence, in the Edict of Compiègne of 1557 he expanded the role of secular courts to include all cases which involved any public scandal; and he commanded that there be a single penalty for heresy—death (in June 1559 further specified as death by burning).

Nevertheless, the Reform movement continued to grow. Its adherents in Paris, braving the king's displeasure, held regular meetings in private homes. It was one of these that triggered the next incident. On 4 September 1557 some Calvinist worshippers (contemporary sources claim three to four hundred of them, but this figure probably is exaggerated) were gathered in a house on the rue St. Jacques, where they were discovered by some students from a nearby college. The authorities were alerted, and a crowd gathered, surrounding the house. Some of the Protestants fought their way out and fled; others escaped through back gardens and alleys. But one hundred and thirty-five, among them many women, were arrested. Several had their tongues cut out and were burned, including one young woman granted the "mercy" of being strangled first—but only after her feet and face were "seared with a torch."

This "Affair of the rue St. Jacques" soon acquired international significance. Not only did Calvin write letters of encouragement to the Paris Reformed congregation and especially to the prisoners, but he and other prominent Evangelical leaders also succeeded in persuading several of Henry's Protestant German and Swiss allies to intercede on behalf of those arrested. They asked the king to moderate his policy, and in November he did order the release of some of the surviving prisoners. Naturally the monarch was not at all pleased with this turn of events. While he was able to bury the immediate issue in protracted discussions, this development may have been significant in his decision to end his foreign wars and to focus upon domestic problems.

Certainly French Protestants saw international peace as a threat to themselves. Already in 1558, when peace talks had just begun, Calvin received a letter from France which claimed that if peace were made the king would "turn all his strength against the Protestants, a fact which he does not hide." A pastor writing to Calvin in July 1559, three months after the peace had been signed, claimed that the king had a long list of persons to be arrested as soon as the royal marriages which were a part of the treaties had been accomplished. It is possible that Protestant fears were exaggerated, of course; but it is significant that the prominent Cardinal of Lorraine told the Parlement of Paris that the king was determined upon peace so as to be able to exterminate heresy in his own kingdom.

The king's foreign policy was not decided only by his domestic religious goals. In the late 1550s many circumstances combined to make peace both more desirable and more feasible than it had been for many years. Most important were the transformation of the Habsburg position, the changing role of England, and fiscal pressures.

Though an intelligent, hard-working ruler, Charles V nonetheless was given to grandiose dreams of universal empire that were in conflict with the rising national consciousness that animated many sixteenth-century Europeans. He was, moreover, a dedicated Catholic quite unreconciled to the establishment of a legal position for heresy. As a result, his ambitions outstripped his resources, especially as he also had to contend with the Turks on his eastern frontiers. By the 1550s he was stretched to the breaking point. In 1551 an army of German Protestant princes defeated him in south Germany. The next year French forces on the western borders of the Holy Roman Empire captured Metz, an important city on the Moselle River, and Charles' efforts to retake it failed. Then in 1554 the papacy passed into the hands of Paul IV, who was known to be violently anti-Habsburg. Capping it all, Charles' health was failing as he was increasingly wracked by painful gout. Finally he had to admit that he no longer could carry on. In 1554 and 1555 he abdicated his many titles and sought tranquility in Spain, where he lived in retirement until his death in 1558.

In his German lands Charles was succeeded by his brother Ferdinand I (1556–1564) who was already King of Bohemia and Hungary and often had served as Charles' deputy in Germany. As Charles turned more and more authority over to him in the 1550s, Ferdinand sought compromise with the Lutheran princes. The Peace of Augsburg of 1555 was largely his personal achievement. By allowing the princes to choose between Roman Catholicism and Lutheranism for their states, Ferdinand brought a temporary end to the German religious wars and reduced the opportunities for foreign intervention in the Holy Roman Empire.

In his western lands, the overseas territories, and Italy, Charles V was succeeded by his son, who as Philip II of Spain (1556–1598) was largely to dominate western European affairs for the last half of the sixteenth century. Philip faced a variety of complex problems. He had to grapple with the development of the empire in the Americas; he was the major Christian power on the Mediterranean and had to contend with both Ottoman fleets and Barbary pirates. The war with France left his northern Italian and southern Netherlands territories constantly threatened. As prince consort of Mary Tudor, Queen of England since 1553, he also had a major role in the effort to return England to the Roman Catholic Church.

Such was the situation that Henry II faced. The great Habsburg holdings finally were divided; and Germany was war-torn and exhausted, somewhat easing the pressure on France from the east. However, in Italy Henry's fortunes were at a low ebb as Spanish viceroys governed in Milan and Naples—though the new pope represented some increment to anti-Habsburg interests. Spain remained a great and threatening power, a threat that became real in 1557 when Spanish troops took St. Quentin on the Somme River, not far north of Paris. Fortunately for Henry, he was able to interpose an army that prevented the Spaniards from marching on Paris, and they had to content themselves with burning Noyon—Calvin's old home—before winter ended campaigning. A royal marriage had put England into the enemy camp, with Queen Mary declaring war on the King of France in 1557. The first round in that struggle went to France in the form of the capture of Calais, the last English stronghold on the Continent.

On balance, Henry II was momentarily secure, but the future was uncertain. His German allies had little incentive to fight further; the Spanish position in Italy, if not impregnable, was very strong; the Spanish forces in the Netherlands were always dangerous; and England might mount a major offensive at any time. Furthermore, Henry had run out of money. Hence, the military situation and financial exigencies as well as the goals of the king's religious policy pressed him to make peace. The result was the Treaty of Câteau-Cambrésis, signed in April 1559.

It is impossible to estimate how great an effect Henry's desire to move strongly against religious dissenters had upon his foreign policy. However, it is indisputable that he quickly took advantage of foreign peace to prepare a new campaign against heresy. Moreover, the mood of confrontation was further embittered on 25 May—just seven weeks after the conclusion of the Treaty of Câteau-Cambrésis. On that date French Evangelical Christians opened a four-day national synod in Paris, during which they adopted a common Confession of Faith and a set of Rules of Discipline, modeled on Geneva. It was an undercover meeting, of course, supposedly very secret, but so large and significant an assembly could not maintain absolute security, and the king heard of it.

Henry II made the next move. After years of ferocious persecution a moderate party had developed in the Parlement of Paris. Its adherents appear to have been a mixed lot—Evangelical sympathizers, Catholics who believed in toleration, and members of the judiciary less concerned for religion than for the traditional jurisdictions and roles of the high court. In any case, the Parlement seemed no longer to share the king's ardor, and he reacted quickly.

In early summer a debate developed in the Parlement concerning the severity of measures to be undertaken against heresy. On 10 June Henry II—accompanied by French cardinals and high officers of the Crown—entered the court and commanded that the discussions continue in his presence. One of the moderates, Anne du Bourg, son of a former chancellor of the realm, with perhaps more courage than wisdom opposed the persecutions. He observed that it was "no small thing to condemn those who, amidst the flames, invoke the name of Jesus Christ." After a brief consultation with his advisors, the king ordered du Bourg and several of his colleagues arrested; others made their submission or fled. It was, in effect, a royal *coup d'état*. The king had decided upon enforced conformity, and he would tolerate no opposition. Expressing himself unreservedly, in the first days of July he wrote to his ambassador in Rome that he hoped "to punish, chastise, and extirpate" heresy. In December, in obedience to the king's command, du Bourg was burned at the stake.

By the time of du Bourg's execution, however, the situation had changed drastically, for Henry II was dead. The Treaty of Câteau-Cambrésis had included provisions for marriages of French princesses, one to the King of Spain (Philip II being a widower after the death of Mary Tudor in 1558) and one to the Duke of Savoy. On 30 June, among the festivities celebrating these marriages, Henry II took part in a tournament. In the course of it his opponent's lance shattered, and a splinter penetrated the king's left eye; he fought for his life for several days, but in the small hours of 10 July Henry II died. In France as on the international scene, a new era had dawned.

# Chapter Four

# The Reformed Church Emerges

IN MANY WAYS 1559 was a pivotal year for France. It was marked by the achievement of peace in the seemingly endless struggle between the French kings and the Habsburgs. It witnessed the unexpected death of the King of France and the confusion resulting from the succession of a young prince in the keeping of a foreign Queen Mother and ambitious and competitive aristocrats. It also was the year of the first national synod of French Evangelicals. Until then they could hardly have been called a Church but only a diffuse movement of disturbed Christians who recognized one another as sharing certain vague concerns. These included the clarification and purification of Christian doctrine on a Scriptural base, reform of the morals and standards of Church practice, and greater involvement of the individual layman in personal religious experience. Hence, 1559 is a good point at which to pause to consider in greater detail the evolution of the French Reform movement—its adherents, its principles and its organization.

As previously noted, a vast restiveness, a sort of religious hunger, had permeated western Christendom since the thirteenth century, and the established Church had been able to contain and channel only some elements of it. For those who desired to give themselves entirely to the religious life, monasteries of varying degrees of severity offered opportunities for withdrawal to prayer, hard labor and contemplation. For those moved by Christian char-

51

ity and love to serve their fellow man, the mendicant orders—
primarily the Dominicans and the Franciscans—offered different
possibilities. But for those who desired to live as involved and
committed Christians in a workaday world—with the usual responsibilities of household and family, of job and taxes and war—and
who sought in that world the peace and solace of religious conviction, the Church's offerings commonly were rather shallow and for
many were unsatisfactory.

Christianity is by no means alone among the world's great
religions in experiencing a conflict between order-power relationships on the one hand and love-experience relationships on the
other. The former are built around authority, hierarchy, reason,
and stability, the latter around individual commitment, personal
experience, intuition, and ferment. The Roman Catholic Church of
the late medieval era was committed almost wholly to the first of
these approaches. Historically it had proved to be both comprehensible and satisfactory to a laity and clergy mostly caught up
in a world of hierarchical relationships of peasant and lord and of
lord and overlord, of priest and bishop and of bishop and high
prelate.

But by the sixteenth century the religious ferment first notable
in the late twelfth and early thirteenth centuries had reached crisis
proportions in an ever more complex world of burgeoning towns
and merchants classes, of overseas explorations and discoveries,
and of cultural and linguistic developments that accentuated the
emergence of national societies. Among these increasing uncertainties, many people, both lay and clerical, sought a closer relationship
with God, a religion at the same time demanding and reassuring,
inspiring but comprehensible. By contrast, the established Church
offered only mysteries and miracles celebrated in a language incomprehensible to most, interpreted by an anointed and especially
garbed elite set apart from the rest of mankind, and presented in an
atmosphere of pomp and mechanical ceremony that reduced the
worshipper to an observer rather than a participant. Compounding
the malaise arising from all this, increasing mobility and improved
communications throughout European society resulted in disturbing whispers—and sometimes outcries—of malfeasance in high
places: of priests who did not know the meaning of the Latin they

mumbled, of bishops who bought their positions, and of popes with mistresses and illegitimate offspring. In both doctrine and practice the early sixteenth-century Church posed problems to excite the concern of many Christians. Nowhere was this so more than in France where the staffing of the Church had just become a part of the royal system of patronage, and the pope appeared interested only in his revenues from the French dioceses.

Not surprisingly, then, French critics and reformers found an eager audience. They ranged from intellectually and Scripturally oriented Christians sensitive to the interpretive challenges posed by Lefèvre d'Etaples, or at least eager to read and ponder the Biblical texts that he made available in a language they could comprehend, to those who hungered for the direct experience of guilt, repentance, forgiveness, and hope that could be evoked by the sermons of preachers like Farel.

A major element in the growth of the reform movement appears to have been priests and monks won over to the new ideas. They were, after all, more acquainted than the society at large with problems and abuses; and many of them were in orders in the first place because of sincere religious commitment. Moreover, many of them were in a position to preach and teach and to attract audiences easily. These men were reinforced, especially from about the middle 1540s, by scores of preachers of unquenchable zeal who had trained abroad. Their existence was difficult, their lives always in danger. Despite this, they swarmed across France. At first they preached and taught in forest glades and obscure country houses. Then they became bolder and entered the cities, occasionally even preaching publicly. They are difficult to follow, for they were pursued by the authorities and consequently changed their names often or went underground. But they do seem to have been very numerous.

Backing up these personal missions were books, pamphlets, letters, and placards. Printing with movable type was a relatively new craft, at most a century old. Its invention as a technique for mass-producing reading materials usually is attributed to Johann Gutenberg of Mainz, about 1440, though he was only one of the most successful of many independent experimenters in Germany, the Netherlands, Switzerland, France, and Italy in the mid-fifteenth century. In fact, rapidly expanding university populations and the constant growth of a literate middle class had created a considerable market demand just as technical progress in metallurgy and paper-making made the essentials of print and printable surfaces more available. Consequently, the printing trade expanded rapidly. Such cities as Basel and Venice earned Europe-wide reputations for the quality of their work. Thus, the sixteenth-century critics and reformers found ready to hand a weapon not available to many of their predecessors, and they seized upon it with enthusiasm.

That the establishment quickly recognized the potential power of the printing press is clear. Reacting to the "Night of the Placards," in January 1535 Francis I ordered that all bookstores be closed and that all publishing cease. He only permitted resumption of the book trade a month later when a mechanism for censorship had been created in the Parlement of Paris. In December 1547 Henry II reinforced this censorship law and also fulminated against illegal imports from "Geneva, Germany, and other foreign places": and in 1551 his Edict of Châteaubriand further tightened controls. Moreover, these major pieces of legislation were supplemented by a host of lesser official actions: administrative regulations banning the import of published materials without a license; censure of undesirable books by the Sorbonne; and the public burning of "dangerous" works by order of the Parlement. Nonetheless, illicit reading material circulated widely, some of it published secretly in France (as was Servetus' book, for instance) and some of it smuggled into the kingdom from foreign presses.

In March 1549 unlicensed books from the presses of two French publishers were seized in Paris to prevent their distribution. Notable among these were some works of Erasmus, some French translations from the Bible and a collection of Psalms. As the only really subversive item was a translation of some of Luther's tracts, the authorities do not appear to have gone beyond simple confiscation in this case. Three years later in Toulouse, however, some confiscated books were burned. About the same time, in the Garonne Valley not far east of Bordeaux, a bookseller and his brother-in-law were sentenced to death for handling forbidden works. Subsequently, there were seizures of books, often including the *Geneva Catechism*, in many towns of the south. In Montpellier a wandering bookpeddler was imprisoned because of the material he carried.

CAROLVS V. DEI GRATIA ROMANORVM IMPERATOR;
HISPANIARVM, INDIARVM, NEAPOLIS ET SICILIÆ REX;
DVX BVRGVNDIÆ, BRABANTIÆ; COMES FLANDRIÆ, HOLLANDIÆ etc.

Charles V von Habsburg, Holy Roman Emperor

Francis I de Valois, King of France

Charles VIII de Valois, King of France

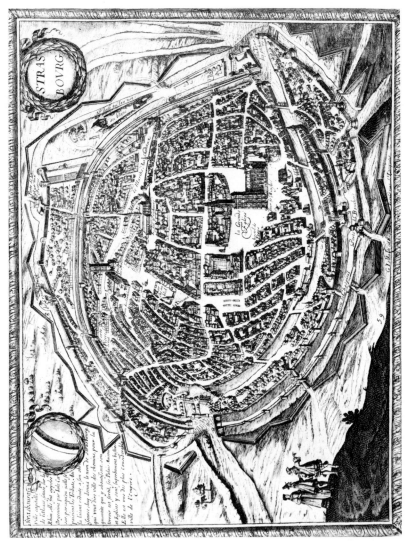

Plan of Strasbourg

Death of King Henry II, 30 June 1559

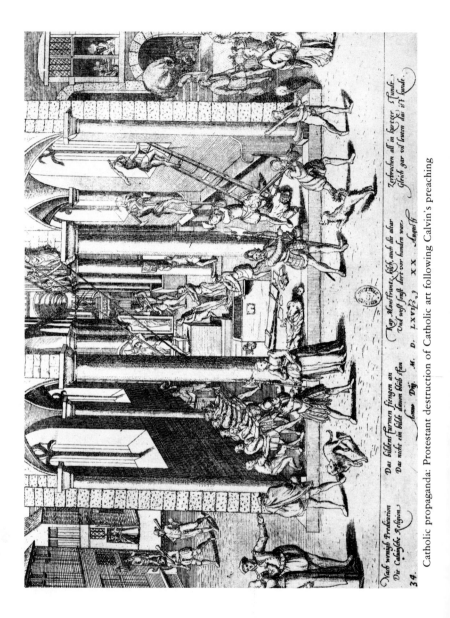

Nach wenig Prediation     Das bildens sturmen fiengen an     Key Monstrantz, Kelch, auch die altar     Zerbrechen all in kurtzer Stunde,
Die Calvinische Religion          Das nicht im bildt seinen bleib stan     Und weiß sonst dort vor hinden war.     Gleich gar vil leuten das ist kunde.

34.                                              Anno Dñi. M. D. LXVI₃₃   xx Augusti

Catholic propaganda: Protestant destruction of Catholic art following Calvin's preaching

View of Geneva: The large church at the upper right is St. Pierre, where Calvin preached

Execution of Anne du Bourg, December 1559. As it was found that heretics burned at the stake died too quickly, by the late 1550s it became common to suspend them over the fire by a rope or in cages so they could be dipped in and out of the flames.

Marguerite de Valois, née le 11 Avril
1492. Elle était sœur de François 1er
et femme de Henri d'Albret.

Marguerite de Valois, duchesse d'Angoulême, Queen of Navarre

•24•

Louise of Savoy, duchesse d'Angoulême, Queen-Regent of France

Jacques Le Febvre d'Etaples

Guillaume Budé

Protestants burned in front of Notre Dame de Paris, 1549

Guillaume Briçonnet, Évesque de
Meaux, & Abbé de St. Germain
des prez les Paris

Guillaume Briçonnet, Bishop of Meaux

Michael Servetus

Catholic propaganda: Horrible cruelties perpetrated by Protestants, burning churches and desecrating tombs

William Farel

John Calvin

*ncta dolans ad amuſſim, examino cuncta Dolet*
*Me tamen & rurſus Muſica turba dolat.*

Etienne Dolet

Theodore de Beza

Henry II de Valois, King of France

NEC SPE NEC METV.

Titianus pinxit.

PHILIPPE 11. du nom Roy d'Espagne et
femmes, mais il n'eut enfans suruiuans
qui estoit ELISABETH de Valois, fille
CLAIRE EVGENIE, mariée a ALBERT
EMANVEL, Duc de Sauoÿe. Sa quattriesme
PHILIPPE V. Mourut en l'Escurial de St.

IV. des Ducs de Brabant, eut quattre
que des deux : asçauoir de sa troisieme,
du Roy de France, il eut ISABELLE
d'Austriche, et CATHARINE a CHARLES
femme ANNE d'Austriche luy engendra
Laurent l'an 1598.

Pet. de Iode sculp.

Philip II von Habsburg, King of Spain

The theater also came under suspicion, in at least some instances apparently justly as playwrights mocked debauched clergy and made jokes about lazy and ignorant monks—all to the great delight of their audiences but to the displeasure of the authorities. In the 1550s controls were extended to drama by regulations of the Parlement requiring that scripts be submitted to royal officers and local bishops before performances were authorized. Municipal magistrates were held responsible and were susceptible to heavy fines if they allowed "scandalous performances." Repression in the theater does not appear to have gone much beyond these formal pronouncements, however, though occasionally a playwright was burned in effigy. Apparently they were not so careless as to await arrest if their performances caused a stir.

For an overall picture of the spread of the Reform, one really ought to look to the local level, but this is extremely difficult. Obviously, faced with violent repression, the adherents of the Reform usually sought to hide themselves. As they had no national organization, there were no registers or central archives. Among the most commonly used sources for the growth of French Protestantism are judicial records, listing arrests and prosecutions; but they pose some problems. Only eight of the French provinces had regional high courts, parlements. Probably these have attracted disproportionate attention, while areas where lesser courts and administrative officers operated on a day to day and case to case basis are underestimated. In addition, there is no guarantee—quite the contrary—that there was any evenness of application of the law from one of these courts to another. One region could suffer fervent persecutors, and therefore see much litigation, while another experienced tolerant or even sympathetic judges.

Happily there are other sources, though they sometimes defy integration. These include diaries and personal papers, and letters to and from Calvin (especially after about the mid-1540s), as well as the correspondence of other prominent reformers; but these depend too heavily upon the accidents of survival to allow confident generalization. The student of these problems is endlessly indebted to the many local historical societies in France for the publication of numerous regional studies, and even more to the Society for the History of French Protestantism whose *Bulletin* is without parallel for such interests. And yet, when all is said it is still necessary to admit that where patterns of growth are concerned precise statistics remain out of reach and that even conclusions of a general nature are rather tentative.

Until the early 1540s, or even the middle of that decade, persecution outside of Paris was too sporadic and the instances of it too scattered to permit any confident generalizations by region. The tendency of authorities to lump all religious dissenters together as "Lutherans" further clouds the picture. During the reign of Henry II, however, incidents became much more frequent. While this development might be explained to some extent by the king's zeal for persecution, the wide distribution of cases across the kingdom precludes offering this as a total explanation.

In the persecutions of the late 1540s and the 1550s some patterns become discernible. The high rate of activity in the area of Paris and the Loire Valley doubtless indicates the greater effectiveness of the king's will in those central areas of his domains, but it also reflects the rather heavy concentration of intellectual life that characterized the northern Renaissance. In Italy intellectual and cultural activity had developed in several cities, of which Florence, Rome, Venice, and Milan were only the most important. In France, as in England and later in Scandinavia, monarchical centralization and royal domination of patronage tended to focus cultural life in those areas where the king's government sat and where his Court moved.

In France, of course, that meant the Paris region, where the king's principal residences stood. These include Fontainebleau, which Francis I built in the beautiful woods some thirty-five miles southeast of the capital, and the stunning Renaissance châteaux of Chambord and Chenonceaux on the Loire. Hence, even if this part of the kingdom, under the persecuting monarch's own hand, was one of the most dangerous for religious dissenters, it also was one where they gathered thickly. There were great universities—Paris and Orléans most notably—which attracted restless, questing minds. There the king and some of the great nobles who clustered around him had the means and the will to support artists and writers, architects and printers, poets and musicians. Some of these then as now were radicals and rebels against accepted truths. There the law courts and many administrative offices offered employment to the literate, to hundreds of clerks and scribes, many of them dull scribblers but some with intellectual pretensions, and all of them capable of reading the controversial new religious material. Some highly developed provincial centers experienced comparable phenomena, though usually to a lesser degree. The important university towns of Grenoble and Toulouse both suffered continuous religious turmoil through the late 1540s and the 1550s; and in such scattered places as Rouen, La Rochelle, Bordeaux and Nîmes, Church authorities complained constantly, and the numbers of cases brought before the courts lend credence to their complaints.

Away from the Court and notable university centers, if there is any single factor that might be linked tentatively with enthusiasm for Reform doctrines, it is a high level of commercial activity. Ever since the eminent German social scientist Max Weber first published *The Protestant Ethic and the Spirit of Capitalism* in the early years of the twentieth century, volumes have been written concerning the relationship of Protestantism in general and Calvinism in particular to the growth of capitalism. There are extremists on many sides of the argument. Some would make the predestinarian mentality and Calvinist business ethics the creators of capitalism. Some would present Calvinism as a sort of spiritual rationalization of capitalism, the almost inevitable cult of the business classes. Yet others find no more relevance between capitalism and Calvinism than between capitalism and Catholicism. Some of these arguments are rather trivial; some are basically sensible but overextended. Happily it is not necessary to re-examine the whole controversy here.

Part of the problem is, of course, a matter of definition. The acquisitive urge seems to be at least as old as mankind, but capitalism is more complex. A basic working definition of capitalism, to be meaningful, must include at least some concept of acquisition not for consumption but for reinvestment and some idea of a business enterprise as a sort of organic entity to be nurtured for growth and not merely drained of profits. Under such a definition it is difficult to avoid the conclusion that Calvinism and capitalism were highly compatible. It is not so much a question of which fathered which as it is of their being complementary modes of thought.

Lutheran and Roman Catholic intellectuals were as aware as their Evangelical rivals of the socio-economic evolution taking place in their world and of its implications for both social and personal ethics. But Roman Catholic thinkers, deep-rooted in scholasticism, and followers of Luther—who was fundamentally very conservative—tended to view change with suspicion, innovation with hostility. After all, the Catholic Church treasured tradition. And Luther sought no novelty; he claimed to be *restoring* the faith to its pristine form. Both Catholicism and Lutheranism thus were part of what might be called the traditional agrarian-aristocratic society. By contrast, Calvinism was much better equipped to cope with a changing world.

The importance of the fact that Calvin was French already has been noted. It is equally important that he was urban, that he came from a busy commercial town and spent most of his life in such towns—Noyon, Paris, Orléans, Strasbourg, and Geneva. This does not mean that Calvin was limited to a middle-class view of society or that he easily accepted all of the goals and practices of townsmen; far from it. It does mean, however, that he did not find town life and commercial activity strange, did not think that because they differed from the older relationships of lords and peasants they were dangerous and should be regarded with suspicion.

Thus, while Catholic and Lutheran thinkers tended to regard the socio-economic evolution of the sixteenth century with a certain hostility, Calvin never doubted that these changes, like everything else in the world, could be bent to God's service. Consequently, Calvin could join with more conservative Christian thinkers in opposing usury—loansharking in modern parlance—but could distinguish between usury and the business of lending at interest, recognizing the latter as legitimate commercial activity within certain conditions. He could damn the *arrivist* behavior of social climbers as roundly as anyone, but he could admire the successful businessmen who continued a modest Christian life.

Congeniality rather than cause and effect, then, is probably the best explanation of the relationship between Calvinism and capitalism, and it was profound. Calvin's predestinarianism divided mankind into the Elect, whom God intended—for his own mysterious reasons—to save, and the rest, who were damned. This proved to be a powerful dynamic. The individual could never *know* that he was of the Elect, but he could seek signs of it; and if he enjoyed material success he might hope it was a mark of God's blessing upon one of His chosen. Thus, one should live frugally and work hard, not for security or comfort but to bear witness, to demonstrate to the ungodly the power of God's blessing, and to find some encouragement for hopes of salvation.

Both Catholic and Lutheran social ethics certainly endorsed hard work; but they tended to the view that a man should content himself in the station to which he was born, should fulfill himself and meet his Christian obligations by honest labor *within* that place. By contrast, Calvinist conceptions of vocation clearly could justify considerable social mobility so long as the reasons were proper and the life-style appropriate. Not surprisingly, then, Calvinism appealed strongly, though not exclusively, to middle-class people. It spread rapidly along the trade routes from Geneva, which probably accounts for its early strength in the towns along the Rhône Valley and the highways of the south of France.

It is difficult to establish the founding dates for Protestant churches, as distinct from irregular meetings of Evangelical believers for worship, Bible readings, or sermons by itinerant preachers. In fact, there is even some problem in determining what constituted an early "church." In his extensive correspondence with French congregations, Calvin stressed the importance of organization, not just to present a stronger opposition to enemies and oppressors but also to promote better internal order and to further propagation of the faith. He even expressed some disapproval of the ministration of the sacrament to Evangelical congregations that were not organized into "churches" in which purity of faith and propriety of morals could be disciplined. But while Calvin outlined clearly what should be the ultimate organizational goals of a Calvinist congregation, he never specified at what point short of these goals it qualified as a proper church.

The ideal organization prescribed by Calvin was, not surprisingly, the Geneva model. He proposed that a congregation should elect a consistory composed of elders and deacons. The former were to establish the rules of morality and to enforce discipline, the latter to bear much of the church's social responsibility such as visitations to the poor and the sick as well as assisting the minister. This consistory should then select and arrange a stipend for a minister, or pastor, with assistants if the size of the congregation warranted it. Ministers were expected to preach often, administer the sacraments regularly, oversee education, social welfare work and community organization and preside over meetings of the consistory. Thus, the "church" would be tightly organized, self-contained, and self-sustaining.

In fact, however, early French Calvinist churches often fell far short of this goal. They lacked consistories, depending upon ministers whom Calvin sent to them, and were unable to undertake much by way of welfare work or education beyond simple catechizing because of the necessity to remain hidden. Thus, when sixteenth-century Protestant sources speak proudly of the foundation of a new church, they may mean only that a loosely structured Evangelical community finally had recruited a regular minister, or had been sent one by Calvin. Often they continued to meet in private homes, changing location often, while the full burden of instruction and discipline fell upon the new pastor.

Nonetheless, despite these uncertainties, it is clear that organized churches proliferated during the 1540s and especially in the 1550s. In Meaux, which had a very early connection with the Reform, of course, the arrests and sentences of 1546 appear to have fallen upon a well-developed church. While it was set back by the terrible persecution of 1546, it was reorganized and flourishing in 1555. In the Loire Valley the earliest incontestable foundation was the church of Orléans in 1557, with a half-dozen others in nearby towns by 1559, but there were very active irregular congregations well before that.

In the south, there was a Reformed congregation at Nîmes as early as 1547 which quickly established correspondence with Calvin and developed its organization along the lines he advised, a pattern repeated a few years later at Castres. And in Montauban the Reform was so successful that by the early 1550s even the local clergy had joined the new church.

Meanwhile, in the north an official in Noyon claimed in 1549 that there were Reformed congregations scattered all across Picardy. Organized churches in both Noyon itself and in Amiens can be dated from 1555, with another dozen emerging in surrounding communities in the latter half of the decade.

In the west, the congregation of Poitiers was corresponding with Calvin about organization as early as 1554, and the next year he sent them a minister from Geneva. By 1559 there also was a well-developed church at Limoges. Persecutions and executions blocked a first effort at organization in La Rochelle in 1552, but in the autumn of 1558 a church complete with consistory was formed. In Normandy, Rouen saw a very early foundation—some time in the middle 1540s. A decade later several more had emerged. In Brittany, while there appears to have been little activity until the late 1550s, by 1559 two ministers from Geneva were well established.

Paris posed a situation of particular complexity. As the administrative and cultural center of the kingdom it probably supported the most intense cultural and religious activity. But it also was the heart of the opposition—represented by the king, the Sorbonne, the Parlement, an efficient Catholic parish organization, a hostile municipal government with an effective police force, and a rather fanatically Catholic and potentially violent urban population. Despite all this, Evangelical Christianity won many supporters. In the mid-1550s they finally acquired some organization. In 1556 there were the rudiments of a church, with pastors sent from Geneva; and by 1557 there was the full apparatus of elders, deacons and consistory.

The Paris church was particularly controversial, of course, as it was situated in the stronghold of the opposition, and it experienced considerable overt conflict, some of which its members seemed to invite. Despite the "Affair of the rue St. Jacques" in September 1557, for instance, and its terrible sequel of public executions, in May 1558 there was a new confrontation. Amid crowds strolling the open area of the Pré-aux-Clercs, a popular gathering place on the left bank of the Seine beyond the city walls, Calvinist demonstrators began chanting Psalms, in which they were joined by many in the crowd. Afterwards they marched off in a sort of impromptu parade, in which a number of well-born gentlemen participated.

Church authorities were scandalized and organized Catholic processions; disturbed university officials ordered the student body to special prayers; the Parlement issued a new injunction against such demonstrations; and the king was said to be infuriated. It was a brave public witness and a bold show of strength but hardly wise.

The national organization of the Reformed Church, which was to come to maturity in 1559, thus grew naturally out of developments of the late 1550s. The rapid expansion of congregations, Calvin's frequent exhortations concerning organization and discipline, the emergence of a common pattern of ministers and consistories on the Geneva model and often in regular contact with Geneva, and mounting opposition and persecution all pushed French Evangelicals toward the creation of some sort of national framework.

The first step toward a single, national representation came from Calvin, who in November 1557 sent Henry II a "Confession of Faith" outlining the doctrines of Calvinism. He argued that they were not in conflict with any Christian principle maintained by the Catholic Church and begged a sympathetic consideration from the king and his council. This action was, of course, entirely in keeping with Calvin's effort to win royal toleration for the Reform two decades earlier, when he had included the same sort of plea to Francis I in the dedicatory preface of his *Institutes*. This time the motivation was more immediate. In late 1557 organized and disciplined Evangelical churches existed all over France, with more appearing all the time. With the nation ruled by a king far more fanatical and oppressive than Francis I, and with religious clashes multiplying within France, the growing likelihood of an early international peace increased the probability of intensified persecution. In brief, a confrontation was looming, and perhaps Calvin hoped to head it off.

In addition, Calvin may have felt his leadership of the French Reformed churches threatened. There was no apparatus linking the French churches with one another, no mechanism to resolve doctrinal disputes within or among them other than reference to Calvin himself. This was a slow and cumbersome procedure but one which assured his detailed supervision. There were, however, some informal visits of ministers from one congregation to another, sometimes on invitation to mediate disputes. This mechanism was used to settle a particularly serious quarrel about predestination in the Church at Poitiers in 1558, when a Parisian minister mediated. It appears that these contacts, the disagreements, and the increasingly threatening political atmosphere evoked discussions of the desirability of a general assembly to draft an official Confession of Faith and to establish a national organization. When correspondents communicated this idea to Calvin, however, he replied only that he found the enthusiasm misplaced and the idea displeasing. Perhaps his acquaintance with a quarter century of theological fragmentation in central Europe and the ultimate failure of such men as Melanchthon and Bucer to unify the German and Swiss Reformations caused him to fear an assembly of French theologians and to believe that the French Reform was safer in his own hands. In any case, he opposed the notion initially.

Nonetheless, in May 1559, apparently on the initiative of the Paris Church, ministers and elders from many parts of France gathered in a house in a suburb of the capital, the Faubourg St. Germain, and Calvin sent three delegates. Besides Paris itself, eleven congregations—mostly from northern and western France—have been identified. However, many others were represented, perhaps as many as fifty, though the total of seventy-two given by one contemporary document is almost certainly exaggerated.

On 29 May, the fourth day of deliberations, a Confession of Faith of forty articles was adopted. Though the synod agreed that it should be a confidential document, as it would be likely to aggravate religious tensions, before the year was over it had been printed and was circulating widely. In fact, it was very much the "Confession" which Calvin had written and sent to the king in 1557, with some additions and a few minor modifications, such as a statement of submission to civil authority and a declaration of loyalty to the crown. The source of its inspiration is not surprising, for most of the ministers in attendance had trained under Calvin in Geneva. The assembly also adopted a set of "Rules of Discipline." As might be expected, the Geneva model of local organization was endorsed. Provision was made for provincial and general synods—with unequivocal assertion that no church should enjoy any special superiority or privilege over others.

The adoption of the "Confession" and "Rules" marked the emergence into maturity of the French Reformed Church. After four decades of a growing Reform movement, the Covenant was made, and the Evangelical Christians scattered across France truly had become "Covenanters," *Huguenots.*

To this point the French Reformation had been unique in Europe. It had engendered no rebellion, had engaged in no political action. It had not depended upon princes—as in Germany, nor upon the Crown—as in England, nor upon popular patriotism—as in Switzerland. The Reform movement comprised many small congregations made up mostly of commoners, though in the very late 1550s it began to win the adherence of a few aristocrats. It recognized no leader except Calvin—whose leadership was spiritual and moral. It had no large-scale organization beyond the general provision for regional and national synods. Despite mounting persecution, it did not even have a plan of defense.

The national synod of 1559 was a significant step forward, but its achievements were hardly more than a beginning. Very shortly much, much more would be needed, for political and social crises were fast overtaking religious development. Mid-sixteenth-century France seethed with problems. Economic development was undercutting many of the traditional feudal bases of society. Royal policies of domestic patronage and foreign war had proved ruinously expensive. Ambitious aristocratic factions jostled for position and influence all across the kingdom and especially at Court. Thus, the controversial growth of French Protestantism was but one of many factors in a highly volatile and potentially explosive situation. As was not unusual in a tradition-oriented monarchy, the stabilizing force that maintained some sort of equilibrium amid these uncertainties was the king. But less than six weeks after the first national synod adjourned, Henry II was dead.

# Part Two
## The Age of
## The Civil Wars

# Chapter Five

# Scenario: The Reign of Francis II

DURING THE YEARS just following the death of Henry II the whole nature of the French Calvinist movement changed, as it became a political force with enormous ramifications on both the domestic and foreign scenes. The chief factor in the Huguenots' involvement in larger crises was their entanglement in the 1560s in the ambitions and rivalries of the turbulent French nobility just when France's problems, both religious and political, were beginning to be subsumed in a broader international struggle.

Only recently have scholars begun to re-examine the sixteenth-century nobility seriously. For too long it has been obscured by interests in the Renaissance, in nascent royal bureaucracies, in economic evolution and urban growth and in emergent national consciousness. But sixteenth-century society owed far more to the legacy of the past, in which the nobility was the central element, than to a nebulous vision of a future comprising bureaucratized royal absolutism, mercantilism, and nationalism.

The French nobility about the middle of the sixteenth century was primarily an elite of men who fought and governed. Their chief ambitions were to win repute as soldiers and to exercise political power. Often brave to a fault, they tended to be aggressive, competitive, and extremely sensitive on matters of honor—too often ready to risk their lives and the kingdom's peace at swordpoint or to turn a minor clash into a vendetta.

Among such people, the king's role depended enormously
upon his capacities for leadership and domination. He truly had to
be "the first soldier of France" and "the first gentleman of France"
to maintain his primacy. On the other hand, the great nobility also
depended heavily upon the king. The place of honor was at the
sovereign's side. An invitation to accompany him or a dismissal
from his presence in disgrace were matters of tremendous importance. Moreover, the nobleman had great need of the king's patronage, not only for his own career but to see his children settled
securely. For the eldest son there were his father's estates, and for
the eldest daughter probably a dowry could be found sufficient to
arrange a good match. But for the support of other children the
noble often had to look to the army and the Church, the king's
commission or the king's nomination.

As medieval society waned, this nobility, especially the lesser
nobles, found themselves threatened by several developments. An
inflationary economy bore hard upon land rents fixed by long
leases. New weapons and the entry of university-trained experts
into government endangered their ancient monopoly of military
and political power; and the expeditions into Italy, in which the
nobles had to participate in order to avoid forfeiting royal favor and
patronage, proved ruinously expensive. As a result, by the middle
of the sixteenth century there had emerged what historians generally describe as "bastard feudalism."

In contrast to earlier medieval hierarchies based upon fief
lands, this transformed feudalism was a vast client system composed of a few great men and hordes of dependents. For despite the
difficulties and disasters suffered by much of the nobility during the
early sixteenth century, a few men close to the king had prospered.
Commanding royal armies, they had shared the booty and ransoms
of rich Italian cities, and they and their relatives had been rewarded
with titles, honors, and power. The lesser nobility had then flocked
to them—accepting posts and pensions in their households and
bodyguards, recommending cousins and neighbors from the provinces, and building whole hierarchies of dependents. As a result,
masses of the French nobility came to be organized under the
leadership of a handful of great families. After Henry II's death

the Huguenots found themselves caught up in the maelstrom of their rivalries and jealousies.

OF THE GREAT families prominent at the French Court, in the mid-sixteenth century the strongest was the House of Guise. Relative newcomers to the French scene, its members had shown enormous talent and energy, and with royal favor they had enjoyed a mercurial rise to power. The family was founded in 1508 when the County of Guise passed to the second son of the Duke of Lorraine, Claude, comte and later duc de Guise (1496–1550). He fought with distinction for Francis I, especially in Italy, where three of his brothers died also fighting for the same cause. Another brother, John, became first cardinal de Lorraine and a prominent member of the French Church. Thus, a whole generation of Guises served the French Crown well.

Claude, the eldest, reaped the benefits. Francis I made him governor of the wealthy provinces of Champagne and Burgundy. After the king's capture at Pavia he was a member of the regency council that worked with Louise of Savoy; and in 1527, shortly after Francis I's return from captivity, he became a duke and peer of the realm. Of the thirteen children he sired, the most important was his eldest legitimate son, François, who became duc de Guise after him. But many of his other sons achieved important positions in the Church. They included two cardinals, an abbot of the powerful Order of Cluny and a Grand Prior of the Knights of Malta in France (a military order). Claude's daughter Mary married King James V of Scotland.

François, second duc de Guise (1519–1563), called *Le Balafré* ("Scarface"), also had a distinguished military record and enjoyed great political influence. No doubt his career was aided by his marriage to a granddaughter of King Louis XII, which made him a cousin of the royal family of France as well as brother-in-law to the King of Scotland. He was Lieutenant-General of the Kingdom for several years, almost a viceroyal appointment. It was he who succeeded in expelling the English from Calais, their last position in France. In 1558 his niece, Mary Stuart, married the heir apparent to the French throne; so the next year he found himself uncle to the Queen of France. Thus, in two generations the Guises had risen from obscurity to occupy first place at the king's side.

The family that might reasonably have expected to hold highest honors next to the king was the House of Bourbon, but in the mid-sixteenth century it was in eclipse. The Bourbons, who could trace their lineage to the tenth century, were cousins by male line to the Kings of France. As princes of the royal blood their influence normally was considerable. But early in the sixteenth century disaster struck the family in the person of Charles III, duc de Bourbon and Constable of France (1490–1527).

After some distinguished military exploits, at the age of twenty-five Bourbon was named constable, supreme commander of the king's forces, by Francis I. Then his relations with the royal family deteriorated. Early in the 1520s Francis I began a lawsuit against him. Resentful of such treatment, and apparently convinced that the king was determined to ruin him, the constable went over to the Emperor Charles V, thus becoming one of the most famous traitors in French history. He served in the emperor's forces for a few years and then died, without sons, in the attack on Rome in 1527. So leadership of the family passed to the scion of a collateral branch, Bourbon-La March-Vendôme.

Antoine, duc de Vendôme (1518–1562), was weak and vacillating, sometimes willing to intrigue but rarely willing to make a commitment. His major achievement was to get the family a royal title by marrying Jeanne d'Albret, heiress to the kingdom of Navarre. Though circumstances later catapulted Antoine into a position of considerable power, his irresolution and his early death gave a large share in directing the fortunes of the House of Bourbon to his wife and to his younger brother, Louis, first prince de Condé (1530–1569). These two showed considerable determination and ability, but despite their efforts the future of the family remained uncertain until the maturity of Antoine's son, Henry, who was only nine years old when his father died in 1562.

The other family of great power and influence at the French Court in the mid-sixteenth century was the House of Montmorency. Also able to trace tenth-century origins, the Montmorencys claimed no kinship with the royal family but rather prided themselves on a tradition of loyal feudal service. Indeed, before the family's extinction in the 1630s it gave the Crown six constables and twelve marshals.

The great figure of the middle sixteenth century was the Constable Anne de Montmorency (1493–1567), an enormously wealthy aristocrat reputed to own six hundred fiefs. A contemporary and companion-in-arms of Claude de Guise, the Constable de Bourbon, and of Francis I himself, Montmorency outlived them all. He died of wounds sustained in his last battle at the age of seventy-four.

In 1522 Montmorency was promoted Marshal of France and was received into the distinguished Order of St. Michel. Then he was appointed to the royal council and became one of the most important men in the kingdom for a decade and a half. In 1538 he was named Constable of France. But he had made potent enemies during his career, and in 1541 he was forced to retire. He retained the friendship of the crown prince, however, and with the change of reign in 1547 he was recalled to the royal service and in 1551 was named duke and peer. So by the time of Henry II's death, Montmorency was a towering figure at Court—a man in his middle sixties, with a respected military reputation, who had survived the fluctuations of royal favor to arrive at even higher honors in the new reign.

AFTER 1559 RESPONSIBILITY for defending the Crown's authority and the interests of the royal House of Valois fell largely upon Catherine de Médicis (1519–1589), widow of Henry II and mother of young Francis II. Like most royal matches, hers had been a marriage of political convenience. It reinforced the French alliance with the papacy and tightened the French connection with the wealthy and influential ruling house of Tuscany in north central Italy. A bride at fourteen, Catherine remained childless for a decade and then produced ten children in rapid succession, of whom four boys and three girls survived the terrible infant mortality of that time. However, Catherine had very little political influence.

Except for a brief appointment as regent, with limited powers, in
1533 while her husband was off campaigning, she rarely exercised
authority before 1559.

Both during her lifetime and afterwards Catherine de Médicis'
reputation suffered from growing anti-Italian sentiments among the
French, who more and more resented the domination of Italian
taste, the primacy of Italian artists and, finally, anything Italian. In
addition, nineteenth-century historians—who showed a peculiar
fascination for plots and conspiracies—enveloped her in a legend of
mystery and intrigue. In fact, she was an intelligent, courageous and
determined queen mother, caught up in very difficult circumstances. A woman and a foreigner in a masculine and ever more
xenophobic environment, she was a neophyte in the most viciously
sophisticated political arena of the kingdom. Despite these hand-
icaps, for three decades Catherine coped so effectively with noble
ambitions, religious turmoil, and foreign threats that the whole
epoch of 1559 to 1589 is known as "The Age of Catherine de
Médicis."

ANOTHER PERSON WHO played a major role in French affairs, but
from a distance, was Philip II, King of Spain. Though clearly
intelligent, pious, and hard-working, Philip sometimes has been
portrayed as a religious fanatic who subordinated all other interests
to his championship of the Counter-Reformation. Modern studies
challenge such a narrow interpretation of him. Certainly he de-
tested heresy, and as monarch of Europe's most powerful Catholic
state he felt a responsibility to defend the Church. But he also was
very much aware of political and dynastic interests, and he pursued
them with equal vigor. Moreover, he was particularly drawn into
the affairs of France. On his deathbed Henry II had written to
Philip begging his friendly concern for Francis II; and on every side
Philip's other interests were affected by the affairs of France.

As former king-consort in England, Philip had a personal as
well as a religious interest in English affairs, and Queen Elizabeth's
succession to the English Crown posed problems. As she was
conceived of a marriage considered illicit by Catholics, because
they did not recognize Henry VIII's divorce, Elizabeth's claim was

insecure. If it could be negated, her strongest rival was Mary Stuart, daughter of James V of Scotland. Mary Stuart was Catholic and could be expected to continue the effort to return England to the Roman fold. But she was also the niece of the duc de Guise and wife of the heir to the French throne. So her accession in England would represent the establishment of a French position in England as well as Scotland, which was quite unacceptable to Philip for secular reasons.

Comparably, in the Netherlands, part of Philip's domains, religious and political issues were closely entwined. The Evangelical Reform had flown swiftly along the great trade routes, recognizing no political boundaries, so heresy was as pressing a concern in the great textile cities of the Netherlands as it was in France. Though the evidence is fragmentary, it appears that Protestants in the southern Netherlands had close contacts with the French Huguenots as well as with Calvin.

In trying to reverse this religious development, however, as well as in administrative reforms, Philip clashed with the strong particularism of the Netherlands. Both the bourgeois patricians who dominated the towns and the old nobility were deeply committed to their traditional privileges. Though they generally had little sympathy for heresy, they were not prepared to bow to unrestricted royal authority. Through a combination of impatience, inflexibility, and incompetent agents Philip's efforts aroused more and more hostility until, in the late 1560s, open rebellion flared. He then had to consider the possibility of foreign intervention.

Hence, Philip found himself in a very awkward position in trying to assess his French interests. Domination of the Crown by the Guises, whose Catholic commitment was beyond question, would minimize the likelihood of any French aid to the Protestants in the Netherlands; but it would increase the likelihood of French involvement in the British Isles. On the other hand, the ascendancy of Protestantism in France not only was personally repugnant to Philip but would raise the spectre of French aid to Netherlands Calvinists and of an Anglo-French combination against Spain. Ultimately the chief result of Philip's French policy was the maintenance of civil strife. He aided the French Catholic party consistently but never in such strength as to assure it a definitive victory.

One consequence was that as the Netherlands revolt intensified and Anglo-Spanish relations worsened, French religious affairs became ever more closely tied to international interests.

THE ATTRACTION OF noblemen to French Calvinism was a gradual and largely unrecorded process which allows neither confident attribution of motive nor precision of dating. The experience of Scotland, the Netherlands, and eastern Europe as well as France, suggests, however, that in the sixteenth century Calvinism exercised a special appeal to social groups that felt themselves repressed, threatened, or in some way frustrated. This description could be applied to much of the French nobility by the middle of the century. Certainly the large numbers of noblemen who turned out to fight for the Huguenot cause shortly after 1559 suggests long recruitment.

The absence of noble names from early lists of victims of persecution proves nothing. On their own lands and in their own châteaux noblemen were relatively independent. In fact many enjoyed "rights of justice," so were more likely to appear as the judges than the judged. Probably in religion as in most things, those nobles who were financially secure did as they pleased while those who were dependent tended to follow the lead of their patrons. The presence of a few noble names in the Genevan refugee lists of the 1550s indicates that sincere personal belief certainly was part of the process and that some noble converts had to give up home and property to maintain their faith, and were willing to do so; but the evidence simply does not permit further generalization concerning the lesser nobility before the 1560s.

In the case of the great nobility the situation is clearer. The House of Guise was unwavering in its commitment to the old Church. When Henry II had proposed to bring the Inquisition to France in 1557, the cardinal de Lorraine was one of the churchmen whom he had intended to direct it. Both the cardinal and his brother, the duc de Guise, were fervent advocates of persecution; and for three decades following Henry II's death the religious dedication of the House of Guise was a major factor in French political life.

The highest ranking aristocrats to be won over to the Calvinist cause were the Bourbons. Antoine de Bourbon's marriage drew him strongly toward the Reformed Church, for Jeanne d'Albret not only continued her mother's policy of protecting religious refugees at Nérac and Pau but professed the Reformed faith herself. As early as 1555 Antoine was reputed to have allowed Calvinists to preach freely in the castle chapel at Nérac. During the next year or two he was reported to have joined a Calvinist procession, carrying a candle, and to have held late night discussions with a Calvinist missionary; and in 1558 he attended some Protestant demonstrations at the Pré-aux-Clercs in Paris. So while his hesitations made his exact position difficult to define, contemporaries clearly counted him a sympathizer of the Reformed Church.

More open in his adherence was Antoine's younger brother, the prince de Condé, who was reared among people with Evangelical sympathies. His marriage in the 1550s to a professed Calvinist confirmed his own commitment. Moreover, despite loyal service in the king's army he had been offered little reward or favor, while the Huguenots were eager for a spokesman and protector more reliable than Antoine de Bourbon. So, from whatever mixture of causes, at the end of Henry II's reign Condé—*Monsieur le Prince,* as the Huguenots called him—generally was considered and sometimes designated himself "Protector of the Reformed Churches."

During the 1550s the new doctrines also won important adherents from a junior branch of the House of Montmorency. Though the old constable himself remained a staunch Roman Catholic and a determined opponent of heresy, three of his sister's sons became Calvinists: Odet, cardinal de Châtillon (1517–1571); Gaspard de Châtillon, comte de Coligny (1519–1572); and François de Coligny, seigneur d'Andelot (1521–1569).

Already in the early 1550s the oldest of the brothers, Cardinal Odet, was reputed to be a sympathizer of the Evangelical Reform. He was popularly called "the Protestant cardinal." The youngest of them, d'Andelot, took so firm a stand for the Reform in 1558 that Henry II had him arrested—which moved Calvin to send his congratulations for the courage to bear witness. Though d'Andelot recanted and temporarily returned to the mass, he eventually made a public commitment to Calvinism. Indisputably, however, the most prominent convert of the three brothers was Gaspard, comte de Coligny, one-time Colonel-General of the Infantry and after 1552 Admiral of France. As early as the middle 1550s he had expressed sympathy for the religious reformers. Then, when he was taken prisoner by Spanish forces in 1557 he sought comfort in Evangelical literature and in correspondence with Calvin. Although he did not profess Calvinism publicly until after Henry II's death, his conversion almost certainly dates from this period of imprisonment. At the opening of the new reign he came forward almost immediately as a vigorous champion of the Huguenots, a policy which quickly led to a clash with the Guises.

As they were closely connected to one of the greatest and wealthiest families in France, it would require a rather extreme cynicism to argue that worldly ambition motivated the conversion of the Châtillon brothers. Quite the contrary, in fact: after playing roles of some importance in the first religious wars of the 1560s, Odet and d'Andelot faded into relative obscurity. Only Coligny enjoyed a prominent political career, and as Admiral de France and a nephew of the great Montmorency he seemed destined for that well before his conversion.

THE ACCESSION OF Francis II (1559–1560) greatly strenghtened the Guises, and they were quick to consolidate their advantage. Montmorency was forced to retire to his estates, with his son's promotion to Marshal of France as a minor consolation. Then the duc de Guise—uncle of the new king's wife—assumed the post of Grand Master of the Royal Household, and with it effective control of the young king's person and government. Within a month he also was given charge of military matters while his brother, the cardinal de Lorraine, undertook the direction of finance and foreign affairs. The Princes of the Blood were neutralized too. Antoine de Bourbon, weak and uncertain, posed no immediate threat; Condé, who had never managed to win favor in any case, was sent abroad on a diplomatic mission; and their brother, the cardinal de Bourbon, was sent off on another errand. However, the Guises, through their arrogance and aggressiveness, soon embittered old rivalries and made new enemies.

The duc de Guise behaved as autocratically as though he were king, issuing brisk commands and signing royal orders himself. Meanwhile, the cardinal de Lorraine worked to draw France into a great Catholic coalition dominated by Philip of Spain, aimed at isolating Protestants in the Netherlands and Scotland and putting pressure on Elizabeth of England as well as crushing heresy in France. The Guises also maintained the vigorous domestic persecution of the former reign. The parlementarian Anne du Bourg was burned in December of 1559 and a whole series of new edicts threatened dire penalties for various dissenting practices.

In addition, to reduce expenses the Guises disbanded several military units rendered superfluous by the Peace of Câteau-Cambrésis, thus destroying the livelihood of many lesser nobles as well as common soldiers. Almost inevitably these moves evoked a reaction, as many nobles motivated more by political than by religious grievances rallied to the Huguenots. This was not a new phenomenon, for the phrases "religious Huguenot" and "political Huguenot" already were used fairly commonly; but Guise policy accelerated the process. These new adherents to the Huguenot cause were, of course, class-conscious members of the military caste. Their influence began to erode the traditionally rather pacific and submissive character of the Reform movement.

Soon an anti-Guise plot began to take shape. There is little doubt that Condé was behind it, though he kept well in the background. He used as organizer a Calvinist nobleman, La Renaudie, who simply spoke vaguely of "a greater man" who would reveal himself later. There is also some evidence that French refugees in Geneva played some role in the planning. The plotters seem to have intended to seize the royal family as the court was moving about in the Loire Valley in the late winter of 1559–1560. They planned then to form a new government while in control of the king; to drive out and probably to kill the Guises; and to establish religious toleration. However, the conspiracy was too large and security too imperfect. The plot was revealed to the Guises, who moved the royal party into the strong château of Amboise and brought up reinforcements. When a desultory attack was launched on 16 and 17 March it failed miserably, and many prisoners were taken.

Guise moved swiftly to punish the plotters. He had the king

name him lieutenant-general to deal with the crises and then unleashed a slaughter which eventually claimed over a thousand victims. A manhunt swept fugitives from the surrounding woods and countryside. After quick trials many were hanged, and when there were not enough gibbets the battlements of the château were pressed into service. Others were bound and cast into the Loire to drown. Then officers were sent to various parts of the country armed with warrants and letters of authority to deal with those who had escaped. And though no firm evidence could be produced against Condé, he was held at Court for several weeks and suffered suspicion and insults. But the violence with which the Guises reacted to the "Tumult of Amboise" heightened the opposition to them. Montmorency suggested publicly that their greed might have endangered the king. Finally the queen mother moved into the scene.

A French king was considered to reach majority at fourteen, so despite his youth and obvious dependence there was no regency for Francis II; and Catherine de Médicis, like Montmorency and the Bourbons, had been excluded from the new government by the Guises. Had there been a regency, tradition and precedent—though a bit vague—would have demanded some sorts of roles for the Princes of the Blood (the Bourbons), the queen mother (Catherine) and the great officers of the Crown (Constable Montmorency and Admiral Coligny at least).

The Guises probably had underestimated Catherine, however. Despite her personal inexperience, she came from a family famous for political talent, she was ambitious, and she wanted to preserve the independence of the Crown. In the spring of 1560 she began to assert herself. She arranged the appointment as chancellor—head of the French judiciary and an important officer of state—of a moderate whom she trusted, Michel de l'Hôpital (c. 1505–1573). A former member of the Parlement of Paris, a fiscal administrator and a member of the Privy Council, l'Hôpital had considerable experience and commanded wide respect. The Guises did not oppose the appointment. In fact, they probably expected l'Hôpital's support, as he had always cultivated good relations with them, and they later berated him for his "betrayal." Then Catherine persuaded the king to issue a rather broad amnesty to recent offenders, followed shortly by an edict restricting the jurisdiction of secular courts in religious matters. Finally she launched a sort of inquest into the disturbances in the kingdom. This the Guises found disquieting, for she managed subtly to emphasize their provocations.

At this point Guise interest suffered a serious setback abroad. In Scotland Mary of Guise, regent for Mary Stuart, had promoted her family's aggressively Catholic religious policies so forcefully that she had evoked a serious rebellion by the Scots Protestant lords, supported by Elizabeth I of England. In the spring of 1560 Catholic forces were crushed. On 11 June Mary of Guise died; and a treaty signed in July made Scotland practically a protectorate of the English queen. The Guise position in Scotland was in shambles, and Mary Stuart's royal rights appeared jeopardized.

Amid these circumstances, in an atmosphere made more tense by continuing pamphlet attacks upon the Guises and by violent religious clashes in the provinces, Catherine arranged the summoning of an Assembly of Notables (important persons gathered by royal invitation) for Fontainebleau in August. The meeting quickly became a forum to consider the religious crisis when Coligny, apparently with Catherine's approval, made an impassioned plea to the king for toleration. Not only was he warmly applauded, but the liberal archbishop of Vienne added an appeal for genuine reform of the Church. Suddenly on the defensive, the duc de Guise replied angrily, but the cardinal de Lorraine counseled patience and broader consultation. Hence, it was agreed that if the pope did not call a general council first, a French national assembly of the clergy, with Huguenot representation, should be held early in 1561. There was a further suggestion that the Estates General—the elected consultative assembly of clergy, nobility, and commons—should be convened, and this met with approval, so the king called it for December 1560.

In the autumn Guise prospects brightened perceptibly when Mary Stuart was thought to be pregnant, and they launched another blow at the Bourbons. The latter had been supporting the vicious pamphlet attacks; and they were suspected of being behind an insurrection in Lyons as well as open religious rioting in which Protestant bands were sacking Catholic churches. At the request of his wife's uncles, the king summoned Antoine de Bourbon and the prince de Condé to Orléans, where the Court had moved for the upcoming meeting of the Estates General, to give an account of themselves. Though Antoine was allowed the liberty of the Court, Condé was arrested and confined immediately upon arrival. In late November a hand-picked special judicial commission found him guilty of treason and pronounced his death sentence.

The Guises had cause to rejoice. Montmorency was in retirement; the Bourbons appeared about to lose their only effective leader; and the queen mother, after her first assertiveness, seemed hesitant again, inclined to caution. Moreover, the extremism of the pamphlet attacks weakened the credibility of the Huguenots as peaceful reformers, and they were compromised in open revolts—especially in the south. There was a strong possibility that if the Estates General could be led to some solidly royalist and Catholic resolutions, not likely to be too difficult, the king might be persuaded to turn the whole force of the royal army against the heretics—accepting civil war as the price of maintaining Francis I's old dictum of *un roi, une loi, une foi,* "one king, one law, one faith." In such a campaign of extermination both the military and political power of the Guises was likely to be confirmed beyond challenge.

At that point disaster struck. Reports of Mary Stuart's pregnancy proved to be unfounded, so the future suddenly was less secure. Then in mid-November Francis II, always in poor health, became gravely ill, and tension gripped the Court. No action was taken on Condé's condemnation; the duc de Guise was reported to be threatening to hang the doctors if they failed to save the young monarch; and the cardinal de Lorraine ordered processions and public prayers. But all was in vain. On 5 December 1560, after a reign of only a year and a half, Francis II died.

# Chapter Six

# The First
# Civil Wars

THE DEATH OF Francis II was a serious setback for the Guises. His brother and successor, Charles IX (1560–1574), was only ten years old, so a formal regency was necessary. A fierce competition for power quickly developed, in the course of which the Huguenots' prospects improved at first.

Both Catherine de Médicis and the Guises sought the support of the old Constable de Montmorency; but relations between the Guises and the Montmorencies had been embittered beyond easy repair, and he agreed to support the queen mother. Equally as important, Antoine de Bourbon accepted Catherine's invitation to join her in a co-regency. Each was to keep one of the two keys needed for access to the royal seal. The queen mother was to have sole possession of the king's person, and requests to the king or the Privy Council were to be forwarded through her, making her the focus of the new government. Within two weeks after the beginning of Charles IX's reign the Venetian ambassador noted that the Guises and their supporters no longer were seen near the king, and shortly after that they withdrew from Court.

Thus it was Catherine who devised policy late in 1560 and early in 1561. It is impossible to say whether she already had identified the goals she was to pursue for the next thirty years—pacification, reconciliation, and affirmation of royal authority; but these were the directions in which she began to move almost immediately. In religion this meant a policy of limited toleration. Catherine was not attracted personally to Evangelical Christianity, and she knew the fundamental Catholicism of the French Crown— running back to the fifth-century conversion of Clovis. But she feared the civil discord that persecution was certain to cause and struggled grimly to avoid having it forced upon her as Crown policy.

The Estates General opened on 13 December, only a week after Charles IX's accession. Almost immediately Catherine confronted a challenge from some of the nobility who objected to the moderate government that she was building around herself. Catherine outfaced them by demanding that they put their objections into a written and signed petition. When they lacked the courage to do so she was able to order them to proceed with business. Their submission, and the estates' subsequent dealings with her government, constituted an important *de facto* recognition of the regency.

At the opening session of the estates Chancellor L'Hôpital sought to circumvent the explosive Huguenot issue with a speech that stressed secular problems, called for administrative and fiscal reforms and blamed religious unrest on lazy and dissolute clergy— carefully avoiding doctrinal considerations. However, the controversy could not be suppressed so easily, though it quickly became evident that there were not one but several complex "religious questions."

The nobility, who entertained a lively nostalgia for the feudal past, did not address themselves to religious matters in much detail; but some argued that all important decisions belonged to their class and that noble lords should be allowed to determine religion on their lands, as had been established in Germany by the recent Peace of Augsburg. The first estate, the clergy, called upon the Crown to suppress heresy, of course. The other major religious problem that its members identified was outside interference in the French Church's appointments and revenues. They argued that such visible problems as clerical abuses and the alienation of the laity were rooted in papal and royal rights established by the Concordat of Bologna and would be cured if the Gallican Church were allowed self-government under its bishops. The commons, on the other hand, wanted participation of the local laity in clerical appointments and also some controls of finance to assure that contributions of the faithful were not diverted to secular purposes or "sent abroad." Overall, the tenor of the religious debates suggests a mood of concern, of anti-papalism and of assertive Gallicanism rather than bitter fanaticism.

Both the Huguenots and the government had cause to be pleased. Despite occasional clashes—some vituperative argument whether the Huguenots should be allowed to build churches and some hot words between Coligny and the chief officer of the clergy—the assembly passed rather quietly, devoting most meetings to taxes and the king's finances. A spirit of moderation seemed to prevail. In combination with the departure of the Guises from Court, this spirit could allow the Huguenots to feel a bit more secure. The government further reassured them with significant concessions: a general pardon to all those accused of religious offences, without any requirement for a new profession of faith, and the promise of a national religious council if the pope did not summon a general council before June.

Catherine's policy of pacification and conciliation appeared well launched, but it was soon in difficulty as her relations with her aristocratic allies deteriorated. Already in February 1561 Catherine and Antoine de Bourbon were beginning to quarrel. He seemed unoffended that she had allowed him little real power in their joint government, but he was aggressively eager to advance family interests. There were disagreements over political appointments and over support for his claims to Spanish Navarrese lands (when the last thing Catherine wanted was to agitate Philip of Spain!); but the major issue concerned Bourbon's brother.

Though Condé had been released from arrest after Francis II's death, the charges of treason and conspiracy against him had never been settled. He and Antoine apparently hoped not only that Catherine might force the courts to exonerate him but also that the Guises might be humiliated by a judicial criticism. Instead, not without jurisdictional difficulties with the Parlement, Catherine invoked the young king's "personal" judgment and persuaded the judges that the charges should be dropped because of some irregularities in the evidence. Though somewhat disgruntled, the

Bourbons accepted this solution, probably because of other "gratifications" which soon followed. In March both Condé and Coligny,
who was considered an ally, were admitted to the Privy Council;
and at the beginning of April Antoine was appointed Lieutenant-
General of the Kingdom, giving him control of military affairs.

No sooner was this dangerous rift resolved, however, than
Catherine's position was weakened seriously by the defection of
Montmorency. The old constable may have been a bit jealous of
the Bourbons, but his primary motive was religion. Born in 1493,
Montmorency was a grown man—commander of armies and
shortly to be a Marshal of France—when the doctrinal challenges of
Luther and Lefèvre d'Etaples were first heard. He had experienced
the religious dissension under Francis I, Henry II and Francis II;
and despite the conversion of his nephews, for whom he had a
genuine fondness, as he approached seventy he was a conservative
old man and still a staunch Catholic. The Guises had been making
conciliatory approaches to him for some time, and in the spring of
1561 he agreed to join them for the preservation of the Church.
Their association usually is called "The Triumvirate" after its three
leading figures—Guise, Montmorency and Marshal St. André, the
latter a prominent military figure—though in fact it also involved
many others, such as the cardinal de Lorraine.

Despite the loss of Montmorency's support, and the ominous
contacts that the Triumvirate quickly developed with Philip II of
Spain, Catherine pressed on through the summer of 1561 with her
efforts to find compromise solutions and to maintain the peace. She
hoped that the conference between the two religions scheduled for
the autumn, the Colloquy of Poissy, would be able to establish a
basis for mutual toleration. She realized that if civil war broke out
the Crown would have to support the established Church. This
would almost surely deliver her government into the hands of
Catholic extremists, making the Guises supreme again. For
Catherine peace was the essential condition of the maintenance of
her authority.

The drift of events worked against the queen mother, however. Since Francis II's death thousands of Huguenot refugees had
flocked back into France. They tended to be militant and uncompromising, eager for security based on real power after the bitter-

ness of exile. At the same time Catholic opinion was hardening, stimulated both by extremist preaching and by Huguenot desecration of churches and disruption of Catholic services. All over the country confrontations occurred, armed clashes multiplied, and civil war became more imminent.

To make matters worse, the ever-unreliable Bourbon began to vacillate again. He was listening to the blandishments of the Spaniards, who held out hopes of a favorable settlement of his Navarrese claims. These hopes were entirely unrealistic, for it was unbelievable that Spain would abandon hard won frontier territory, especially on the French border. But Bourbon negotiated eagerly.

In the late summer of 1561 Catherine's fortunes took a turn for the worse. Jeanne d'Albret's arrival in Paris in August was the occasion for unrestrained Huguenot demonstrations that greatly heightened popular tensions in the capital. Another assembly of the Estates General, dealing with matters left over from the Orléans meetings, proved very anti-clerical and forced the clergy to take over the king's debts. This financial relief was obtained at the price of more deeply offending the Catholic party. Montmorency remarked that the author of the scheme should have been hanged. Then the Colloquy of Poissy failed utterly as questions of papal authority and the Eucharist completely blocked any compromise.

In the meantime, while Catholic forces sought the support of Spain, the Huguenots—especially after Condé's rehabilitation— had agents soliciting help from England, Denmark, and the Protestant German princes. They received some encouragement; so the possibilities of foreign intervention also were increasing. To give immediacy to the threat, in October a rumor reported Philip II to have remarked that if Catherine declined his offer of assistance "to correct religious abuses" he would give it to whomever asked it.

For a few more months Catherine was able to press on, balancing factions, calming tempers, and somehow avoiding a general state of war despite many localized clashes. Then, on 17 January 1562, with the advice of L'Hôpital, Condé, Coligny, and d'Andelot, she brought forth her greatest effort, proclaiming an edict of toleration and tried desperately to de-escalate the issue.

Under the new edict, the Calvinists were to be known as the *Réligion Prétendue Reformée* (R.P.R.), the "Religion Calling Itself

Reformed," not excessively prejudicial. They were to be allowed liberty of conscience and outside of major towns free religious practices (especially *outside* of fanatically Catholic Paris). As concessions to Catholics, the Protestants were not permitted to erect churches, they were forbidden to preach anything contrary to the Scriptures or the Nicene Creed, and they were prohibited from using vituperative language concerning the established Church.

Catherine hoped that the Edict of January would content both sides. Instead, it satisfied neither. Catholics objected to granting any sort of legal position to heresy; and Huguenots, who might once have accepted such concessions gratefully, now argued that the edict did not go far enough. Calvin himself remarked that it was inadequate. Subsequently, Catherine's hopes collapsed rapidly.

Abandoned by Montmorency, unable to depend upon Bourbon and confronted by adamant Catholic opposition to any religious compromise, the queen mother became more and more dependent on the Châtillons, who still sought only toleration for Huguenot worship. It was not so much that she favored Protestants as that only among them could she find support for her moderate policies. The situation was polarizing rapidly, with increasing militancy on both sides. Religious rioting spread through provincial cities, and the danger that sporadic violence might become generalized into civil war was well recognized. The decisive confrontation occurred on 1 March, as the duc de Guise and his party were passing through Vassy, about a hundred miles east of Paris. There they encountered a Protestant worship service in a barn just outside of the town. Fighting broke out, and Guise's soldiers killed many of the Huguenots. Word of the "Massacre of Vassy" spread rapidly, and when Guise arrived in Paris two weeks later the capital received him as a hero, the city government offering him a subsidy in support of the Catholic cause.

The situation then began to deteriorate rapidly. Condé arrived in Paris shortly after Guise. Finding the duke in armed control of the city he proposed that they both withdraw. When Guise brought up more troops instead, Condé moved to Meaux, where Coligny and d'Andelot joined him. Catherine's interests suffered another blow when Bourbon finally came to a decision. On Palm Sunday, 22 March, he attended mass, and soon he joined the Triumvirate.

Without any support left among the foremost aristocrats, Catherine appears to have become fearful that the young king might be taken from her. She proposed to move the Court to the Loire Valley. However, confronted with loud protests from the Guises, the Spanish ambassador and the reconverted Bourbon, the queen mother agreed to Fontainebleau instead. From there she soon allowed the Guises to move her and her son to nearby Melun, which was more defensible.

With Guise, supported by Montmorency and Bourbon, in control of both the royal family and the capital, Condé and the Châtillon brothers moved to Orléans and began raising troops. Condé assumed command, and on 8 April 1562 he issued a manifesto proclaiming that he was taking up arms to defend the authority of the king, the government of the queen mother, and the Edict of January. The civil wars had begun, and for the next thirty years the state of war was to be more or less constant, despite several interruptions by short-lived settlements.

The so-called "first civil war" lasted just under a year, from the spring of 1562 to March 1563. It did not go well for the Huguenots. The Crown's armies succeeded in retaking several towns, though at the price of the Triumvirate's figurehead, Antoine de Bourbon. Though the only pitched battle, fought on 19 December at Dreux, west of Paris, was indecisive, the Catholic forces were left in possession of the field. In this last fight another member of the Triumvirate was killed, St. André; but Guise earned such great credit that he was named Lieutenant-General of the Kingdom again. Nonetheless, a few months later the war ended in compromise. On 18 February 1563, just eight weeks after the battle of Dreux, a single shot eliminated the Catholic party's most effective leader when the duc de Guise was assassinated. Catherine de Médicis had long been negotiating with Coligny, and the assassination removed the last obstacle to a general accord. A month later, on 19 March—ironically, the day of Guise's funeral—she issued the Edict of Amboise.

A group of tentative and sometimes unenforceable concessions, the new edict was an appropriate result of an inconclusive war. The government recognized Condé as first Bourbon prince (Antoine's son being still a boy). It granted amnesties for the rebellion. It agreed to pay the costs of the Huguenot army. And it guaranteed Protestant religious practice in at least one town in each district and on the estates of noblemen who so wished. The rather feudal nature of the concessions, based upon personal clauses and social rank, reflects clearly the ascendancy of noble elements in the Huguenot party and the continuing de-emphasis of religious issues.

The next year the queen mother tried further to strengthen the position of the Crown. In March 1564 she set out with the young king, whose minority had just ended, upon a two-year tour of the provinces—trying to rally the strong royalism always latent in the populace. She also tried to persuade Philip II to a personal conference somewhere on the Franco-Spanish frontier. This did not eventuate, but Philip did send his wife (Catherine's daughter) and some of his confidential advisors to meetings in Bayonne in the spring of 1565, though nothing concrete came of their discussions.

Despite Catherine's efforts, the peace proved unstable. In many parts of France, Catholics refused to accept the concessions to the Huguenots. Some even formed regional Catholic leagues to facilitate resistance. Neither party would lay down arms, and both sides increased their recruitment of German and Swiss mercenaries in obvious anticipation of renewed war.

Attempting a quick coup, Condé tried to seize the king in September of 1567. When this failed he undertook a siege of Paris. In response, Constable Montmorency led a force against him, and on 10 November, at the battle of St. Denis, he broke the siege. Montmorency was gravely wounded, however, and with his death two days later another of the great figures disappeared. Condé then led his forces away from Paris, desultorily pursued by the king's brother, Henry, duc d'Anjou; but neither side showed much keenness for further fighting. So in February 1568, with some initiative from the king himself, a new pacification was announced: the Treaty of Longjumeau, really a reconfirmation of the Edict of Amboise.

The second civil war appeared to have achieved nothing, and neither did the treaty. In the provinces bitter fighting continued and soon grew into a third civil war. Though a scarcity of money impeded large operations by either side, a few major battles were achieved. In the west, at both Jarnac on 13 March 1569 and at

Moncontour in the autumn, Protestant forces suffered serious re-
verses. The credit went to Anjou, though it was more likely de-
served by the veteran Marshal Tavannes who was at his side. Then
in June 1570, at Arnay-le-Duc in Burgundy, the Huguenots won a
small victory. The most important effect of these three clashes was
upon Protestant leadership. Condé was killed at Jarnac, leaving
Coligny the undisputed chief of the Huguenots—especially after
his brother d'Andelot died two months later. Henry of Navarre,
Antoine's seventeen-year-old son, fought his first battle at Arnay-
le-Duc, adding to his growing reputation as a future Huguenot
leader.

By 1570 Catherine de Médicis and Charles IX were growing
impatient with the arrogance of the cardinal de Lorraine and the
ambition of his young nephew, Henry, third duc de Guise. Henry's
attentions to the king's sister, Marguerite, had become rather pre-
sumptuous. Since spring the king and the queen mother had been
negotiating with Coligny, and the Protestant success at Arnay-le-
Duc resulted in another compromise peace in early August, the
generous Edict of St. Germain.

After the usual amnesties and restitution of honors and
confiscated property, the new settlement provided for freedom of
conscience throughout the kingdom and public Protestant worship
wherever it had existed before the war as well as in the suburbs of
two towns of each district and in noble houses. The Huguenots also
were granted control of four fortified towns as "security places";
and the king recognized and forgave the Netherlands Protestant
princes who had assisted the rebellion against his government—
politically significant since those same princes were the leaders of
the Netherlands revolt against Philip II.

The armed peace established by the Edict of St. Germain
lasted only two years. Across the country unorganized violence
continued, while at Court the edict's future clearly depended upon
the rivalries of the factions. The Guises appeared to have an ally in
the duc d'Anjou, whose relations with his royal brother were ever
more strained. The policy of toleration, the restoration of Coligny's
honors, titles and influence, and the government's recognition of
the Netherlands rebels were anathema to Spain—whose ambassador protested at length. So the most significant effects of the new

settlement, other than once more affirming a legal right of existence to the Huguenots, likely were further to politicize the religious issue and to tie it ever more closely to international questions. As all of these trends came to an explosive climax late in the summer of 1572, it is necessary to consider their development apart from the events of the wars.

Although Philip II's fear of an international Protestant conspiracy was exaggerated—for many issues divided the several Protestant factions—there were some international contacts and personal connections. John Knox, who led the Reformation in Scotland, had studied and worked with Calvin in Geneva, as also had many French pastors. Theodore de Beza, Calvin's disciple and eventual successor, returned to France for the Colloquy of Poissy; and William of Orange, leader of the Netherlands revolt, eventually married a daughter of Coligny. Moreover, the Huguenots sometimes got military assistance from some of the German Protestant princes. On the other side, international relationships were more centralized, as most Catholics looked to Philip of Spain for support of their efforts in England, Scotland, and the Netherlands as well as in France. Thus, the religious struggles all over western Europe inevitably had far-reaching political ramifications. Probably 1568 was the crucial year.

In May 1568 Mary Stuart was overthrown in Scotland and fled to England. She had claims upon the English throne that could have been awkward had Queen Elizabeth's search for accommodation with her Catholic subjects deteriorated into confrontation. She was a natural focus for any opposition—which she sometimes was willing to encourage. Hence, plots both for her restoration in Scotland and for her usurpation of Elizabeth's crown abounded. Around her "Catholic cause" swirled agents, messengers and rumors linking her to the King of Spain, to Alva—his governor in the Netherlands—and to her uncle, the cardinal de Lorraine.

In early June 1568 Alva began a bloodbath in the Netherlands with the public execution of persons who had resisted his authority, including high-ranking aristocrats. One result was a movement of Protestant refugees to France, strengthening the connections between the Netherlands Calvinists and the Huguenots. As another consequence, William of Orange prepared for war and sought to coordinate efforts with Coligny and Condé. In August they signed a treaty of cooperation. Protesting that their princes were the victims of evil counsellors (Alva and Lorraine) from which religion and the rights of the nobility suffered, they announced their decision to take up arms and agreed that if victory were achieved by either group, it would come to the aid of the other.

Despite increasing international involvement, however, domestic issues—and especially factional and personal rivalries—continued to be important to Huguenot prospects, entangled as they were in Court politics. To some extent death had greatly simplified the situation, removing Antoine de Bourbon, the elder Guise, Montmorency, Condé and d'Andelot. About 1570 the sons of Bourbon, Condé and Guise were just approaching the age of twenty. Montmorency's sons, though grown men, did not have their father's stature; and though d'Andelot left four sons, none of them acquired great distinction. So Coligny and the cardinal de Lorraine, while not the only important leaders, towered above the rest as they confronted one another.

Catherine de Médicis, with the support of Charles IX, was trying as always to maintain the independence of the Crown. The threat from the Guises was renewed civil war, until heresy was crushed. But internationalization of the religious struggles added to the dangers of too-close involvement with Coligny, for such an alliance easily could draw France into a foreign war. To Catherine both wars were repugnant. Not only would she likely lose her freedom of maneuver but military necessity would impose great commanders upon her, and she would lose her authority. So in the early 1570s Catherine's policy was not so much the balancing of factions, as often has been alleged, as the avoidance of domination by either of them combined with desperate efforts to escape the military commitments that both wanted. And in addition she had to cope with the disturbing ambitions of her younger sons, Anjou and Alençon, both of whom seemed eager to seek military reputation and were showing jealousy of their reigning brother.

As always, Catherine's program was negotiation. To escape the Guises and at the same time avoid dependence upon Coligny, she sought to marry her daughter Marguerite to the young Henry of Navarre, son of Antoine de Bourbon and Jeanne d'Albret. This proposal may have originated with the Montmorencys and was supported enthusiastically by Charles IX. At the same time she sought to settle her younger sons advantageously. When proposals that Elizabeth of England should marry Anjou broke down, Alençon was substituted, despite the discrepancy in ages. (Elizabeth was twenty-two years older than the young prince.) And in 1572 Catherine began negotiation for Anjou's election as King of Poland, to give him honor of his own and remove him from the French scene.

Coligny was unenthusiastic about making Huguenot security so largely dependent upon the Crown. Of course he must have seen the implicit diminution of his own role. Nonetheless, he much preferred a French government with Protestant alliances to one with only Catholic connections. He hoped to lead an army in support of William of Orange (if not a national army, at least a Huguenot force), so he supported the marriages.

Lorraine's faction was bitterly opposed to the new alliances, as was Spain whose ambassador worked tirelessly against them. But Catherine found some support from a relatively new source, some prominent Catholics tired of the endless unproductive civil strife and fearful of foreign influence. Calling themselves *politiques,* they began to encourage the policies that Catherine and l'Hôpital had advocated a decade earlier—toleration of religious dissidents who would obey the laws and support the Crown, and opposition to extremists on both sides. Nothing came of the proposed English match, but the Bourbon marriage was scheduled for the late summer of 1572. At the same time the Polish plans were developing promisingly.

Probably the queen mother's expectations were modest. With talk of war on every tongue, and a widespread conviction that the only choice was between civil war and war with Spain, Catherine seems to have preserved her hopes to contain a confrontation, if not actually to preserve the peace. A spirit of friendly neutrality had emerged from the negotiations with England. If Coligny simply were allowed to raise a Huguenot force for service under William of Orange, without participation of the French Crown, it was likely that Spain would be too occupied in the Netherlands to intervene in France without greater provocation. And without Spanish support, French extreme Catholics would not be able to attempt much. So it just might prove possible to avoid both civil war and national war with Spain.

By 1572 the Catholic-Spanish party must have felt a growing sense of desperation. Already in September 1571 Philip II had written to Alva that he believed the security of the Netherlands ultimately would depend upon the overthrow of Elizabeth of England. Now it appeared that the French Crown was moving toward supporting her. Moreover, in the spring of 1572 some of the Netherlands rebels, the Sea Beggars, captured the port of Brille, establishing seaborne connections to their sympathizers abroad. Thus the prospect of a Protestant and largely anti-Spanish bloc of England, Scotland, France, and parts of north Germany was entirely believable—encouraging heresy, supporting the growing Netherlands rebellion, and endangering the entire Habsburg hegemony.

Assassination and political murder were accepted policies in the religious strife of the 1560s and 1570s. Already in 1560 the Guises had shown their ruthlessness with the arrest and extralegal condemnation of Condé, whose life probably was spared only by the death of Francis II. In the spring of 1561 the newly formed Triumvirate vowed not just the defeat but the elimination of the Bourbons, an intention confirmed in subsequent Guisard-Spanish communications.

Ironically, though, the first notable assassination came from the other side when the duc de Guise was shot by a Protestant nobleman in 1563. His death added a personal note of vendetta to the factional animosities as his thirteen-year-old son and successor, Henry, insisted ever after on blaming the murder on Coligny—though there is no persuasive evidence to support this charge. Subsequently, as tensions increased towards the end of the decade, so did some evidence and many rumors of murder plots in both France and England, soon substantiated by more deaths.

Alva's slaughter of the opposition in the Netherlands in June 1568 has to be considered judicial murder. During that same summer so many plots against French Protestant leaders were uncovered that in August Condé and Coligny, with their families, sought refuge in the Huguenot stronghold of La Rochelle. In mid-March 1569 Condé was almost certainly murdered after being

captured and disarmed at the battle of Jarnac. When d'Andelot died
in May of the same year of high fever, he was widely believed to
have been poisoned—though this tale can be neither proved nor
disproved. At the same time, informers and captured correspondence left no doubt that there were serious plots, probably
inspired by the cardinal de Lorraine, aimed at Coligny and perhaps
also at Condé's son and at the young King of Navarre. In the winter
another assassination, though foreign, was felt in France: in January
of 1570 the Protestant Regent of Scotland, Murray, was murdered.

Such was the background to the marriage of the King of
Navarre to Catherine's daughter on 18 August 1572. His followers
had flocked into Paris, their heretical religion and their provincial
manners flaming irritants to the Catholic fanaticism and self-
conscious sophistication of the capital, adding popular resentment
to the Guisard-Spanish opposition to the marriage. Inevitably,
when Jeanne d'Albret died suddenly in June, just two months
before the wedding, rumors of poison again seemed credible.
Then, on 22 August, four days after the marriage, an attempt on
Coligny's life just missed succeeding. Shots were fired at him from
a window as he was passing in the street, and he was carried to his
quarters lightly wounded.

It is impossible to say with certainty who was responsible for
the attempt on Coligny. Naturally the Guises were blamed, and
that is a possibility. One cannot ignore the established Guisard-
Spanish policy of "elimination." But the meager evidence points
more strongly toward Anjou, who also seems to have had rather
close contacts with the Spaniards about this time. In any case, the
incident triggered panic. There were hundreds, perhaps thousands,
of Huguenots in Paris, many of them armed noblemen; and the
populace clearly feared their vengeance. The Court and the government were frightened too, and the next thirty-six hours witnessed frantic activity. The king visited Coligny to offer his condo-
lences; the militia was called out, and the gates of the city were
guarded. Messengers scurried back and forth, and council sessions
and impromptu meetings were convened. Out of it all came a
decision in favor of a preemptive strike against the Huguenot
leadership on 24 August, St. Bartholomew's Day.

Early in the morning of the twenty-fourth the killing began.

Coligny was one of the first victims, as Guise's men invaded his house and killed him in his bed. At the Court the King of Navarre and Condé made rapid conversions to Catholicism and were spared; and a few prominent Huguenots managed to flee the city. For the rest it was a bloodbath. As word of what was happening spread and the populace joined in the hunt, locked city gates prevented escape. The estimates of the slaughter are generally unreliable and vary enormously, from one thousand to ten thousand. Observers likely to be reasonably well informed and not excessively biased suggest two to three thousand in the capital. As the news was disseminated, however, the massacres spread to provincial towns. There the figures are even more vague, but probably another six to eight thousand died.

A great deal of nonsense has been written about the St. Bartholomew's massacres. Contemporary Catholics clearly accepted the likelihood of a Huguenot "fury" and perhaps a long-planned rising. The pope and other Catholic powers wrote to congratulate the French government on having blocked a Protestant coup. Some Protestant historians have suggested a well-developed Catholic plot, perhaps conceived as early as the Bayonne conference of 1565, with the Bourbon marriage as bait. They have held Catherine responsible. In fact, the affair seems most likely to have begun as a preemptive assassination plot aimed at a limited number of important Huguenot leaders, rather hastily organized after the failure of the first attempt upon Coligny created a panicky concern about possible consequences. These planned murders appear to have ignited the volatile and bloodthirsty fanaticism of the Paris populace to a slaughter which afterwards spread across the kingdom.

# Chapter Seven

# The Three Henrys

THE MOST STARTLING thing about the St. Bartholomew's massacres is that their effect was so slight. With Coligny dead and Navarre and Condé virtual prisoners at Court, of course any aggressive policy was out of the question; so perhaps the immediate purposes of the assassins had been achieved. But after the first shock, the Huguenots recovered quickly, arming themselves and strengthening their defenses. The royal government made some effort to negotiate, but it had lost its credibility, and the Huguenot towns and nobility refused to disarm. Hence, while the freedom to practice their religion continued to be the ostensible justification of their defiance, St. Bartholomew's Day had completed the Huguenots' transformation into a group of armed insurgents. The only party to profit significantly from the affair was the King of Spain. Deprived of their established leaders and forced into a defensive posture, the Huguenots were unable to undertake the foreign expedition that Coligny had desired. So William of Orange was denied support, and the prospects of the Netherlands revolt darkened considerably.

In France the key to the Huguenot position was the town of La Rochelle. An old port on the west coast, it is first mentioned in late tenth-century documents. By the twelfth century it had become a chartered self-governing town. By the fifteenth century it was a well fortified, highly independent port; and in the mid-sixteenth

century, like many other commercial centers, it had welcomed
Calvinism. Its wealth, independence, and shipping connections
soon made it one of the bastions of the Reformed religion.
Throughout the winter of 1572–1573 La Rochelle was subjected to a protracted siege. Several peace proposals were rejected
by the city. On one occasion Catherine de Médicis was told bluntly
that the Huguenots had no faith in the king's word after St. Bartholomew; and in the spring and early summer of 1573 a series of
bloody assaults failed to penetrate the defenses. Consequently,
when the royal army was faced with deadly camp disease and
serious desertion, it was the Crown that made concessions. At the
end of June the Edict of La Rochelle promised amnesties, allowed
liberty of conscience throughout the kingdom and free Protestant
worship in three security towns as well as in some noble households. It authorized two Protestant regional assemblies in the south
and granted other lesser privileges. This settlement fell short of the
Edict of St. Germain of 1570, but it was the best that La Rochelle
was able to wrest from the government.

The Protestant south continued its resistance, organizing politically. In fact, developments in the south during the next two years,
1573 to 1575, were to have important long-term effects for the
Huguenots. A Protestant Union was formed and acquired the habit
of regular political meetings, general assemblies, in contrast to the
synods which concerned themselves primarily with doctrine and
discipline. Here lay the foundations of the famous "state within a
state" which the Huguenots often were charged with desiring.

The situation in the south depended largely upon an ever more
important figure, the sieur de Damville (1534–1614), second son
of the old Constable de Montmorency. He was appointed Governor of Languedoc in 1563 and was promoted to the rank of Marshal
of France in 1566. As a young man he had been somewhat identified with Catholic extremists. In the middle 1570s family interests
and the new ascendancy of the Guises pressed him toward both
religious moderation and more aggressive political action—
especially after May 1574 when the duc de Montmorency, his older
brother, was imprisoned in the Bastille, where he spent the next
two years.

Such was the situation when Anjou departed to assume the

crown of Poland in the summer of 1573: armed truce in the north and west and continued fighting and virtual autonomy in the south. The Bourbons were neutralized, the Montmorencys in opposition, and the Guises again dominant at Court. However, on 30 May 1574 Charles IX died of tuberculosis, and suddenly there were new fears. It was whispered that Alençon was plotting with the Montmorencys to block Anjou from the throne of France, that Huguenots and *politique* Catholics were allying and would rally to Alençon. In this atmosphere, in accordance with Charles IX's last wishes, Catherine formed a new regency to govern while awaiting Anjou's return. This time her government lasted seven months, until the beginning of 1575.

About this time Damville began to act more assertively. On 1 August 1574 he contacted the Huguenot Assembly at Millau, which represented a great many of the Protestant communities of the south, to suggest an alliance between the Huguenots and *politique* Catholics, just as the rumors had predicted. After some discussions the basis of an accord was worked out: Damville would not attempt to re-establish the "papist cult" in any Huguenot garrison towns; otherwise there would be free exercise of both religions everywhere that the alliance ruled. With religious concerns thus quickly dealt with, the agreement turned to practical military and political arrangements. Damville was to be chief of any combined operations, though the prince de Condé (who had escaped from Court) was recognized as nominal leader and protector of the Huguenots. In addition, the Protestants imposed upon him a council of a half dozen of their members. Thus, Damville further strengthened his role as *de facto* sovereign, or at least viceroy, of the south.

When Anjou arrived back in France at the beginning of 1575 he seems to have been as strongly opposed to toleration as ever, and this time Catherine appears to have agreed with him. Perhaps she feared growing Huguenot strength, or a threat from the Montmorencys backed by the Protestant-*politique* alliance. Or perhaps she underestimated the still potent threat of the Guises, as the cardinal de Lorraine had died quietly at the end of December of 1574: for she still had to deal with the duc de Guise and his younger brother, the cardinal de Guise, both able and ambitious.

On 14 February 1575, the day after his coronation, the new king—
then properly styled Henry III (1574–1589)—married a lady of his
own choice, a cousin of the Guise brothers. In any case, in the
autumn of 1575 the Crown began military operations against the
Huguenots once more, opening a new struggle which quickly became another Guise-Montmorency fight.

In September Alençon escaped from Court and joined the
rebellion, and Condé busied himself hiring German mercenaries,
while Damville raised the Languedoc. Opposing them, the king
himself led an army into the Rhone Valley. His campaign went
badly, with desertion and lack of money offering little hope for
improvement in the spring.

Meanwhile, the young duc de Guise, now twenty-four and
showing something of his father's flair for leadership, led an army
into eastern France to contest the passage of Condé's hired Germans. In a short clash in October he succeeded in turning back
Condé's forward elements, which were under the command of a
relative of the Montmorencys. This achievement was exagger-
atedly celebrated as a great victory by the Catholic party. In the
course of it Guise was wounded in the left cheek and ear, acquiring
a scar remarkably like the one his father had borne, though less
disfiguring. This only added to his popular appeal and promptly
won him his father's old nickname, Le Balafré.

Elsewhere military operations achieved nothing, and as ad-
vancing winter halted campaigning the situation offered a familiar
appearance. Civil war had once more enhanced the position of the
extremist Catholics, and consequently of the House of Guise. In
opposition to the Guises, alleging concern for both religion and
class rights, stood the Montmorencys and the Bourbons. In February 1576 the latter were strengthened when Navarre escaped
from the Court and fled to La Rochelle. There he promptly abjured
his forced conversion and was recognized as Protector of the Reformed Churches.

Thus, by the spring the position of the Crown had deteriorated
drastically. Two princes of the blood, Navarre and Condé, stood at
the head of a vast rebellion, supported presumably by the imprisoned duc de Montmorency and certainly by his powerful brother,
Damville, and other nobles of their family. Altogether the rebels

had as many as 30,000 men in the field, a formidable threat. Henry III was left with little of the kingdom under his control except the Ile-de-France, Champagne, and Burgundy. For much of that as well as for whatever military force was left him he was dependent upon the Guises. With startling suddenness he appeared to have been reduced to the condition of his ancestors, confronting a fragmented realm dominated by great princes. Recognizing that it was time to make peace, the government freed the duc de Montmorency—a conciliatory gesture—and the queen mother undertook to negotiate terms. The result was the Edict of Beaulieu, more commonly called the Peace of Monsieur, promulgated in the first week of May 1576.

The terms of the Peace of Monsieur reflect clearly the diminishing significance of religious issues in the so-called religious wars, as concessions to Navarre, to Alençon and to the *politiques* in general loomed far larger. There was a religious settlement, of course. As might be expected with Huguenots so strong in the field, it was much more generous than the Edict of La Rochelle of 1573; but there was little in it that was novel.

Protestant worship was to be allowed everywhere except in the immediate vicinity of Paris and of the Court. Reformed Christians were to have access to all offices and honors without prejudice. A somewhat innovative aspect was provision not only for Protestant membership in provincial parlements but also for a new mixed chamber in the Parlement of Paris, an effort to achieve less biased judicial processes. And this time the Huguenots were to have eight security towns. Finally, there were the usual arrangements for amnesties and restitutions.

Interestingly, the only religious provision that the Huguenots contested was the definition of the buffer zone around Paris, where free religious practice was denied them; for it excluded them from some established sites, especially Charenton, just southeast of the capital. Otherwise, the most controversial issue was the matter of security towns, to be garrisoned and governed by the Huguenots. They wanted two in each district, which would have made a total of twenty-eight; but Catherine insisted that regions ceded politically to the control of the Huguenots' noble leaders also constituted places of guaranteed security, and finally she persuaded them to agree to eight. Thus, after a little tinkering with the much-revised religious arrangements of the preceding decade and a half, the important provisions of the treaty were those which established settlements with the Huguenots' noble leaders and *politique* allies.

Navarre was, of course, the most important of the Huguenot princes to be gratified. At the age of twenty-three he was the scion of the senior branch of the Bourbons and first prince of the blood. Moreover, he possessed a royal title in his own right. His demands were a bit breathtaking: all monies owing to his family from the French Crown, assistance to reconquer Spanish Navarre, and such autonomy in his lands in southwestern France as would effectively make him independent of the Crown. But Catherine was a very experienced negotiator, and the ties that bound the anti-government forces together would not stand too much strain; so he settled for restoration of his own and his family's possessions and honors as they had been in 1574, before the recent troubles.

Of the Huguenots' *politique* allies, Alençon got the most extensive gratifications. Perhaps this was not surprising. Not only was he Catherine's son but also heir apparent to the throne until such time as his reigning brother might sire a son. His settlement amounted almost to a feudal appanage from the middle ages: a vast sweep of lands and towns in central France including the entire provinces of Anjou, Touraine and Berry. Thereafter he styled himself by the king's former title, duc d'Anjou. Damville was confirmed in his governorship of Languedoc, and there were lesser gratifications for other nobles; but the major concession to the *politiques* was the government's agreement to convene the Estates General within six months.

Especially because of this last provision, the second half of 1576 was filled with intense political activity. Under the leadership of the duc de Guise many of the regional Catholic associations were fused into a Catholic League. Its purposes—beyond "defense of religion and the Church"—were a bit vague but variously rumored. Certainly it opposed toleration in general and the Peace of Monsieur in particular; and it campaigned vigorously to elect conservative Catholics to the Estates General and to exclude heretics. But there were also rumors of secret approaches to the pope to disqualify the *politique* Anjou (formerly Alençon) from the French throne. While such reports probably were exaggerated, the sudden appear-

League Violence in Paris, November 1591

The Murder of François duc de Guise, 18 February 1563

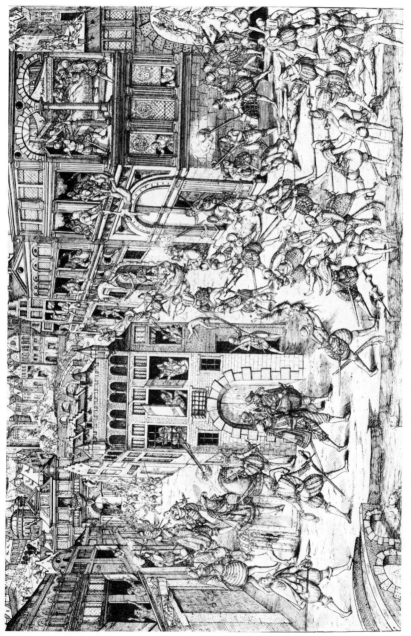

St. Bartholomew's Day Massacre in Paris, 24 August 1572

The Battle of Jarnac 13 March 1569

The Battle of Coutras, 20 October 1587

The Massacre at Vassy, 1 March 1562

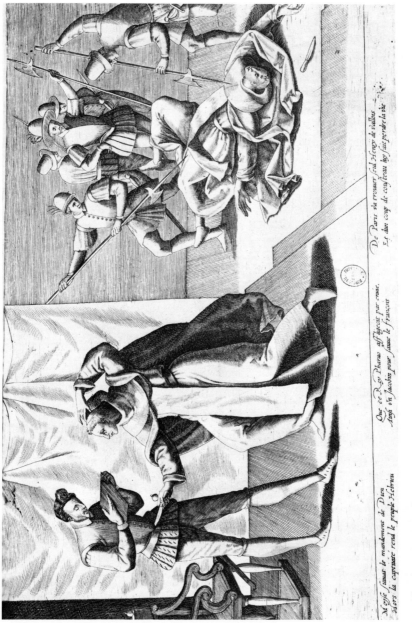

Moysé fumur le mandement de Dieu     Que ce Roy Pharao affligeoyt par cruë,
Hors sa captiue remit le peuple Hebrieu     Ainsi vn Iacobin pour sauue le françois

De Paris vm reuuer feul Henry de Vallois
Et dun coup de couteau hoy fait perdre la vie

The Assassination of King Henry III, 31 July 1589

The Assassination of Henry I, duc de Guise, 23 December 1588

Henry IV de Bourbon, King of Navarre and
later King of France (from the author's collection)

Marguerite de Valois, sister of Henry III and first wife
of Henry de Navarre

Henry I de Lorraine, duc de Guise

Mary Stuart, Queen of France and Scotland

LVDOVICVS VON BOVRBON
PRINCE VON CONDE.

Louis I de Bourbon, prince de Condé

Henry III de Valois, King of France

Antoine de Bourbon, King of Navarre

Charles IX de Valois, King of France

Catherine de Médicis, Queen-Regent of France

Anne de Montmorency, Constable of France

Francis I de Lorraine, duc de Guise

Francis II de Valois, King of France

COLLIGNEI FRATRES·

The Coligny Brothers: Cardinal Odet, Admiral
Gaspard, Francis

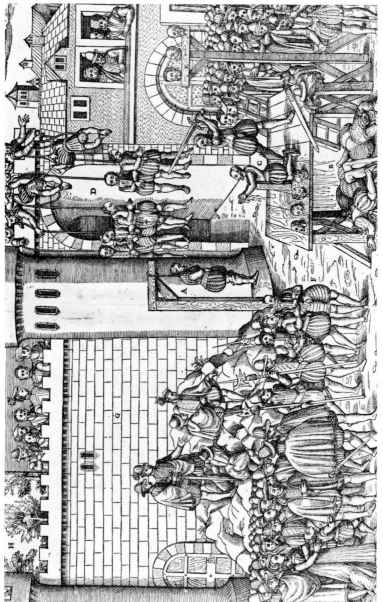

The Executions at Amboise, 15 March 1560

ance of pamphlets lauding both the religious and national service of the Guises and tracing the origin of their parent House of Lorraine to Charlemagne lent some credence to the suspicion that they were beginning to aspire to the crown itself.

Whatever may have been the Leaguers' broader, long-range goals, they certainly enjoyed considerable success with the Estates General, which the *politiques* had hoped would be their instrument. When the assembly opened on 7 December it quickly became clear that the League dominated the two upper houses overwhelmingly. Even though the third estate was divided, a majority there also favored Catholic conformity and renewed civil war. Significantly, though, none of the estates showed any eagerness to provide the money necessary to implement such a policy.

On 1 January 1577, Henry III, announcing that he was responding to the desire of the nation as expressed through the Estates General, issued a new edict revoking the settlement made the previous spring and promising the extirpation of heresy. He also announced that to better achieve these purposes he would assume leadership of the Catholic League himself. Despite the king's attempt to thus guard his authority, however, the effective leader of the League continued to be Guise, supported from the late 1570s by a pension from Spain.

Not surprisingly, the Huguenots quickly formed a sort of counter-league, which obtained promises of aid from England, some of the north German principalities, and the Scandinavian kingdoms. By the spring of 1577 war had broken out again and was to continue intermittently for years, despite occasional short-lived settlements; but it would require considerable imagination to call it religious war. In 1584 the struggle was even further secularized by sudden deterioration of the anti-Catholic, anti-Spanish international position and by the threat of a succession crisis in France. Both crises were the result of princely deaths. In the Netherlands William of Orange was assassinated and in France the duc d'Anjou died.

THE PROBLEM THAT loomed over the French throne after 1584 would have been unbelievable if predicted a quarter century earlier. The venerable Salic Law limited the royal succession to eldest male blood lines, but ever since the Valois had inherited the throne early in the fourteenth century they had produced young princes to maintain the inheritance. As Henry II lay dying of his lance wound in 1559 four of his seven surviving children were males, so again the future of the House of Valois appeared quite secure.

This was an ill-starred generation, however, and one after another Henry II's sons died without offspring for the crown—Francis II in 1560, Charles IX in 1574, and Anjou (Alençon) in 1584. Unexpectedly, then, the survival of the Valois direct male line depended upon the reigning Henry III, who in 1584 was nine years married and still childless. Ironically, should the line die with him, the heir under the Salic Law was his distant cousin Navarre, who was descended—like the Valois—from the mid-thirteenth century St. Louis. As Navarre was also the most prominent Calvinist in France, and leader of the Protestant faction, the succession question inevitably drew the Huguenots more deeply into politics.

The next phase of the military struggle, which became known as the "War of the Three Henrys," is best understood through consideration of the protagonists: Henry III de Valois, King of France; Henry de Bourbon, King of Navarre; and Henry de Lorraine, duc de Guise. All three were in their early to middle thirties, proud scions of ancient lineage, but there the similarities stopped. Their personalities, abilities and ambitions differed enormously.

Henry III remains one of the least comprehensible personalities of his day. Delicately handsome and clearly intelligent, as a youth he appeared deeply religious, energetic, and ambitious. But there was a shallowness to his character, and the promise of youth was never fulfilled as he matured. His religiosity soon degenerated into occasional devotional excesses, such as fasting and joining processions of flagellants. His energy proved equally sporadic, showing itself chiefly in explosive outbursts, often following moods of depression. His ambition seemed to drain away into nothing more than a desire for distraction and amusement. Surrounding himself with young men in rouge and ribbons, his *mignons*, and a whole menagerie of lap dogs, Henry III maintained a Court generally considered degenerate and debauched even by the easy standards of the time.

Probably Guise profited greatly from comparison with Henry

III. Tall and athletic, with rugged good looks romantically scarred from battle, he was a superb horseman and swordsman and a brave soldier. Reared in the family traditions of Catholic intolerance, fierce pride, and unlimited ambition, he seems to have been wrenched suddenly into manhood in his early teens when his father was assassinated. Ever thereafter he appears two-dimensional, almost too predictable. Though an able battlefield commander, he showed no great political skills, for he liked nothing short of total victory and never learned to compromise. There are some grounds to believe that Guise aspired to the crown. This hope was not altogether chimerical if the Valois male line died with Henry III, if the Bourbon princes could be excluded on grounds of religion and if the good will of Philip of Spain could be preserved. In any case, he was a political power; for his handsome figure, his reputation for bravery, and his uncomplicated commitments made him the natural leader of the Catholic League and the idol of the Paris populace.

Probably the ablest of the three Henrys was Navarre, though the reality of the man sometimes disappears behind a sort of mythology that Huguenot propagandists and Bourbon apologists developed around him later, a sort of image of all virtue perhaps slightly flawed by a sensual weakness for women. A portrait in such superlatives is unpersuasive, of course, but he was so talented and so colorful that often it is difficult to sift fact from fancy.

Jeanne d'Albret seems to have had a marked influence upon the formation of her son. Though Henry never acquired her deep religious convictions, he showed her firmness and determination in contrast to his father's constant vacillation. But he also was as susceptible to anger and jealousy as any of his contemporaries and quite capable of petty revenges.

In battle Navarre certainly showed the bravery usually attributed to him, but a careless gallantry was expected and generally found in men of his class. Whether he had military talent is a more debatable matter. Bourbon historians almost certainly have overpraised him. On the other hand, the derogatory opinion of the Duke of Parma, Spain's commander in the Netherlands, likely was exaggerated; for Parma was the greatest commander of the age and held no high regard for any of his adversaries.

Legend and history clearly agree, however, that Navarre had

great political ability. Although he sometimes made a display of the southerner's Gascon bravado, he also showed considerable capacity for shrewd analysis. A popular touch and a flair for leadership let him always get the best effort from his followers. Such talents enabled him to field armies with almost no money, to win battles when badly outnumbered, to retain loyalties even through defeat, and to make friends of former foes. The real Navarre is perhaps more impressive than the product of the myth-makers. As susceptible to human foible as other men, and vulnerable to deep discouragement, he used his talents and his courage with great perseverance. His ultimate victory was due in no small part to his own determination and effort.

The "three Henrys," then, are a study in contrasts. Henry III appears the weakest, but he was the anointed King of France and possessed an authority that neither of the others could command. Both Guise and Navarre were men of action—Guise the more direct and Navarre the more subtle. Henry III probably held the most sincere religious convictions, shallow and demonstrative though they were. Guise, for all his fiery intolerance, seems to have been a more conforming than a deeply devoted Roman Catholic; and Navarre clearly showed that he could adjust his religious commitments without crises of conscience when necessity demanded. The contemporary historian J. A. de Thou (1553–1617) observed acidly that Guise and Navarre made an equal "parade" of religion to encourage their followers. Clearly he found both unconvincing.

The death of Anjou, on 10 June 1584, made Navarre heir apparent to the throne. Henry III immediately tried to persuade him to convert, but he refused. Perhaps he had scruples; more likely he recognized the danger of alienating Huguenots without really winning Catholics. The reaction of the Lorraine princes was predictable. There were meetings and discussions, envoys to Philip of Spain and the pope, and even approaches to Navarre's uncle, the cardinal de Bourbon. The Catholic League, first formed in 1576, was reconstituted with papal blessings and Spanish subsidies. It recognized the cardinal de Bourbon as heir apparent, Navarre and Condé being declared ineligible by reason of heresy. Obviously, this was a stop-gap measure as the cardinal was old and childless, but it gave the Catholic princes a figurehead of the royal blood.

At the end of March 1585, the leaders of the new league issued a manifesto from Péronne, in Picardy. The format went far beyond the goals originally declared. Dangers to the Catholic faith were cited as justifications for their resort to arms, but religious concerns then gave way to drastic political and fiscal programs. The princes attacked Henry III's favorites, the ducs d'Epernon and de Joyeuse (both Catholics) and demanded their dismissal. They complained that the king had not waged a vigorous war for the restoration of the Church but that nevertheless the nation was crushed by excessive taxation, which should be reduced. They called for the re-establishment of the "liberties" of the nobility and the prosperity of the people. And finally they demanded that the Estates General be convened every three years. Then they began raising troops in Germany and Switzerland as well as in France. Several towns declared in their favor, and they soon controlled most of the kingdom except the south and the west. Without money and without an army Henry III's options were very limited. He formed a new royal bodyguard, and he sent his mother to negotiate with Guise.

Catherine tried to make the best of a bad situation, but she had nothing to bargain with, so the princes got everything they asked. In a treaty signed on 7 July 1585 the king agreed to ban heresy, to assume many of the military expenses of the princes, and to grant them governorships of several important towns. A contemporary parlementary diarist noted that the king remarked upon the irony of his position. Earlier, he said, he had registered edicts of toleration, against his conscience but willingly, for the security of his people; now he found himself abolishing toleration, in keeping with his conscience but unwillingly, for he foresaw the ruin of his people. The new edict revoked all previous grants of toleration, forbidding all Protestant religious practice, ordering all Reformed ministers out of the kingdom immediately, banning Protestants from public offices and requiring all Reformed Christians to convert or depart within six months. It was the most severe edict of proscription that the Huguenots had faced in years. Given the king's military weakness, any attempt to implement it clearly would require the League's forces and would again deliver the state into the hands of the Guises.

The king once more sought Navarre's conversion, and again Navarre refused, but courteously, saying that conscience cannot be forced. Unlike Guise, he never gave offense gratuitously; and he acted with careful respect toward the royal authority that he hoped to inherit. But on 10 August he and Condé met with Damville and renewed the old Huguenot-*politique* alliance. Then, on 9 September 1585 Pope Sixtus V affirmed the League's position, declaring Navarre and Condé relapsed heretics who forfeited all rights and claims. This action raised a storm of protest, and not only from Protestants. When Huguenot pamphleteers rushed to reply, they found they were supported by Gallican Catholics appalled by such papal pretensions in France.

Finally, however, the war of words gave way to a war of soldiers. For two years, from the autumn of 1585 to the autumn of 1587, there were no decisive engagements. Then on 20 October 1587, at Coutras in the west, Navarre destroyed a large League army, killing many prominent Leaguers in the battle. Subsequently he did not exploit his victory and march upon Paris, for which he has been criticized severely. While this may have been poor military judgment, it also may have been the sound judgment of an able politician who did not want to ravage or divide the France he hoped to govern or to humiliate the king whose goodwill he desired.

A month later at Auneau, southwest of Paris, the duc de Guise achieved a victory against an army of German and Swiss mercenaries who were marching to reinforce the Huguenots, so the successes of Navarre and Guise in 1587 appeared to balance. Unlike Navarre, however, Guise was eager for acclaim. In the spring of 1588 he decided to go to Paris to accept the adulation of the capital, thus setting in motion events that were to lead to disaster.

Paris was tumultuous, its traditional intolerance further stirred by fanatical popular preachers. Placards and pamphlets treated Henry III contemptuously; Leaguers dealt openly with the Spanish ambassador; and it was rumored that there would be some sort of Catholic coup to coincide with the descent of Spain's Great Armada upon England. In such circumstances the king judged Guise's presence to be inflammatory and forbade him to enter the city. But with further League demands to press and with a confidence born of recent victory, Guise came anyway and was cheered through the streets by the crowds. Angered and humiliated by this open defiance, Henry III controlled himself and received Guise coldly, but worse was to come. Rumors spread that Guise would be arrested, that the city was to be punished, that there would be a slaughter of League leaders. On Thursday, 12 May, the Parisians began barricading the streets, prepared to do battle with royal troops to defend the League and Guise. It was only Guise himself who was able to calm them and extricate some of the king's soldiers from a threatening massacre. Recognizing that his case was lost in Paris, Henry III slipped out of the Louvre palace next day and fled the city with only a small guard.

The queen mother remained in the capital to negotiate with the Leaguers, and by mid-summer they had agreed upon the terms of an Edict of Union. It was a complete royal surrender: all heresy proscribed, all actions in Paris in May forgiven, all earlier gratifications confirmed and new ones promised, the Estates General to be convened, and Guise appointed Lieutenant-General once more.

When the Estates General opened at Blois in October 1588 the League dominated it. Guise was everywhere received with deference while the king was virtually ignored. Once more the deputies demanded war against heresy while refusing subsidies. But except for some critical remarks in his opening speech, Henry III endured several weeks of this treatment with disarming tranquility. It is impossible to determine exactly when he made his decision to act forcefully, perhaps as early as the Day of the Barricades in May or perhaps only under the sting of further humiliations at Blois. But the decision he took ought not be surprising in a prince who probably had a hand in planning Coligny's murder and certainly took part in the St. Bartholomew's massacre, a man with a record of brooding and lethargy mixed with frenetic activity. On 23 December, when Guise was in the royal apartments for a special council meeting, the king summoned him to his private quarters. As soon as he entered he was attacked by members of the new royal bodyguard and stabbed to death. Then, in a well coordinated operation several of his associates were quickly arrested, including his brother the cardinal de Guise (who was murdered in prison next day) and the cardinal de Bourbon.

Henry III was ecstatic at the success of his plot. Announcing that now he was king in fact, he apparently expected that without

Guise the opposition to him would collapse. His mother was less optimistic, warning that he would find himself "King of Nothing." This proved to be the case. The Estates General refused further business and broke up in mid-January. Paris was incensed, and the popular preachers raged. The Sorbonne condemned the king's action. To complete his isolation, on 5 January 1589 Catherine de Médicis died at the age of seventy.

Nor was the League broken. The duc de Guise and the cardinal had another brother, the duc de Mayenne, who had not been at Blois and consequently had survived. As Guise's eldest son was only seventeen, leadership of the League fell to Mayenne. Though time was to show that he was both militarily incompetent and politically inept, under him the League survived.

There remained only one source from which Henry III might draw support, the Huguenot-*politique* alliance. With the League now openly hostile to him and ever more dependent upon the Spaniards, he had nothing more to lose. Further encouraging him, in March of 1589 Navarre published an appeal for peace, vigorously asserting his devotion to the king and the Crown and promising that he would never deny Catholics the liberty that he had fought for himself. At a meeting in April a pact was arranged, and together the two kings swept aside League resistance and advanced upon Paris, where they arrived at the end of July. Establishing their camp at St. Cloud, just west of the city, they began a siege with every prospect of success, but once again unexpected violence transformed the situation.

On 1 August Jacques Clément, a monk in his early twenties, appeared at St. Cloud claiming to bear letters and messages from within Paris. No sooner was he received by Henry III, however, than he drew a knife and stabbed the king in the abdomen. At first the doctors thought the king would live, but in the evening he began to sink. He was visited by Navarre, whom he blessed and recognized as his successor, begging him to convert. After receiving absolution he was given the sacrament and then he died, murmuring prayers. Of the three Henrys, only Navarre remained, and the fate of the kingdom was in his hands.

# Part Three

## The Huguenots
## and the
## Bourbon Kings

# Chapter Eight

# The Edict of Nantes

THE ASSASSINATION OF Henry III in the summer of 1589 greatly complicated Navarre's position. It transformed him from the heir apparent, recognized by his sovereign whom he was assisting against a rebellious nobility and an insurrectionary capital, into an heretical claimant of the throne of France, opposed by numerous powerful elements in the kingdom he wished to govern. Many religious and political questions were involved, but after Henry III's death the single question of the Bourbon succession gave them focus.

Navarre immediately claimed the French crown, styling himself Henry IV (1589–1610), and moved promptly to consolidate as strong a position as possible. Still refusing to make a conversion that might appear too opportunistic or too forced, he nonetheless repeated his promises to protect the Catholic Church and once more suggested the possibility of future conversion. His manifesto, which was widely distributed, had the lengthy descriptive title characteristic of the time: *Promise Made by King Henry IV Upon His Accession to the Crown to Maintain and Preserve the Roman Catholic and Apostolic Religion in Its Entirety, Desiring Nothing More Than to Be Instructed by a Good and Free Council.* He also confirmed the practice of the Reformed faith "in towns and places where it has been customary" to reassure his Huguenots. And he wrote separately to several important people, guaranteeing their honors and

113

privileges, and to the Parlement of Paris (that part of it which had obeyed Henry III's order to transfer to Tours when the capital rebelled) confirming the judges' appointments and again promising to maintain the Church "without innovations."

The result was that in addition to his Huguenots, some *politique* nobility and some towns supported him, and the royalist (Tours) section of the Parlement of Paris wrote quickly to promise obedience. But some Catholics who had followed Henry III in hopes that Navarre would convert abandoned him for the League. Others withdrew into a sort of neutrality until events should clarify issues of conscience or of self-interest. In November the League section of the Parlement (still in Paris) named the cardinal de Bourbon King of France as Charles X. Actually the role of the cardinal was most equivocal. Though he remained a prisoner in Navarre's hands, generally he was a pawn of the Leaguers. A few weeks before his death on 8 May 1590, he was persuaded or intimidated into issuing an appeal to the great nobility to support his nephew. Thus, on his accession Henry IV was able to claim the loyalties of some Catholics, but his promises were not enough to overcome the opposition of a broad range of aristocratic, popular and corporative interests without which he could not hope to rule effectively.

The year following the death of Henry III was a critical time for his successor. Though his Huguenot support in the south was reasonably secure, north of the Loire he could depend upon only a scattering of Huguenot and *politique* governors of towns and fortresses, and both Paris and the northeastern regions were quite solidly with the League. Moreover, there was always the possibility, which sometimes became reality, that Parma's forces would intervene against him from the Spanish-Netherlands and threaten to occupy the whole Channel coast. This would jeopardize his communications with England, whence he expected some help from Elizabeth. Thus, Henry IV appears to have considered the area west and northwest of Paris, Normandy, the critical theater of the war. He made it the chief focus of his personal efforts, though fighting also continued in several other regions.

In September 1589, with only a small army, the new king was trying doggedly to conquer the lower Seine Valley, where both

Rouen and Havre supported the League. To meet his challenge the duc de Mayenne marched west from Paris with an army about three times the size of the royal force. Henry IV had to give way, but instead of retreating toward the west or south where he might find friendly forces, as probably was expected of him, he fell back northward onto Dieppe, which was held for him by a *politique* governor.

This was a dangerous gamble, and Henry's decision to chance it probably owed something to Elizabeth's commitment to support him. It was to Dieppe that she had promised to send both money and troops, and abandonment of Normandy might have caused her to change her mind. Success against Mayenne would secure Henry's communications with England and increase the likelihood of actually receiving the promised reinforcements. However, the possible consequences of defeat were awesome—loss of his army, which would have no place to retreat; a humiliating personal flight by sea, if indeed he escaped capture; and the probable collapse of all his support in the north. But the king won his gamble. Mayenne pursued him and after three weeks of skirmishing attempted to assault his prepared defenses at Arques, where a narrow front negated the League army's numerical advantage. Henry's victory was complete, and Mayenne withdrew to Amiens to lick his wounds in the reassuring shadow of Parma, while the king made a quick raid on Paris and then fell back into the Loire Valley.

Henry IV pressed a modest offensive through the winter of 1589–1590. He successfully besieged a number of small towns in Normandy and made himself master of almost all of that province south and west of the Seine Valley—where Rouen and Le Havre were still held by the League. Then in March, Mayenne determined to halt his progress and sortied from Paris with another League army, reinforced by Parma. On 14 March the two forces met at Ivry. Though the king was again outnumbered, this time with no advantage of terrain or prepared positions, he won a stunning victory, scattering Mayenne's army and capturing his battle standard.

Once more the road to Paris lay open, and this time there was no relieving force lying at Amiens as had been the case after Arques six months before. But again the king refrained from delivering a coup. When he invested the capital in May he allowed noncombatants to depart, and his subsequent desultory siege was raised by Parma in September.

In the summer of 1590 Henry appears to have assumed that victory was in sight. His successes at Arques and Ivry and his military promenade through the Loire had discredited League claims to be able to halt him in the field. And recognition by the Venetian Senate, a Catholic government, was encouraging, for the political astuteness of the Venetians was famous. Consequently, he refused compromise and summoned the League to obedience in various letters to the League council in Paris and to individual League nobles. Meanwhile, Mayenne was discouraged and unsure of himself. In his correspondence with Madrid he seemed to have no notion what he would do next, and Philip II's replies offered only noncommittal reassurances.

By autumn, when Spanish troops intervened and forced the king to raise the siege of Paris, the situation was clear. Henry IV had proved his military capacities and controlled most of France. He offered legitimacy of blood, peace, support of a sort of status quo in religion and an appeal to French national consciousness against the foreigner. At the same time, the League was much weakened. Except for the single important issue of religion, the Leaguers were in the unhappy position of innovators supported by a foreign power and pledged to a continuation of civil war. They had succeeded, with Spanish help, in keeping Henry IV from his capital, and various provincial towns would not recognize his authority. But no permanent exclusion of his claims had been achieved. With neither side able to win a total victory, the only alternative to civil war was some sort of compromise.

The king grew stronger with each passing month as more and more provinces and noblemen submitted to him, but he also suffered setbacks. In the winter of 1591–1592 he reluctantly undertook a siege of Rouen, which Queen Elizabeth had made a condition of continued support. In the spring his misgivings were justified when Parma once more intervened and saved the town. It is significant, however, that it was the Spaniards and not Mayenne who thus frustrated his efforts. The leadership of the League—never firmly united—was cracking. The condition to which the League had been reduced was described tersely by Parma in

January 1592. He wrote to Philip II that Mayenne and young Guise had become bitter rivals, that Mayenne was "withdrawn and suspicious" and that Guise was "full of complaints" about both Mayenne and Spanish help. Parma's pessimistic analysis of the prospects of the League was echoed by the Venetian resident in Paris who reported to his government about the same time that Mayenne's relations with the Spaniards were deteriorating and that they "made little account" of him.

To advance League aims Mayenne had to try to discredit Henry IV and then find a permanent solution for the succession, to dispose of the Salic Law and then to legitimize the selection of a new king acceptable to the League. He hoped to find the solution in a new convocation of the Estates General. If the estates would accept the League's theories of religious qualifications for the crown, declare the throne vacant, and elect a king, the League's fading strength might revive, and it might be possible to get more help from Spain. The convocation of the estates was, however, a reluctant decision and a last resort. Mayenne hesitated to offer his rivals such an opportunity to criticize his leadership and to appeal for popular support. His concern for his position was not exaggerated, for Parma had speculated in a letter to the King of Spain whether they would "need" Mayenne much longer. Only when the Estates General seemed the sole alternative to complete disaster did Mayenne summon the body for January of 1593.

On the eve of the assembly of the estates Mayenne published a *Declaration* in which he lucidly summed up the position of the League on the question of pretensions to the crown. He asserted that had Henry of Navarre been Catholic, all loyal Frenchmen would have supported him because of the Salic Law. But, he claimed, "the perpetual and inviolable observation of religion and piety in this kingdom since the days of Clovis [which was] reaffirmed by the Estates General of 1576 and 1588" made it impossible to accept him. Thus, Mayenne wrote: "One may not justly blame Catholics who have followed the law of the Church, the example of their predecessors, and the fundamental law of the kingdom which require of a prince who pretends to the crown of this monarchy that he be a true son of the Holy, Catholic, and Apostolic Church. . . ."

According to Mayenne, when the Salic Law and the religious qualification were irreconcilable, the latter took precedence for two reasons. First, the promise to protect and defend the Church "is the first oath of our kings on which is founded the obedience and fidelity of their subjects" and without it there would be no obligation of the subject to the Crown. Secondly, religion must always transcend politics for "the Church does not exist within the state but the state within the faith." Mayenne's repudiation of heresy and even, implicitly, of Gallicanism, was thus both vigorous and persuasive. It also was potentially dangerous to the extreme Leaguers' ambitions; for if Henry IV should be converted, there would be no justification for continued resistance.

With a certain candor Mayenne also demonstrated his understanding of Henry's position, observing that he resisted conversion despite many promises, "so as not to be constrained by his subjects." To this the duke objected that the religious condition was not a simple question of wilfulness of subjects but a profound matter of conscience that could not be compromised, and he invited the king to a conference to make arrangements for his conversion.

This *Declaration* posed a real threat to the public image that Henry IV was attempting to project. He had long contended that the crown was his by right of blood, that the League was simply an alliance of malcontents, and that once the civil disturbances were quieted he would receive instruction in Catholicism. On these grounds he had stood aloof from the public debate and had worked grimly at the military reduction of his foes. Now he was challenged to demonstrate his good faith.

The convocation of the estates was an even greater threat to Henry's pretensions, but opposing it also raised embarrassing problems. He dared not simply ignore the meeting. The mystique of the "voice of the nation" could be dangerous if the assembled deputies took a fervently anti-Bourbon position, and could make Mayenne appear to have the widespread support that he sought. Such an appearance might even persuade Philip II to increase his aid to the League. On the other hand, if the king attacked the assembly too vigorously, he risked lending credence to its claims of legitimacy by the seriousness of his concern. However, such an assembly of League supporters also offered opportunities to negotiate with the opposition and thus weaken its foundations. The king's reactions to the assembly of the estates appear to have been weighed carefully. He made no move until the deputies who had been drifting into Paris for some time actually gathered on 27 January 1593 for a formal opening session. Then, contending that it was simply a rebellion under the pretext of religion, he had the Parlement of Paris (Tours) issue an injunction "against the assembly to be held in Paris under the name of the duc de Mayenne." This move set a pattern which was not to be broken. Henry IV never dealt directly and personally with the assembly, and he never conceded the name of Estates General to it.

The Leaguers proceeded as though confident of their authority, nonetheless, and a defense of their position was published anonymously in 1593 under the title of *A Notice to the Deputies of the Estates.* The unidentified author claimed that the estates could play the role the League desired of them, citing many arguments and precedents for such extraordinary action; but finally he showed himself to be a thorough monarchist at heart, writing:

> One must regulate and reform what is disordered and deformed, but a king is necessary for the execution of it. This state is monarchical and can no longer remain without a king. Everything languishes for lack of such a power! The Catholic religion perishes for lack of it; . . . the first prince of the blood of France, our enemy, is a relapsed heretic, and by this misfortune we are without a king.

This was no idle ranting or emotional fanaticism. It was a lucid attempt to argue the legitimacy and authority of the Estates General, to derogate Henry IV's claims and at the same time to maintain the authority of the Crown against aristocratic usurpations. The pamphlet well illustrates the irresolution and some of the contradictions of the League in 1593—Catholic, anti-Bourbon, willing to set aside the Salic Law, but at heart monarchical.

Actually, the authority of this assembly of the estates was open to attack on practical as well as theoretical grounds. In addition to the usual problems of difficulty and expense of travel and lodgings, exaggerated by convocation to Paris, the deputies faced the uncertainties of civil war and the danger of passing the king's lines, which were drawn around the city. Consequently the attendance was very limited, and the distribution of representation was very uneven.

No deputies appeared from Languedoc for the opening session (though a deputy from Toulouse arrived later). Paris, on the other hand, provided twenty deputies and the surrounding Ile-de-France another sixteen. The only other areas well represented were the League provinces of Champagne and Burgundy. Obviously only men in sympathy with the League were likely to defy the difficulties and dangers of attendance, but more than that, most deputies came from those areas that the League actually controlled and governed. Even had Mayenne succeeded in drawing from the estates the decisions he desired, the moral force of such an assembly might have been less than he hoped. But the independent course taken by the deputies underscored dramatically the lack of popular support for the anti-royalist and anti-national implications of the League's opposition to Henry IV.

A week after the opening of the Estates General the king's Catholic supporters wrote to agree on the need for a reconciliation and to propose a conference lest the kingdom fall completely "to the insolence of the Spaniards." After much debate and many delays active negotiations were opened in the spring. Meanwhile, the Duke of Feria, a special emissary from Philip of Spain, arrived in Paris in early March. During the next few months, while the estates were negotiating with both Bourbon and the Spaniards, a pattern emerged which was fundamentally national and monarchical.

The discussions between the estates and the royalists were amicable and produced results in mid-May, when Bourbon made a considerable concession. Apparently satisfied that most Leaguers were willing to accept him if he changed his religion, and perhaps convinced that they would never willingly accept him otherwise, he allowed his supporters to announce that he had been "converted in his heart" and that he was proceeding immediately to formal public conversion. As evidence, he wrote an open letter asking the bishops and prelates of France to attend him on 15 July. Ever conscious of the power of persuasion, he allowed his Catholic supporters to send an official announcement of these moves to the assembly in June, together with a proposal for a truce.

This suggestion triggered vituperative debate, as the deputies of the third estate and of the nobility pressed for agreement, while the clergy resisted, threatening ecclesiastical penalties against anyone who dealt directly with the heretic. The clergy finally succeeded in having a truce deferred until the king's promised conversion actually had taken place, but the quarrel divided the estates bitterly. The issue was significant. Henry IV accepted the political necessity of conversion, but he wanted recognition and the truce first. Committed Leaguers, on the other hand, especially the clergy, insisted that the conversion had to take place first. At issue was the question whether Henry would recognize religion as a qualification upon his hereditary claims or only as a political concession to peace after his claims had been accepted.

While the deputies' negotiations with the royalists were proceeding through the early summer of 1593, discussions also were in progress with the Spaniards. The difference was startling. In mid-May Feria advanced claims for the *Infanta*, Isabella, who was Philip II's daughter by Elizabeth of France and thus a granddaughter of Henry II. And from then into July there was a whole series of Spanish proposals and League counter-proposals that finally proved fruitless. The Spaniards first suggested that the estates should recognize the *Infanta*'s claim as a birthright through her mother. When the estates objected that a woman could not inherit the French throne, Feria proposed that they should elect her queen. Then the deputies raised the question of a husband for her. At first they were told only that Philip would make a wise choice. When they objected to this answer, they were promised that he would choose a French prince. Finally Feria conceded that they might submit a list of names from which Philip would select. Satisfied on these points, the estates then shifted ground completely and announced that they would consider no election until promised Spanish reinforcements actually were at hand.

The contrast between the sincere and amicable negotiations with the royalists and the petty, bickering discussions with the Spaniards suggests very strongly that by the summer of 1593 most of the deputies, this rank and file of the League, had no desire for an alternative to Henry IV. Rather the discussions with the Spaniards have the air of a grim charade intended only to keep Spain in the game as a club to force the king to the baptismal font. Traditionally it has been assumed that Henry's victory was due at least in part to the rigidity and unrealistic behavior of the Spaniards, whose tool the League was supposed to be. But Feria, though sometimes clumsy, appears to have been flexible, accommodating, and quite ready to meet the estates' requests. And far from the League being Spain's tool, as was perhaps the case earlier, in the 1590s it appears that Spain was used by the League; for the Spanish threat remained poised should the king fail to fulfill his promises, while the deputies gave Spain nothing in return except empty hopes for a crown for the *Infanta*.

As the summer advanced, the king's support continued to grow. At the end of June the League section of the Parlement of Paris, which should have been one of the staunchest defenders of the League's positions, produced an injunction on the Salic Law, and one of its chief justices announced to Mayenne:

> The court has charged me to inform you that it has declared and declares null and void everything that has been done or may be done in the assembly of the estates to the prejudice of the Salic Law and [other] fundamental laws of the kingdom.

After adopting such a position the parlement could, of course, accept no alternative to Henry IV, though the judges showed no indication of being willing to accept him before conversion.

On 25 and 26 July Henry publicly renounced heresy and made a profession of faith in the Catholic Church. On 31 July the truce that had long been under discussion was signed. For all practical purposes the civil war was over, though it was February 1594 before the king proceeded to his coronation and March before he entered Paris. Officially Henry was not absolved of heresy until September 1595 when the pope accepted his conversion. Mayenne remained in arms and made his final surrender only after the papal decision. But nonetheless, towns and nobles hurried to make their submissions.

While most of Catholic Europe received news of the king's

conversion with joy, understandably most of his Huguenot subjects and his Protestant allies reacted adversely, though there were exceptions. His old companion-in-arms and financial advisor, the duc de Sully (1560–1641), though he remained a Calvinist himself, not only approved the king's action as a necessity of state but later claimed in his memoirs to have been a fervent advocate of it; and some Calvinist nobles followed the king's example and converted. But to a great many of the Huguenots there were no causes that justified the compromise of religious principles, and they felt betrayed and fearful of new repression.

Queen Elizabeth of England also declared herself scandalized by the conversion, disdainfully calling it "a notable mutation." Likely, though, she exaggerated her surprise, for her agents kept her well informed. In any case, there can be little doubt that Henry's decision aggravated already worsening Anglo-French relations, contributing to the effective end of English aid shortly thereafter.

The situation continued to be dangerous. Philip II, who had felt so near to dominating the French crown, did not give up his hopes. After the collapse of the League, war broke out between France and Spain in 1595. Moreover, not only did English aid taper off, but Henry's disgruntled Huguenots also refused him significant help, and he largely blamed them for the Spanish capture of Amiens in 1597. So the international conflict continued, and the domestic scene was far from tranquil during the half dozen years following the king's conversion, despite the advantages that accrued from it. Only in 1598 did he finally achieve a resolution of both problems.

In the spring of 1598 the aging Philip II finally resigned himself to the new realities in France. His own power was greatly diminished by repeated naval failures against England and an apparently irresoluble rebellion in the Netherlands. In 1596 he had been forced to declare bankruptcy for the second time. Henry IV was immeasurably strengthened by papal recognition and by the submission of almost all of those who had opposed him in France. Thus there was no prospect for significant Spanish gains from the war. On 2 May 1598 France and Spain agreed to the Peace of Vervins, which restored things as they had been after the Treaty of

Câteau-Cambrésis in 1559. Four months later, on 13 September, Philip II died.

More complicated was the domestic religious settlement that Henry IV designed, usually considered one of his greatest achievements. For nearly a decade following his accession, the Crown's relations with the Huguenots had been uncertain. He had reaffirmed their eligibility for public office only after considerable hesitation. He had revoked the repressive edicts of the late 1580's only "provisionally" and had referred often to his intention to establish a general settlement without actually doing anything about it. Naturally, the Huguenots felt that his conversion made their position even more insecure. Their concern was heightened by the favor that he showed former opponents in his effort to eradicate old animosities. By the late 1590s the situation was rather tense.

Once Henry felt he had the Spanish situation under control, he turned his full attention to negotiations with the Huguenots, and after much haggling, a settlement was agreed upon. The result was the Edict of Nantes, which the king signed on 13 April 1598. Its preface declared the king's intent that it be "perpetual and irrevocable."

Actually, there was little foundation for a permanent religious settlement, for both Catholics and Huguenots still dreamed of total victory. The apparent recognition of Protestantism as a permanent force in French society was abhorrent to the former, while the limitations imposed upon Protestant worship were deemed humiliating by the latter. Catholics had not yet learned the futility of trying to enforce conformity, and the Huguenots still aspired to the overthrow of the established Church. Toleration in France was a royal notion, politically motivated.

But from another point of view, Henry IV really had no alternative to granting the Edict of Nantes. His former co-religionists were too strong to be coerced and too militant to be ignored. The king's correspondence of this time shows that he understood this clearly. Any estimate of numbers for this period is highly speculative, but one Italian diplomat suggested that a contemporary census showed one and one quarter million organized into almost one thousand congregations, about one quarter of these

attached to noble households. Since internal peace was a necessary
precondition for the re-establishment of the royal authority, the
only solution was a limited toleration enforced by the Crown. Since
the royal armies could not be everywhere at once, this necessitated
allowing the Huguenots both legal rights and the capacity to defend
them. The means by which Henry sought these goals, however,
clearly indicate that he had no intention of creating for Protestants
a permanent independence of the Crown.

The Edict of Nantes was divided into two parts, the first
containing ninety-two general articles and the second fifty-six "secret" articles. Though the edict did not give Protestants equality
with Catholics, it improved their situation immeasurably. They
were to have complete freedom of conscience, might reside in any
part of the kingdom, and might perform the public acts of their
religion in noble households and in a generous number of specified
areas. They were to be allowed the enjoyment of public office,
control and education of their children, and decent burial.
Moreover, special courts were created in which the presence of
Protestant judges offered hope for equitable justice; and though
they still had to pay tithes for the support of the established
Church, they were to be compensated by a royal subsidy for the
support of their ministers and schools. Obviously Henry had drawn
heavily upon the precedents set by his predecessors, especially
Catherine de Médicis. But there was one important difference; this
settlement was to be permanent.

The issuance of the Edict of Nantes exposed Henry IV to
severe criticism. Papal denunciations were scathing. The French
Catholic clergy rebuked him vehemently. The parlements fought a
delaying action against registering the new law. The Parlement of
Paris held it up for ten months of argument and that of Rouen
stalled its implementation in Normandy until 1609. Even the
Huguenot governing bodies showed little gratitude. They had
complained that the edict in its original form did not go far enough.
After the king had made some concessions to their opponents, they
liked it even less and agitated continually for its reissue as originally
drafted. This unenthusiastic reception was indicative of a real division between the moderate desires of the great mass of the
Huguenots and the extremist sympathies of the ministers who

controlled their councils. The moderates no longer could be goaded to "fight or die" and the desire for office, or simply for a quiet life, encouraged many to accept the settlement gratefully.

The Edict of Nantes contains no reference either to "security towns" or to military subsidies. These privileges, which formed an important second half of Henry's concessions, were granted by letters patent—official letters with the royal seal affixed but not part of the edict itself. The distinction is important, for the military arrangements did not come under the "perpetual and irrevocable" guarantee and clearly were regarded by the king as a temporary measure. The letters patent of 1598 were valid for eight years. In 1606 Henry renewed them for five years, and this became the pattern for future renewals. But unlike the religious provisions of the settlement, these military privileges were never granted without term.

Henry clearly assumed that his guarantee of the position of the Huguenots removed their excuse for the maintenance of a strong military and political organization, and the frequency of his consent to Protestant political assemblies and the amount of his subsidy to their garrisons diminished continually. He was willing to allow meetings of the National Synod, which dealt with matters of doctrine and discipline, but the only regular political organization which he permitted the Huguenots was a two-man deputation which they maintained at Court to represent their interests to him.

During the last decade of Henry IV's reign the condition of the Huguenots changed considerably. By 1610 their military resources had been reduced by twelve years of peace and the slow diminution of the royal subsidy to about a third or a fourth of its 1598 level. Their political solidarity had been weakened by the king's continued opposition to political assemblies; and the differences between fanatics and moderates had been heightened by conciliation of the latter. On the whole, the Huguenots were a far less intimidating force by 1610 than they had been in 1598, and there is some evidence to suggest that Henry had foreseen this development.

Also by 1610, with the assistance of the tireless Sully, the king had largely succeeded in rebuilding the French economy, developing the royal army and replenishing the treasury. At the same time, the Habsburg position in Europe seemed to be weakening. The Austrian branch of the family appeared still exhausted from the wars of the preceding century, and once-mighty Spain had been forced to a rather ignominious truce with the Netherlands rebels. Henry IV seems to have decided that the time had come to renew the struggle to overthrow the Habsburg hegemony, and he began preparations for war. However, on 10 May 1610, as he left the Louvre palace in an open carriage, intending to inspect some new weapons in the arsenal, he was set upon by a frenzied assassin who stabbed him. The last of the three Henrys died like the other two beneath the murderer's blade.

# Chapter Nine

# The Last Rebellion

THE SUDDEN DEATH of Henry IV in 1610 was a severe shock to the Huguenots. They had complained about him often, and frequently their leaders had agitated for greater privileges; but the Edict of Nantes had restored their basic trust in him, despite this minor bickering. Such was not the case with the government that succeeded him.

Henry IV's marriage with Marguerite de Valois, the occasion for the St. Bartholomew's massacre, had not been happy, and had produced no children. Consequently, in 1599 he had obtained a papal annulment dissolving their union, and the next year he had remarried. The king selected as his second wife an Italian princess, Marie de Médicis, a distant relative of the famous Catherine. And though this match also proved stormy, it provided the necessary heirs, two boys and three girls. However, Henry's elder son, Louis XIII (1610–1643), was only nine years old when the king was murdered. Once again a regency was necessary, and once again a foreign queen mother would have a prominent role in the affairs of France.

It is no wonder that the Huguenots found the prospect disturbing. Marie was an Italian Catholic, from a family that had given the Roman Church many cardinals and popes. Among her personal friends at the French Court were the papal nuncio (plenipotentiary) and the Spanish ambassador. There was no reason to expect that she would show much sympathy for heretics. To make matters worse, the letters patent which authorized the Huguenots' military privileges were due to expire in 1611.

Actually, the Huguenots were in considerably less jeopardy than they feared. Though the Parlement of Paris had quickly declared Marie regent for her son, she expected—and soon had to face—vigorous agitation from the princes of the blood and great aristocrats who sought power for themselves. And to maintain foreign peace she had to disentangle herself from the anti-Habsburg commitments that Henry IV had made. She had no desire further to aggravate her situation by arousing the wrath of the Calvinists. Consequently, to reassure them, she immediately confirmed the Edict of Nantes; and she authorized them to convene a national general assembly, a privilege that Henry IV had granted only rarely and with reluctance. Nonetheless, the Huguenots continued to mistrust her and feared for their security.

There were several influential figures among the Huguenots in the early seventeenth century, though no one leader dominated the party so much as Coligny or Navarre had done. From Geneva, Beza maintained an extensive correspondence until his death in 1605, advising chiefly on doctrine and discipline. The duc de Duplessis-Mornay (1549–1623)—scholar, theologian, and onetime secretary to Henry IV—played so prominent a role within the French Reformed Church that he sometimes was called "the Huguenot pope." The king's conversion and the end of the civil wars had greatly diminished the number of militarily active Calvinist nobles. The few still notable often were aging relics of an earlier generation, such as the duc de Lesdiguières (1543–1626), who served in the armies of four kings, or the duc de Bouillon (1555–1623). Indisuptably, however, the most prominent Huguenot noble in 1610 was Henry IV's chief advisor, the duc de Sully.

As soon as he heard of the king's murder, Sully, who had been a schoolboy in Paris in 1572 and had barely survived St. Bartholomew's Day, locked himself into the arsenal, apparently expecting a new massacre. It was only with some difficulty that the queen mother persuaded him to come out, and after this inauspicious beginning his relations with her worsened rapidly. A very conservative fiscal planner and a meticulous administrator, Sully proved too inflexible to cope with the changed situation—especially the necessity for Marie to distribute hard-won royal treasure as "gratifications," really bribes, to pacify the princes. Early in 1611, less than a year after Henry's assassination, he was forced to resign his appointments and retire to private life. This diminution of Protestant influence at the Court caused further concern to the Huguenots. There can be no doubt of the sincerity of Sully's religious commitment, nor of his basic integrity, but his resentment of the queen mother and his hostility to the policies of the new government complicated Huguenot affairs during the regency.

The pivotal event in the Huguenots' relations with Marie's government, and one which was to have lasting effects, was the general assembly that she authorized, which opened at Saumur—on the Loire—in May 1611. Ostensibly its chief task was to nominate delegates who would negotiate with the regent the renewal of the military letters patent and any Protestant grievances. In fact, the dominant issue of the meetings was the question of Huguenot leadership, someone to replace Sully as a chief spokesman at Court.

Probably the duc de Bouillon expected the honor to fall to him easily. He belonged to an old and respected French family and had fought with some distinction for the Huguenot cause in the civil wars. Marriage had given him imperial titles and possession of important frontier positions at Metz and Sedan; and he was a member of the regent's council, the most important Protestant at the center of affairs after Sully's departure. But Bouillon was too opportunistic and too obviously ambitious. He encouraged the Huguenots to agitate, arguing that through his credit with the queen mother he would win them a favorable settlement. At the same time he argued to her that only he had sufficient influence with his co-religionists to calm their agitations without massive concessions. Ultimately, he was distrusted by both sides; and most significantly, he earned the animosity of Sully and the suspicion of Duplessis-Mornay. In consequence, while the Huguenot deputies at Saumur could not be persuaded to take up Sully's private grievances as a party matter, neither were they prepared to entrust themselves to Bouillon's leadership. Instead, they turned to a compromise figure, the duc de Rohan (1579–1638).

A relatively quiet man, reserved and unpretentious, at thirty-two Rohan was young to be thrust into a position of such responsibility, but his background equipped him for the role better than might have been expected. Most importantly, he was a sincerely devout Calvinist. In addition, he was a highly intelligent individual, an avid student of history, geography, and mathematics, and the author of a lengthy commentary on Caesar's *Gallic Wars*. He had traveled widely in both Europe and England; and he had military experience, demonstrating something more than average tactical abilities. In 1603 Henry IV had made him a duke and peer of the realm, a high honor, and two years later he had married a daughter of the duc de Sully.

The negotiations between the Assembly of Saumur and the regent proceeded as might have been predicted. The deputies asked much, the queen mother offered little, and a compromise was arranged. Marie would make the final choice of the persons to be the Huguenots' two permanent representatives at Court from a list of nominees drafted by the deputies. She would confirm again their existing privileges and positions. The Huguenots would not pursue the matter of Sully's dismissal (though they promised him support if any legal actions were launched against him), and they would disband their assembly and return to their homes without insisting upon a prior response to several grievances that they had submitted.

More important in the long run was the further development of Huguenot political organization. This was largely Rohan's work. Previously the provincial councils of the party had worked independently of and sometimes in conflict with one another. Rohan foresaw the time when a particular province, wronged by the Crown or other bodies in its religious rights, would require quicker and more proximate support than the cumbersome national organization could provide. He therefore proposed the grouping of provinces into "circles," an idea probably borrowed from German practice. The circles were not to replace provincial bodies but rather to fill the need for regional coordination at a level between local and national organizations. In passing a resolution adopting this idea the delegates stated that the circle assemblies should be nonpolitical and would seek only to offer moral support. However, the clear potential for political and military coordination was realized during later troubles.

The Assembly of Saumur also gave evidence of trends that were to become more important as time passed. Not only were noblemen numerically less significant than in the previous century, but those who continued to be important disagreed on policy and were divided by rivalries. Sully was disgruntled and sought support for his personal grievances. Bouillon was ambitious and tried to manipulate religious issues to advance his own political interests. Duplessis-Mornay was the theologian and patriarch of the party, rather detached from political affairs. And Lesdiguières did not even attend. A few years later these divisions were to become even more serious.

Ever since Henry IV's death in 1610 the prince de Condé, in this generation a Catholic as his family had followed the king in conversion, had been seeking to impose himself upon Marie de Médicis, but without much success. In 1614, the thirteen year-old Louis XIII was declared to be in his majority (under the Bourbons the old pattern was advanced by a year). This made it more difficult to resist royal decisions, even though Marie still made them; and in 1614–1615 an Estates General, which Condé had hoped would support his criticism of the new government, congratulated Marie on maintaining the peace and generally endorsed her policies. Among the latter was an arrangement to marry Louis XIII to a Spanish princess, called Anne of Austria, while sending Louis' sister, Elizabeth, to marry the crown prince of Spain. In defiance, Condé rebelled and invited the Huguenots, who had long connections with his family despite changed religious circumstances, and who also had cause to mistrust the purpose of a Spanish alliance, to support him in military resistance.

The Huguenots of the southwestern regions of the kingdom, traditionally the most militant, took up arms. To maintain the credibility of his leadership, Rohan, who might have preferred negotiation, joined them. But Sully and Duplessis-Mornay held aloof, and Lesdiguières even volunteered to raise Protestant troops for the service of the Crown. In addition, the governing councils of many Huguenot towns opted for neutrality, and it became obvious that the party was greatly divided. As it turned out, Condé's rebellion was generally ineffectual, the princesses were exchanged and the queen mother then undertook to negotiate settlements with the opposition. By the Treaty of Loudon of May 1616 the Huguenots had their military privileges confirmed yet again, and they were promised increases in their ministerial and military subsidies.

More important than these small gains were the divisions that had appeared between those who believed that security was best maintained by a show of strength and a demand for concessions and those who believed that the future of the party was best served by overt demonstrations of loyalty and submission to the Crown and by reliance upon royal favor. Also significant was the growing independence of the middle-class town councils in opposition to the traditional leadership of noblemen—who had so often ended rebellions by making private settlements and leaving the rank and file to bear the brunt of governmental retribution. All of these trends were accelerated by contemporary developments in French government and became extraordinarily important in the new crises of the middle and late 1620s.

With some oversimplification, the transformation of royal government in the 1620s and 1630s can be summed up in one name—the cardinal de Richelieu (1585–1642). Already in 1617 Louis XIII, then in his late teens, had arranged the murder of his mother's favorite counsellor. He had sent her into seclusion in the country and had tried to organize his own government, drawing heavily upon the aging "greybeards" who had served his father. Initially, however, the experiment had not been very successful. The king was a sober young man who took his responsibilities seriously. He was soon to demonstrate ample reserves of both stamina and courage. But he seems to have possessed little political subtlety in his youth and to have had little patience for the daily strains of careful administration. The first men whom he called upon to serve him proved to be either too old and exhausted or too ambitious and self-seeking.

As a young bishop, Richelieu had first achieved some prominence in the first estate of the Estates General of 1614. He had been given a government post in 1616 and then had been dismissed along with the rest of Marie's appointees in 1617. In the early 1620s he served as intermediary in compromising differences between Marie and her son. He was made a cardinal in 1622 and, on the queen mother's urging, was admitted to the royal council in 1624. At first the young king seems to have mistrusted him, though recognizing his talents. However, as Richelieu established his dominance of the council through sheer ability and demonstrated unwavering dedication to the Crown, Louis placed ever greater confidence in him. Eventually the two men grew as near to being friends as was possible between master and royal servant. Together they changed the French monarchy into a much more centralized and enormously more efficient government than ever it had been before. The transformation of the Huguenot position in the 1620s was no small part of their accomplishment.

During the first year of Louis XIII's personal reign he adopted a rather aggressively Catholic policy. When southern Protestants refused to accept the re-establishment of the Catholic Church in Béarn and Navarre, the government resorted to force. Calvinists all over France rallied, and a general assembly was convened at La Rochelle at Christmas of 1620. Honest fears and the government's readiness to resort to military solutions strengthened the position of the Protestant militants, and the assembly resolved upon armed resistance. The religious wars were reborn in La Rochelle that Christmas. They ended, except for mopping up operations, in the city's agony eight years later.

The Huguenot risings of the 1620s were only a pale reflection of the party's strength in the country. Few great nobles participated, and the cooperation of the propertied bourgeois, who had much to lose, was half-hearted. Not surprisingly in these circumstances, despite Rohan's desperate sincerity and real abilities, the Crown won the first rounds in the new struggle. In 1621 and 1622 royal forces gained victories in both the west and the south, and the rebels were forced to negotiate.

The Peace of Montpellier, signed in October 1622, deepened the division among the Calvinists. The militants called it disastrous, for it reduced the number of security towns that the party was permitted to hold and garrison, leaving chiefly La Rochelle in the west and Montauban in the south; and it forbade Protestant political assemblies without express royal consent. Moreover, the peace left royal garrisons deep in Protestant territory, most notably in

Fort Louis near La Rochelle and in positions on the island of Ré, which stood just in front of La Rochelle's harbor. On the other hand, loyalists could point out that the king had been generous. Although almost universally successful in the field, he had confirmed the religious guarantees of the Edict of Nantes, and he had not attempted to restrict religious assemblies nor to disarm the Protestant community. In a word, the Peace of Montpellier resolved nothing.

During the next two and a half years the militants again came to dominate the Protestant party, and some of their grievances were real enough. The Huguenots claimed that the royal negotiators had promised orally that the threatening garrisons at Fort Louis and on Ré would be reduced. Instead they were strengthened; and the Crown did not withdraw its troops from Montpellier as it certainly had promised to do. Moreover, the rapid ascendancy of Richelieu, a cardinal of the Roman Church, caused unease. Early in 1625 Rohan and his younger brother, Soubise, resorted to arms once again, claiming that they sought only to force the government to honor the Peace of Montpellier. This time they managed a few small victories. At the same time the Crown was discovering that it could not get significant help from its English and Dutch allies against Protestant rebels and was involved in quarrels with both the papacy and Spain. Under so many simultaneous pressures, the French government offered peace but only in another inconclusive settlement. The king refused any diminution of his garrisons, only promising not to allow them to interfere with peaceful commerce. Thus, the Peace of La Rochelle, signed in February 1626, was little more than an armed truce. It lasted just over a year.

Under no illusions about the durability of the peace, the Huguenots were seeking any help they might find. In the spring of 1627 the King of England's vain and blundering favorite, the Duke of Buckingham, made them grandiose promises. He offered thirty thousand men in three fleets to land on Ré, at Bordeaux, and in Normandy "to support the Reformed churches." A realist at heart, the militant Rohan promised to raise the standard of rebellion again *after* the English had landed.

Richelieu was not unaware of these discussions, and he quietly strengthened the west coast garrisons. Consequently, when Buckingham appeared at Ré in early July, with only one fleet and a force variously estimated between five and ten thousand men, he met unexpectedly stiff opposition commanded by an able and dedicated officer, the marquis de Toiras. With only twelve hundred infantry and two hundred cavalry Toiras vigorously contested the English landing, inflicting losses. He then withdrew his forces into the citadel of St. Martin de Ré and the fort de La Prée, a few miles south of St. Martin, effectively denying Buckingham sheltered anchorages. These surprises were only the first of many for the English expeditionary force. When Buckingham and the Rohans tried to raise the French Protestants, the sad legacy of distrust, division, and defeat quickly began to manifest itself.

When Soubise went to La Rochelle with Buckingham's envoys to rally the town to rebellion, he found the gates shut against them. This caused Rohan to remark later that the mayor and the council "had been won by the Court, and the people had neither vigor nor courage." Actually the Rohans enjoyed considerable popular support within the walls, but the propertied bourgeois who ran the town had seen enough of active revolt, and they had not failed to notice the quiet escalation of the Crown's strength around the city. In any case, Soubise and the English were admitted only as the result of a pathetic little scene. Learning what was taking place, the old dowager duchesse de Rohan—mother of the ducs de Rohan and de Soubise and a great local personage in her own right— stormed down upon the gates from the inside, insisted that they be opened and personally escorted her son and his friends into town.

The crowd in the streets cheered them, but the mayor and the council gave them a chilly reception. When offered the "protection of the King of England" they replied that La Rochelle was "only a part of the Body of the Reformed Churches" and could not act or respond alone. Pressed by the Rohans and by the mob, the councillors did not dare an absolute refusal, but their ill will was obvious. In the south Rohan was meeting the same attitude. Though he finally persuaded a Huguenot assembly to call the party to arms, his backing remained uncertain. Several city councils rejected the appeal, and the Protestant towns were torn by factional fights. The bourgeois tried desperately to maintain their control and to pre-

serve the peace while the petty nobility and the mob declared for
Rohan. But while moderates and militants debated revolt, the
decision was taken out of their hands.

Determined to put an end to Huguenot revolts, Louis XIII
issued a proclamation against rebels on 5 August 1627 and set his
armies in motion. Troops were dispatched to the south to tie down
Huguenot forces there, while the main royal army was sent to La
Rochelle, where it arrived in mid-August. A few weeks later the
king arrived to take personal command of his troops, accompanied
by Richelieu. The Rochelais bourgeois still hesitated, even though
the Crown obviously considered them rebels. While the king's
troops dug in, the municipal council argued. Only in September did
the town finally declare for the rebellion and the alliance with
England. It proved a disastrous decision, for it evoked a bitter siege
that lasted over a year, until the English were driven off and La
Rochelle was crushed.

The Crown's first efforts turned to relieving the royal garrisons
on Ré, which was accomplished with surprising ease as Buckingham
proved to be militarily incompetent. In early November French
royal forces landed on the island in some strength, forcing Buckingham to evacuate with heavy losses. Having thus disposed of the
English, at least temporarily, the king next turned to the siege of
the city itself, which presented peculiar problems.

Sitting on an outcrop amid marshes, La Rochelle enjoyed
many advantages of terrain. Only about a third of its circumference
was vulnerable to attack, and that third was well defended by
earthworks and flooded ditches. The rest of its landward face was
protected by the marshes, which pushed the attackers' lines well
away from the city and lengthened them enormously. When
finished, the royal army's siege line measured over ten miles long
and was reinforced with eleven forts and eighteen redoubts. But
even this construction was eclipsed by the massive works undertaken to seal off La Rochelle from the sea.

Since the royal navy did not have a fleet capable of maintaining
an effective blockade, and since closing the port was absolutely
essential to the success of the siege, the Crown adopted a startling
expedient—a fortified dike across the outer harbor. The dike at La

Rochelle was one of the most impressive accomplishments of early seventeenth-century military engineering. When completed, it measured almost four thousand five hundred feet long and was fifty feet thick at the base and twenty-five at the top. The strong west coast tide could not be ignored, so in the middle a gap of about two hundred yards was left, closed by floating barriers, including old ships, all fastened together with cables and chains and defended by artillery. By the spring of 1628, after six months of frantic construction, La Rochelle was sealed off from the outer world.

Cut off by land and sea the city could do little for itself, but its resistance was unwavering. Municipal elections in March of 1628 entrusted the mayoralty to the fiery Jean Guiton, who is reputed to have threatened to personally kill the first man to suggest surrender. However uncertainly the rebellion had begun, by the spring La Rochelle was totally committed. Amid growing scarcity the Rochelais stood firm and awaited English relief.

At the end of April spirits rose when an English force of about fifty ships appeared, but they plummeted again when the fleet simply sailed back and forth before the dike without attacking and then, after several days, returned to England. English messengers managed to pass the royal lines to bring word to the city that the fleet would come back later in greater strength, but after this first vacillating performance the message inspired little confidence. In any case time was running out for La Rochelle.

After the departure of the English in mid-May the siege grew more bitter. Earlier it had been possible for messengers to pass in and out and even for small quantities of provisions to slip through. In fact, Pierre Mervault, a diarist who survived the siege within the city, noted several instances of contact between sympathetic common soldiers and townsmen who slipped out to try to gather shellfish or salt. But in June a captain and two junior officers were executed for complicity in smuggling supplies into the city, and in July an entire regiment was punished for allowing a few cattle to be driven through its lines. The besieging army's grip tightened like a vise, and the troops even managed to destroy a crop of beans that the Rochelais had planted between the walls and the siege lines.

As the summer wore on, conditions grew worse and worse in

the city. In early July the diarist noted the slaughter of horses, mules, dogs, and cats, and by the end of the month rats and mice were being hunted determinedly. Some of the Rochelais weakened and tried to escape or to give themselves up, coming out to the royal positions, but the king ordered that anyone approaching the lines was to be fired on. The only surrender to be accepted was that of the whole city.

On the night of 5 July, in one incident alone, the troops fired into a group of civilians estimated to number five hundred. Several were killed, and the rest were driven back into the city. These harsh orders stood until a particularly vicious enforcement of them evoked a change. On 1 September a woman and two small children approached the lines, begging to be allowed to pass. When she refused to go back as ordered, one of the soldiers fired, wounding but not killing her. As she lay screaming a sergeant leaped out of the lines with a knife, cut her throat, and then killed the children. Apparently this was too much even for callous seventeenth-century stomachs, and the story spread through the army like wildfire. As a consequence, the standing orders were changed to specify that unarmed civilians simply should be driven back with whips and sticks. But really it made little difference since many were then hanged in the city, considered deserters for having tried to give themselves up.

As usual, people of "quality" could have the rules bent for them. On the night of 22 July a young woman of obviously good family proposed to marry any young lieutenant who could get her through the lines, offering a dowry of thirty thousand *livres,* a small fortune. A young officer promptly accepted on condition that the king assent and that he agree not to confiscate her property. As Louis granted this petition, the two were married "with great solemnity." Other women, not so fortunate as to have dowries, crept out to the lines at night to prostitute themselves for a bit of food or in hopes of establishing liasons with soldiers who would smuggle them through. By mid-August this practice had become so common that the king proclaimed harsh measures against it. The guilty were to be broken on the wheel, a particularly grisly execution. Informers were to be rewarded, and captains who attempted to cover for their men were to lose their companies.

The summer was also a time of false hopes. On 29 July a great storm struck the coast and raged for two days. Waves five feet high swept over the dike, carrying away chunks of it, and ten royalist ships were sunk and two more driven ashore. But when the storm blew out, it could be seen that the damage to the dike was superficial, and the remaining ships soon crept back into position. Almost every week brought rumors of another English fleet, and the Rochelais scanned the sea eagerly. On 7 August the dawn revealed forty ships standing down the coast, and the city hastened to unfurl its flags and to fire salutes; but they proved to be only Dutch merchantmen bound for Ré to load salt. The Huguenots took down their flags, and the siege ground on.

In late summer two judges from the city were allowed to surrender in return for the information they brought. They revealed that the public markets had ceased to function and claimed that for a month about six thousand of the poorer residents had eaten only grass and a sort of pudding made by mincing, soaking and boiling old leather. According to them many had died of starvation, especially children. But it is Mervault, the diarist, who evokes the real horror of the siege. In late August he was estimating deaths at about fifty each day. On 12 September he noted that grass, snails, and even small shellfish had been entirely consumed, and he estimated that about two thousand people had died of starvation since the beginning of the month.

Hoarding and profiteering made conditions worse. At the end of July, when the two escaped judges were reporting that the poor were living on grass and boiled leather, the dowager duchesse de Rohan had two of her carriage horses killed to feed her household. Presumably her other horses were still alive and still eating. As late as mid-September, when the death rate must have been well over a hundred each day, Mervault mentions that meals "for those of higher condition" normally consisted of bread soup, sugared herbs, and a bit of horsemeat. Nothing was done to control prices, and they escalated wildly. By autumn a dog brought as much on the market as a good steer before the siege. In late September the municipal government ordered a house by house search for hoards of food. The searches unearthed barrels and bales of provisions, apparently the first effort at control of food distribution despite the terrible conditions in the city.

La Rochelle's last hope was that another English expedition

might materialize before winter closed in again. In late September an English fleet did appear, stronger than the previous one, but again it sailed back and forth unaggressively for two weeks. Then it formed up in battle array. The surviving Rochelais lined their walls to watch, but the English only sent in two fireships, without effect, and then resumed cruising. It was mid-October, Friday the thirteenth. A week later Mervault noted that the death rate in the doomed city had passed four hundred each day, that bodies were piling up in the streets and the cemeteries as no one had the strength to bury them, and that there were instances of cannibalism. The silence of death enveloped the city, and another winter was approaching.

After the long agony of the siege, the surrender was quiet and undramatic. On 27 October the surviving Rochelais inquired the terms of peace and were answered that this time there would be no negotiated treaty. The king insisted upon a simple surrender, but he promised clemency. The rebels' lives would be spared. There would be no sack of the city and no property confiscations. Protestant worship would not be prohibited. The city would lose its fortifications and most of its right of self-government, and it would have to accept the re-establishment of the Catholic Church. Harsh as he had been during the struggle, the king showed himself generous in victory.

The terms were agreed to quickly, and on 28 October the ceremonies were completed. On 1 November Louis XIII made his formal entry into La Rochelle. Mayor Guiton surrendered his sword, remarking that he preferred to capitulate to the king who could take his city rather than to flee for shelter to the king who had failed to save it, as some Rochelais had done. Of a prewar population estimated between eighteen and twenty-five thousand, only five thousand remained.

Louis XIII honored his promises of personal clemency and religious toleration, but the political settlement he imposed assured that there would be no repetition of the revolt. About a dozen people, including Guiton, were exiled from the city briefly, but before long they were permitted to return. The king, who knew how to value courage, competence and tenacity, soon granted Guiton a captaincy in the burgeoning royal navy. The walls of the city were pulled down except for the sea-front ramparts which might prove useful to repel invasion. Old churches and church property were restored to Catholicism, and a Bishopric of La Rochelle was created. Richelieu himself rededicated the greatest of the churches and celebrated the first mass heard in La Rochelle for years. The old chartered self-government was broken, and the town was forced to accept a royal governor and a royal garrison.

In the aftermath of La Rochelle's surrender the remaining opposition fell apart. Ever more concerned with problems in central Europe, England made peace on 24 April 1629, abandoning the Huguenots of southern France who were still in rebellion. In desperation, Rohan then negotiated what must be one of the most cynical alliances of a century noted for diplomatic pragmatism. On 3 May he signed an accord with Spain, which by then was embroiled with the French Crown over north Italian questions. To distract French royal armies, the great Catholic champion agreed to provide subsidies to keep alive the Huguenot rebellion. Nonetheless the southern uprising spluttered to an end, and one after another the southern towns asked for terms.

Again Louis XIII and Richelieu refused to negotiate, but they allowed a Protestant assembly to convene to receive the king's offer. At Alès, on 28 June 1629, Louis promulgated the Edict of Grace, offering personal pardon and religious toleration to all who would submit. Once more clemency proved effective. Town governments hastened to surrender, and already by the end of August twenty had accepted royal garrisons and had seen their fortifications destroyed. Rohan made his submission and then chose exile. Crossing into Italy, he entered the service of the Venetian government. Like Guiton, however, he enjoyed the esteem of the king, and in the 1630s he was given command of French forces in the Alpine passes where he fought with distinction against the Spaniards. Through clemency and moderation Louis XIII and Richelieu finally had brought an end to the religious wars that had wracked France for three quarters of a century. The political and military power of the Huguenots was finished.

# Chapter Ten

# The Eye of
# the Storm

FOR ABOUT A half century after the Edict of Grace of 1629 the Huguenots enjoyed peace in relative security. With their armies broken, their fortifications destroyed, and Rohan in exile, at first they certainly were in no condition to undertake aggressive action. But more than that, during further noble agitation in the early 1630s they refused temptations to join new rebellions and held the cities of the south firmly for the king, so that even Richelieu was moved to praise their conduct unreservedly.

In fact, more than simple exhaustion or the effects of the Peace of Alès relieved the pressure on the Huguenots after 1629. One must grant Richelieu's sincerity in being willing to tolerate the Huguenots' religious dissent so long as he could depend upon their political loyalty. Already as an official speaker for the clergy at the Estates General of 1614, his first public role, he had noted that though they were "blinded by error" most Huguenots lived "peaceably under the authority of the king"; and he had observed that "our example, our instruction and our prayers . . . are the only weapons one would wish to use against them." The Edict of Grace, which of course Richelieu had a large hand in editing, expressed the pious hope that the Huguenots would "return to the fold of the Church," and in his will he left a large sum to a missionary effort dedicated to Protestant reconversion. But there is no evidence that Richelieu ever contemplated force as an instrument of conversion.

At the same time, the international situation suddenly had become rather highly volatile again. It made the French government not only once more desirous of domestic peace but also again highly image-conscious *vis à vis* its Protestant allies. Early in the 1620s the truce between the Spanish Crown and its Dutch rebels had expired. That struggle had begun again, setting Spanish armies in motion along the Rhine Valley, just to the east of the French frontiers. About the same time, a Bohemian revolt had spread to become an all-German war, pitting the Catholic emperor against the north German and Rhenish Lutheran and Calvinist princes. The early course of this war threatened to result in a Habsburg unification of the German states. These developments were too fundamentally dangerous to French interests to be ignored, but any attempt to intervene had to take account of the Huguenots within France.

In the 1620s with revolt endemic and the Protestant situation still unresolved, there had been little that Louis XIII's government could attempt in foreign affairs. In fact, the strongly Catholic policy of his first advisors even produced suggestions for aiding the emperor against the Bohemian rebels, though early Habsburg successes quickly put an end to those notions. Nonetheless, so long as France's royal armies were tied down by domestic rebellions, and especially by the final great revolt and siege of La Rochelle, the Crown could do nothing direct in central Europe. Instead, Louis XIII's government had to confine itself to subsidizing allies. These were almost invariably Protestants. A league of eastern Swiss mountaineers could close the passes on which the Spaniards depended for transit from north Italy to Germany and the Netherlands. The King of Denmark rallied the north German Lutheran princes against the counter-reformation policies of the emperor. The King of Sweden, the famous Gustavus Adolphus, led his stunningly effective troops on a march through Germany in support of an indefinable mixture of religious and imperial motives. While the condition of the French Protestants was by no means the only, or even the most important, consideration of these allies, it was a consideration, further impelling the French government toward pragmatic arrangements.

In the middle 1630s the situation became even more tense. Subsidies to the Swiss, the Danes, and the Swedes proved inadequate to halt Habsburg successes. The French therefore moved into fuller commitment with the Swedes and raised troops under their own standard in eastern Switzerland. These troops were entrusted to the duc de Rohan after he had done penance for his role in the Huguenot revolts by way of exile in Italy. These efforts also proved insufficient. Chiefly because of lack of money from France, after initially brilliant campaigning Rohan's efforts collapsed. Late in 1634 the Spaniards succeeded in pushing more than fifteen thousand troops through the Alps to reinforce the emperor. And without the brilliant leadership of Gustavus Adolphus, who had been killed in battle in 1632, the outnumbered Swedish and Protestant German forces were defeated decisively at Nördlingen. Though unwilling and unready, Louis XIII and Richelieu were left without alternatives if they wished to contest the Habsburg ascendancy. In May of 1635 they declared war.

The French government's fear of a full scale war was soon justified by events as 1636 became the "Year of Corbie." In that summer the Spanish force that had fought so successfully at Nördlingen two years before, now reinforced and reequipped, pushed south from the Spanish Netherlands and occupied the province of Picardy. In August it captured the town of Corbie, which commanded the crossing of the Somme River only about seventy miles north of Paris. As Spanish reconnaissance units fanned southward almost to within sight of the capital, there was panic and talk of withdrawal to the Loire Valley. Through it all the king showed cool courage and rallied the nation. He called for contributions and volunteers, and when both were forthcoming he formed a new army which succeeded in retaking Corbie in November. But though the worst danger was past, another half-dozen years of bitter fighting lay ahead before the tide of war turned definitely in favor of the French.

This furious new international struggle had many implications for the Huguenots. On the one hand, it appeared to vindicate the king's and the cardinal's decision in the 1620s to force a military resolution of the old problem of the Protestant "state within a state." In the 1630s France was fighting not for conquest but for survival as an international power, and success was hard won. Simultaneous internal divisions arising from unrest in a large, well-organized, and well-armed minority group could have had disastrous consequences. On the other hand, the renewed anti-Habsburg efforts revived and confirmed the French Crown's pattern of alliance with Protestant states—the north German princes, the Dutch, the Danes and the Swedes, restraining any desire to commit the kingdom to the counter-reformation and to new crusades against heresy.

Finally, this war evoked in France strong popular expressions of national consciousness and strong royal expression of absolutist ambitions, both implicitly hostile to dissenting minorities. Louis XIII appealed to the nation for aid in 1636. The nobility responded in large numbers. The guilds of Paris, that backbone of a proudly independent bourgeoisie, made large contributions for "the defense of the kingdom." Recruiters, who usually had great difficulty in filling their quotas, suddenly experienced a rush of volunteers.

French historians have traditionally referred to this response as the "sacred union." It suggests that ideas of a popular obligation to the state and of the "nation in arms," inconceivable a century earlier, had penetrated many levels of society. About the same time, Louis XIII rebuked the Parlement of Paris for meddling "in affairs of my state." This comment suggests strongly that his views of the royal authority were as absolutist as those held by Francis I or Henry II before the civil wars of the later sixteenth century had so sapped the Crown's power. Such a strengthening national identity personified in a crowned and anointed monarch pointed toward unification, centralization, and elimination of difference and dissent. Many groups were to suffer the consequences: surviving elements of the old feudal nobility, hallowed institutions of provincial and regional autonomy such as the estates and the city councils, and even the semi-independent traditional organs of royal government such as the parlements; but none were more identifiably different and dissenting than the Huguenots.

For several years such threats remained potential rather than real. Excessively zealous local officials sometimes made life difficult for the Huguenots despite the Edict of Grace, but the royal government's attention was almost wholly absorbed by the war. Only in the early 1640s did the French begin to win, after Spain had been engaged against the Netherlands rebels for three quarters of a century and the Holy Roman Emperor had been at odds with Bohemian dissidents, north German princes, Scandinavian monarchs, and a variety of their allies for more than two decades. Even then the affairs of France did not run smoothly. The cardinal de Richelieu died late in 1642, and a few months later, early in 1643, his sovereign followed him to the grave. The king's eldest son was destined for greatness as Louis XIV (1643–1715), "the Sun King," but at the time was only five years old. Once again a regency was necessary, and the queen mother, Anne, was a sister of the King of Spain, with whom France was locked in bitter conflict. Understandably, many mistrusted her. In addition, many who had found the rule of Louis XIII and Richelieu oppressive thought that the time for reaction had arrived.

Meanwhile, across the Channel in England affairs had taken a course that appeared fraught with implications for the French monarchy and particularly for its relations with the Huguenots. After years of religious and political dissension, in 1642 civil war finally had erupted in England. After a long struggle anti-royalist forces not only won the military conflict but captured the king, Charles I, whom they proceeded to try, condemn, and execute at the beginning of 1649. Puritanical Calvinist religious elements formed an important part of the revolution, as they did also in the subsequent new government, justifying their political rebellion by appeal to a "higher" obligation. All of these things were known in great detail at the French Court, for King Charles I's widow, Henrietta Maria, was a French princess, a sister of Louis XIII. She had come home to find refuge with her young nephew, Louis XIV, bringing her two sons who were just a little older than he. Consequently, while it is easy for the historian to observe, with three hundred years of perspective, that the Huguenots were no longer a political danger and that the storms of Louis XIV's regency never really threatened the Bourbon monarchy, at the time the French royal family took them very seriously indeed.

The mid-seventeenth century French upheaval known as the

Fronde cannot be ignored. Queen Anne was not an outstanding political manager, but she had courage and tremendous perseverance. Above all, she was grimly determined to preserve her son's inheritance intact. Through the trials of a difficult regency she also was fortunate to have the support and assistance of the cardinal Mazarin (1602–1661), whom Richelieu had hand-picked to be his successor, a very able politician who fully justified the trust of his great predecessor.

There was unrest from the outset of the regency—criticism of policy, competition for office, and ambition for power. But the dissidence reached its peak in the years 1648 to 1653 just as the English revolution was reaching its anti-royalist climax. First the judges of the Parlement of Paris and then the great aristocrats of the kingdom played at armed rebellion once again. At one time or another they were supported by almost all of France's great soldiers of the day. Divided by social issues and unable to agree upon goals, however, these varied elements of opposition never succeeded in making common cause against the regency government. In consequence, despite several serious fights and occasional humiliations, Anne and Mazarin weathered the storm, finally restoring domestic tranquility through a combination of intimidation, persuasion and "gratification." On the international scene they also managed to reestablish peace, on a basis favorable to France, concluding treaties with the emperor in 1648 and with the King of Spain a decade later, in 1659.

Significantly, throughout this turmoil, both foreign and domestic, the Huguenots remained peaceful and loyal, contributing troops to the king's armies and refusing the blandishments of the rebels. Mazarin praised them openly, calling them his "faithful flock" and referring to their pastors as his good friends. In 1652 the young king, then fourteen and coming into his majority, in a speech certainly approved and edited by Mazarin if not, in fact, written by him, remarked that his Protestant subjects had "given us proof of their affection and fidelity . . . , which have given us great satisfaction"; and he promised to uphold the Edict of Nantes. Thus, the first three decades following the Peace of Alès were reasonably tranquil and secure for the Huguenots, certainly not a common experience of seventeenth-century religious dissidents.

THE FIRST GREAT religious settlement to incorporate the principle of toleration was the German Peace of Augsburg of 1555, but the scope and import of its clauses often are misunderstood, exaggerated and even distorted. That peace was an incident of a centuries-long struggle between the emperor and the princes for political supremacy in the Holy Roman Empire, and it is comprehensible only in that context. Over the years the princes had enjoyed many successes. They had preserved the electoral nature of the imperial crown despite the development of the hereditary principle in the western and northern monarchies of England, France, Spain and Scandinavia. They had prevented the establishment of any authority of the emperor directly to raise either taxes or troops outside his personal lands, making him dependent for both upon princely contributions. And in the early sixteenth century they had profited from a reorganization of imperial governmental and especially military administration into ten "circles" or districts to further tighten their control of German affairs.

The Peace of 1555 simply extended this principle of princely authority to religious questions. It did *not* establish religious freedom in Germany, for it recognized only the Roman Catholic and Lutheran communions, to the exclusion of Anabaptists, Zwinglians and—most significantly, given the increasing dynamics of their movement—Calvinists. Even on this limited basis of two legal communions, it did *not* establish individual freedom of choice. The Latin formula was *cujus regio, ejus religio*, "whose the state, his the religion." This allowed every prince to determine the religion to be practiced exclusively in his state. This simple transfer of decision-making from the emperor to the princes, in a definitely non-mobile society, left most laymen as bound by authority as before. A comparable situation quickly developed in Scandinavia, where state Lutheran churches were established. A few members of the commercial middle class may have been able to change their residence for reasons of religious preference; but for the vast majority of nobles, living in family manor houses and dependent for their livelihood upon their estates, and for peasants, dependent upon their little farms and some still bound by economic and even legal strictures from the past, such a course was impossible. Even a century later, Germany did not have full religious toleration. The Peace of Westphalia of 1648 granted Calvinists equal rights with Roman Catholics and Lutherans, but other dissenters still were not recognized.

Even in England, religious dissidents were less secure than the Huguenots in France. Certainly Henry VIII had allowed no doctrinal radicalism, despite his private quarrel with the papacy. Even under his successors, an official prayer book defined a state cult, adherence to which was formally required by everyone. Queen Elizabeth I encouraged the development of very broad and general definitions of Anglican positions, so as to make them acceptable to as many people as possible, so there was a sort of toleration *within* the English Church. But the state cult remained unacceptable to Roman Catholics, since it denied papal authority, and to Presbyterians and Congregationalists, since it maintained the authority of bishops. These people had no legal position, though in fact Elizabeth's government usually refrained from hunting them down and persecuting them.

In the early seventeenth century, however, the first Stuart kings allowed, and sometimes encouraged, a policy of studied harassment of radical Protestant (Puritan) groups. This became a major issue in the mid-century revolt that overturned the throne and sent a king to the executioner. And even late in the century, the question of religious toleration was an important issue in another revolution that finally toppled the Stuart monarchy and gave the crown of Britain to a petty German princeling.

Probably only one religious settlement of the sixteenth and seventeenth centuries even came close to matching the Edict of Nantes in the humaneness of its postulates and the liberality of its provisions. This was the *Letter of Majesty* issued by the King of Bohemia in 1609. Like the Edict of Nantes, a result of royal-aristocratic struggles involving religious questions, which in this case reached back to the Hussite wars of the fifteenth century, the *Letter of Majesty* also recognized freedom of conscience throughout the kingdom and established limited rights of dissenting religious practice for nobles and royally chartered towns. Unfortunately, it became a major political factor in an insurrection that erupted a decade after its issuance. Not only did it not survive the Habsburg victory of the 1620s, but throughout the Habsburg states of Austria, Hungary and Bohemia and such associated territories as Styria, Carinthia and the Tyrol, Catholic conformity was required once more.

By contrast, in France, though the chief ministers of the state—both Richelieu and Mazarin—were cardinals of the Roman Catholic Church, the policy of tolerating the religious dissidence of otherwise loyal subjects was maintained, a practice by no means common in the seventeenth century. The Huguenots' private rights of belief were fully guaranteed by law, and their rights of religious practice were widely established. Where restrictions existed, they were generally practical matters, established to preserve civil peace. Until Mazarin's death in 1661, the Huguenots probably enjoyed as free and as secure an existence as any religious minority in Europe, where conformity was the rule and toleration certainly was the exception.

EVEN DURING THE three quarters of a century of relative religious peace following Henry IV's accession, it is difficult to estimate the numbers of the Huguenots with confidence, though this period permits many more glimpses of their composition and practices than was possible earlier. As noted previously, a contemporary Italian claimed that in 1598 there were one and one quarter million of them. Modern scholars generally are agreed that during the early part of Louis XIV's personal reign, for which the sources are more adequate, the Huguenots numbered about a million. It is doubtful that anyone ever will be able to establish more precise figures.

By the early seventeenth century, patterns of geographical distributions were more or less fixed. The Huguenots could claim at least some adherents in most parts of the kingdom, but the regions of greatest concentration lay in a sort of southern arc pivoted upon Provence and the Languedoc. Sweeping from Geneva through the southeastern cities of Grenoble and Lyons, their congregations clustered thickly around the southern Rhône Valley cities of Nîmes and Montpellier and around Montauban, farther to the west. They then spread through the old Bourbon lands of Gascony—behind Bordeaux—and northward to the middle Atlantic regions around La Rochelle.

More or less isolated churches have been identified elsewhere, such as in the coastal towns of Normandy. Of course Paris, the intellectual as well as the political capital of the nation, always had its Reformed congregations, though even under the Edict of Nantes, Calvinists had to go outside the city to enjoy free religious practice. In the third quarter of the sixteenth century there had been significant Huguenot communities in north central France and in the Loire Valley, especially in the university towns of Bourges and Orléans. These had been decimated during the civil wars, and while they never wholly disappeared, neither did they ever recover their former strength and vigor. So while no generalization can wholly locate Huguenot communities geographically, a sort of crescent moon curving below the central highlands, with its tips resting in Geneva and La Rochelle, would include most of their areas of greatest strength.

Comparably, patterns of social distribution also defy easy generalization. One may safely say that after about 1600 most Huguenots belonged to the middle class or to the petty nobility, but there are distressingly prominent exceptions. Not surprisingly, considering their dependence upon royal favor, a number of prominent aristocrats followed Henry IV's example in the 1590s and accepted conversion. However, a considerable number maintained their Reformed commitment for another three or four decades— such as Lesdiguières, Bouillon, and Sully. The latter two died in that faith as old men. The Marshal Turenne, Bouillon's younger son and one of France's great soldiers in the middle seventeenth century, long upheld his Calvinist faith even though it displeased the king. He finally accepted conversion only a half dozen years before his death in 1675.

Generally Calvinism did not attract peasants, those conservative country folk clinging to their traditional mass, but among them also one finds exceptions. In the Rhône Valley, a route of heavy travel between the intellectual centers of north Italy and the Rhineland Evangelical communities, and affected as well by numerous Calvinist missionary preachers from nearby Geneva, peasants certainly numbered among the adherents of the Reform. And not far away, in the wild Cévennes, the southeastern slopes of the central highlands where there were old Waldensian traditions, Calvinism was strong among the mountain people. When the Crown attempted to suppress their churches in the 1680s they rose in a bitter revolt that dragged on for years.

Unfortunately, despite the efforts of the Society for the History of French Protestantism, it is dubious whether the history of these years ever can be recaptured completely. After 1629 the Huguenots were permitted general assemblies for the consideration of social and political concerns and discussions of problems common to the whole movement only by express royal consent, which was rarely given. With the revival of persecution in the 1680s and the exile of most ministers, much documentation was lost despite efforts of many exiles, especially in the Netherlands, to rebuild the historical record. So after noting the regions of greatest activity, the waning influence of great nobles and the localized involvement of some peasantry, there is little that can be said of the Huguenots as a national movement.

Within these imprecise generalizations it is possible to describe individual congregations a bit more confidently, as not only accounts but even engravings have survived. Their buildings were simple, usually rectangular in the old basilica pattern, though occasionally round or oval. There were no statues or stained windows, no imposing altars, not even crosses openly displayed. Usually, at the front a sort of raised platform on one side faced the pulpit on the other. Members of the consistory, other church officials, and government inspectors, if they wished to visit, sat in the raised section. The pulpit served for the delivery of the sermon, the heart of the Reformed worship service. "Temples," as the Huguenot meeting houses were designated officially, naturally varied in size depending upon the numbers of the local congregation. The one in the eastern Parisian suburb of Charenton—probably the biggest in the country—was reputed to hold four thousand people.

Services seem to have varied considerably. A sermon was part of any very solemn celebration such as baptism, marriage, and the Holy Communion. Otherwise, there were Bible readings, prayers led by the minister or a deacon—with public responses, the singing of the Psalms and public catechisms. The Communion of the Lord's Supper was offered four times a year, and participation was expected of all members of the congregation. On the whole, the tone of these services was austere.

The major intellectual and theological products of the

Huguenots are more easily recorded, of course, through the writings of their great figures. Calvin, Beza, Duplessis-Mornay, and many others all published voluminously, as well as maintaining extensive correspondence, of which a great deal has survived. But their prominence ought not obscure the less dramatic efforts of the mass of pastors who maintained a vigorous intellectual activity in the Church through innumerable synods and colloquies, debates, letters and tracts and, of course, the composition of thousands of sermons. Their interests ranged over Scriptural interpretation, moral responsibility, civil obligation, ecclesiastical discipline, education, and a host of other topics. In the long run, it was these masses of nearly anonymous and almost forgotten pastors, not the great nobles and probably not the great theologians, who held the Church together through the persecutions, maintaining the courage and commitment of the laity. It was they who undramatically carried on in time of peace—ministering to their congregations, baptizing, teaching, visiting, and always preaching and preaching.

Several great questions absorbed Calvinist intellectuals all over Europe in the late sixteenth and early seventeenth centuries. While the French Reformed Church did not contribute massively to the controversies thus aroused, the Huguenots' intellectual vitality was stimulated by the debates these issues evoked in synods and correspondence and in the Huguenot colleges at Nîmes, Montauban, and Saumur.

Inevitably, after Calvin's death disagreements arose around endeavors to interpret and extend his doctrines. Beza, his successor in Geneva, laid more stress on predestinarian determinism than did Calvin himself. The great Scottish associate and disciple of both Calvin and Beza, John Knox, greatly enhanced the role of discipline, raising it to a level of importance almost equal to that of the Scriptures and the sacraments.

These trends evoked a liberal reaction in the early seventeenth century, usually called Arminianism after Jacobus Arminius, a Dutch Reformed theologian at the University of Leiden. This teacher argued that predestination ought not be understood as divine power operating through sheer force but as God's will operating through divine love. The Arminians, concerned to harmonize free will with Calvinist predestinarianism, resisted the sort of determinism implicit in Beza and his followers. Grossly over-simplifying Arminius, most of them argued for an understanding of the Elect based not upon God's inscrutable will but on His omniscient foreknowledge of every man's acceptance or rejection of His offer of love and grace. Ultimately, the Dutch Arminians were condemned by the Synod of Dort of 1618–1619. Many were banished from the Netherlands, but their ideas continued to be discussed widely in Reformed circles, and the theologians of the Huguenot college at Saumur were reputed to be very sympathetic to them. Though the theological points may be a bit obscure to the modern lay reader, they were burning issues in the seventeenth century and provided enormous intellectual stimulus to Calvinists everywhere.

More directly relevant to the Huguenot experience were the endless discussions concerning the interaction of church and state. Calvin himself was not much help on this matter. By way of theoretical position, he frequently asserted great respect for established political authority. He affirmed the Christian's obligation to give the magistrate not only obedience but also "affection and reverence." On the other hand, in the *Institutes* he observed that if governors commanded anything against the Lord it should be ignored, as "we ought to obey God rather than men," an enormously imprecise exception that rather negates his injunctions to humble political submission.

Nor was the problem clarified by the church-state patterns which evolved at Geneva. The city's small size and its achievement of independence of external authority allowed the more or less simultaneous development of the Calvinist Church and a republican government, with what might be called interlocking directorates. After the early 1540s the two authorities tended to be more complementary than competitive. But these forms were not very transferable. Most of Europe did not consist of small republican city-states but of aristocratic principalities of various sizes and varying traditions, all of them rather authoritarian. Even the Dutch Netherlands—not very large, fighting for independence and primarily a patrician republic in its political organization—found the Reformed Church often a rival to the authority of the state. So it is not surprising that princely governments in England, France, and Germany looked with great suspicion upon the Calvinists, with their high levels of activist consciousness and well developed organizations, their participatory ecclesiastical government, and their great religious exception or reservation to the obligation of civil obedience.

Sixteenth-century French Calvinists contributed notably to these questions. François Hotman, sometime professor in the legal faculty of the University of Bourges, published in 1573 his *Franco-Gallia*, which stressed the importance of institutions representing the nation as a restraint upon royal power. Most obviously this treatise was a reaction to the royal persecutions that had culminated in the St. Bartholomew's massacres, and an appeal to the Estates General and the princes of the blood, where the Huguenots might find some protection. The treatise nonetheless attempted to achieve a theoretical justification by contrasting ancient Germanic and Roman practices; and it managed an affirmation of the rights of subjects sufficiently persuasive to warrant its consideration as serious political theory.

A few years later, in 1579, appeared the *Vindiciae contra tyrannos (Defense against Tyrants)*. Its author remains uncertain but was certainly a Huguenot. This work anticipates the social contract theories advanced by Thomas Hobbes and John Locke in the next century. It stresses the obligations as well as the authority of princes and contends that while individuals may not resist just authority, the officials of the realm possess a right of rebellion in the name of the whole society. After the succession of Henry IV and the promulgation of the Edict of Nantes, which changed the Crown from persecutor to protector, the Huguenots ceased producing these implicitly anti-royalist tracts, interesting themselves more in theological publication, but they continued to follow the church-state debate.

As these controversies continued into the seventeenth century they came to focus around a doctrine called Erastianism named for Thomas Erastus, a Swiss who had taught at Heidelberg in the Palatinate, a west German Rhineland state. Actually, Erastus' chief concerns were the Church's right of excommunication (he believed that the sacrament should be given to anyone who truly desired it) and, by extension, the whole question of the Church's disciplinary powers and rights of self-government. He argued that powers of punishment, in contrast to exhortation and persuasion, ought to lie only with the magistrates. Erastus himself never suggested the subordination of religion to the state, but in the seventeenth century this doctrine came to be associated with his name. It enjoyed particular currency in England during the Puritan revolution of the mid-century, and the church-state question remained hotly controversial.

Thus, it is difficult to sum up the Huguenots in this half century of tranquillity and relative security. They were not permitted to develop an autonomous political structure, but their religious organization seems to have functioned adequately, preventing schism among the churches and supporting an intense spiritual vigor. With the exception of Marshal Turenne and Marshal Schomberg, they did not produce any great soldiers, statesmen, or artists, though their adherents became significant in the business and financial world and many held lesser governmental posts. They did not contribute major works to the great Arminian and Erastian controversies, though they were aware of them and were involved, especially in the latter. Their religious postulates were such that they did not develop any imposing new art or architecture, comparable to the stunning baroque of their Catholic neighbors, or liturgical music to rival the rich body of Lutheran hymns. Rather, after their colorful but stormy existence in the previous century, the seventeenth-century Huguenots appear to have been undramatically loyal subjects of the king. Sober, quiet people, mostly of middle-class backgrounds, strongly entrenched in commerce, they no longer expected to disestablish the Roman Church, no longer supported aristocratic rebellions. Theirs was the modest ambition to be allowed to go their own way, simply to be left alone. In the late seventeenth century they were to be denied even that.

# Chapter Eleven

# The Revocation and the Dispersal

On 7 SEPTEMBER 1651, two days after his thirteenth birthday, Louis XIV proclaimed his majority before the Parlement of Paris. This was, of course, a simple maneuver to strengthen his mother's government amid the troubles of the Fronde. His personal reign really began ten years later, with the death of Mazarin.

The cardinal-minister died on 9 March 1661. The next day the young king, only halfway through his twenty-second year, called together the secretaries of state and the ministers of the Crown to announce that it was time for him to govern his affairs himself. He said that he would welcome their counsel, when he requested it, and that they were to sign or seal nothing in his name without his express consent. In response to a question, he said that they should address themselves to him personally when there was business to be settled. Naturally, there was disbelief, doubt that the new monarch would so limit his pleasures and distractions as to persevere in the hard work of governing a large kingdom after the first thrill of novelty had worn off. Only Louis really knew how committed he was to fulfilling the responsibility to which he had been born, and for which Mazarin and his mother had trained him so carefully. And even he could not suspect that France had just entered upon the longest period of personal rule in her history. From 1661 until his death in 1715, more than half a century, Louis XIV ran France.

161

A recent scholar of the period, of that school of thought which desires to re-emphasize "forces" and "movements" in history, in contrast to the impact of individual roles, has suggested that trying to comprehend the king's religious attitudes is not only difficult and speculative but maybe even useless, arguing that what he did is more important than what he thought. Of course, this assertion begs the question why he did what he did, which is the fundamental question of history as a study of humanity. Attempting to understand the mind and sentiments of any individual so able and so complex as Louis XIV, especially when he has been dead so long, is an intimidating and often frustrating challenge. Even Professor John B. Wolf, in his authoritative modern biography of the king, writes with uncharacteristic humility and reserve when discussing Louis' character and religious feelings. But Louis XIV *was* the king; and he *did* govern personally; and it *was* he who ended religious toleration in France. So, however tentatively, a responsible student of the problem has to attempt some estimate of the evolution of the royal mind that in 1685 revoked the Edict of Nantes.

Louis was but five years old when his father died, and through his formative years the cardinal de Mazarin filled the role of father figure. The king was ten when the Fronde erupted, and during the next four years he was sometimes frightened. He saw his foster father twice driven into exile and he observed his mother often in tears—once reduced to sobbing: "My son will punish them; oh, my son will punish them." These experiences alone might be enough to explain the development of some authoritarianism in his character. In fact the impulses toward absolutist conceptions were far more pervasive.

For whatever it is worth, Louis XIV's inheritance was more Habsburg than Bourbon. His mother, Anne of Austria, was a full-blooded Habsburg princess; and his grandmother, Marie de Médicis, had a Habsburg mother. Perhaps more meaningfully, his cultural inheritance was more Italian and Spanish than French. His father, Louis XIII, was only nine years old when Henry IV was murdered; and it was the Italian queen mother, Marie, who ran the Court and shaped its concepts of proper behavior. Louis XIV was only five when his father died. Thereafter his family associations were Anne and Mazarin, a Spanish princess and an Italian cardinal.

It should not be surprising that the young king learned something of a Mediterranean taste for splendor and formality and perhaps something of an imperial and Spanish concept of the royal authority, to reinforce the memory of his more distant ancestors, Francis I and Henry II.

Further amplifying it all, the atmosphere in which he was reared encouraged him to think in absolutist terms—to reflect upon both the power and the responsibility that God had laid upon him. He learned to detest those who imposed such unhappiness upon his loved ones in an attempt to reduce the power of the Crown, and to give thanks for family love, robust good health, and loyal servants as he attempted to shoulder the burdens of the kingship. From earliest youth he was taught to think of himself as someone special, king of the greatest realm in Christendom. Princes of the blood and ministers of the Crown bowed before him. In his name marshals of France had demanded submission and concessions from much of Europe, and in 1648 and 1659 they largely got what they demanded from the Holy Roman Emperor and the King of Spain.

Louis XIV was taught history, geography, and languages, and was given practical experience of council meetings and the analysis of dispatches. He was required to hold formal audiences and to preside over official occasions while still quite young, all part of a rigorous apprenticeship that Mazarin planned to prepare him for his future duties. He was taught riding and fencing and dancing, that he might ably set the patterns of taste and entertainment for Europe's most elegant Court. Clearly, he found these experiences congenial, and he worked hard. All who knew him as a boy and as a young man noted his poise, his calm, his graciousness, and his regal charm. At the age of twenty-two, upon assuming personal direction of his affairs, it would be astonishing if such a prince had not demanded full obedience of his subjects.

As WITH MOST people, Louis' attitudes and opinions changed with the passage of years and the accumulation of experience. It would be highly speculative to attempt to define the nature and intensity of his piety at any particular time. As a youth, he was punctilious about the formal practices of his religion; but he also had great zest for sport, for fine entertainment, for good food and drink, and for attractive women. As a middle-aged man he governed his personal life more conservatively, listened to Christian moral teachings more attentively and seems to have taken his prayers and other religious observances much more seriously. In his old age, when many of his hopes had been crushed, great numbers of friends and family had died and he found himself rather alone and isolated, he appears to have reflected at length on divine retribution for pride and sin, to have sought consolation in faith and, in fact, to have become just a bit of a religious prude. Until the late 1670s and early 1680s, however, when he was becoming middle-aged, his personal religious feelings were less significant for the fate of the Huguenots than were the role of religion as a public institution and the king's view of that role.

Even in this context, the young king must have felt a great deal of pressure from many directions. The papacy had always taken every opportunity to point out that while toleration might be allowed by a Catholic prince as a necessary expedient, it had to be considered temporary, until proper instruction of the heretics and a revival of royal power permitted its elimination. The French Assembly of the Clergy, which met regularly and every year made an important donation of Church funds to the king's treasury, rarely missed a chance to petition for the re-establishment of Catholic conformity, fulminating against the "Synagogues of Satan" that gave comfort to "rebellious slaves." In a word, the Catholic community seems to have recognized clearly that the important difference between the various edicts of toleration established by Catherine de Médicis and her sons and the Edict of Nantes was not the extent of toleration offered but the fact that the former were designated temporary, while Henry IV set a preamble to the latter which described it as perpetual and irrevocable.

Perhaps the Catholic position was best summed up by Paul Hay, an author of Louis' early reign, whose *Treatise on French Policy* went through many editions, suggesting a wide public acceptance. Hay argued, with a logic perfectly comprehensible in the seventeenth century, that diversity of cult encouraged social divisiveness and that unity of faith bound people together so that they would serve the king "under the same flag." But even on the basis of this popular belief, he did not support forced conversion. Rather, he begged the king to finance more extensive missionary work among the heretics, that they might be persuaded; to interpret the Edict of Nantes as strictly as the law would allow, so as to make heretical recalcitrance disadvantageous, while offering rewards to converts; and to have patience.

To comprehend the controversies of the seventeenth century it is essential to remember that kings and their ministers, at least in western Europe, were violently disrupting the old socio-political organization. Against traditional patterns of decentralized authority, multi-tiered administration and infinitely varied governance by local customs, seventeenth-century royal ambitions to build centralized, linear, consistent royal governments were little short of revolutionary.

In such circumstances, and lacking such ideologies as nationalism or fascism or communism to give credence and justification to the resultant political and social dislocations, religion—the oldest mastic of European society—became an even more sensitive subject. Francis I's dictum of "one king, one law, one faith" acquired renewed significance. As the years passed, Louis spent a great deal of time and energy attempting to subsume most of the institutions of French life into neat hierarchies culminating in the royal will. Naturally, so discordant and so visible a minority as the Huguenots attracted his attention early.

In his memoirs for 1661, which he revised shortly after 1670, the king noted that he had long been troubled by the "anomalies" in the religious situation. Apparently, both his dignity, which might expect subjects to accept the faith of their sovereign, and his neat orderly mind, which sought regular hierarchies without such aberrant exceptions, found the existence of a religious minority abhorrent. But, at the same time, he observed that he rejected "extreme and violent remedies." So, though he desired uniformity, at least at the outset the king seems to have thought along the lines of Paul Hay—persuasion and patience.

From the beginning of Louis XIV's personal reign the Huguenots began to feel pressure, for decrees and administrative orders commanded the narrowest possible interpretation of the Edict of Nantes. After 1661 the government no longer granted the permissions necessary for the convocation of national synods. As the general assemblies already had been discontinued during the preceding reign, this left the Reformed churches without any central organization at the national level. Already by the middle 1660s Huguenot pamphleteers were publishing vigorous protests about the strictness of legal action. Schools and churches were reduced to the size and numbers that they had under Henry IV, as the edict had not guaranteed them a right of growth but only of continuation. Those that could not prove their existence from the late sixteenth century faced closure. Protestant preachers, teachers, and booksellers felt the weight of constant surveillance and regulation and were subjected to frequent inspections. As the program was accelerated, Huguenots were banned from the practice of several crafts and professions, most notably law, and Huguenot doctors were forbidden to tend Catholic patients.

Louis' government did not ignore the more positive side of the great effort. The king supported missionary work, sending priests known for their preaching skills, especially Jesuits, into Huguenot areas. He organized debates between prominent Reformed pastors and Catholic clerics. And he encouraged the clergy at Court to strive for the personal conversion of the few great Huguenots still to be found there. He rejoiced in a notable success in the late 1660s when the eloquent Bishop Bossuet brought Marshal Turenne over to Catholicism. In addition, on the suggestion of an ex-Huguenot who was in his service, the king established a "conversion fund" and recommended that bishops do the same. These funds offered a variety of incentives from cash bonuses through tax exemptions for a number of years to occasional life pensions.

Once again there are no specific figures available, but there is no doubt that these policies made serious inroads upon the Huguenot population. A hard core remained unshakable in their commitment to the Reformed faith, of course. But there were many others who weakened as they heard the pleas and arguments of carefully selected Catholic preachers, as they found Protestant worship service very difficult to attend because the local church had been closed and as they came to fear for their children's education because the school had been closed or drastically curtailed. In addition to all this, they felt their livelihood threatened by the

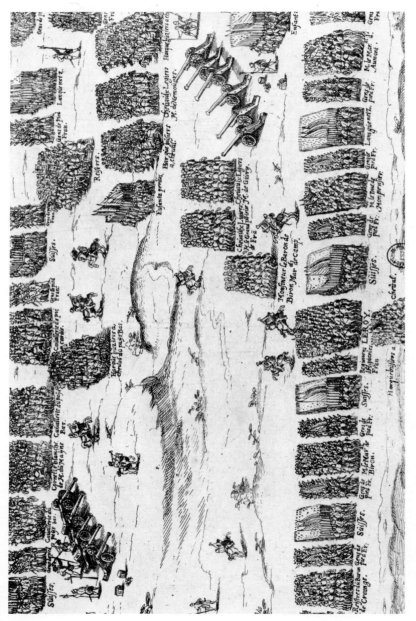

The Battle of Ivry, 14 March 1590

The Siege of La Rochelle, 1628

Proclamation of the Edict of Nantes

The Estates of the League, January–July 1593. An imaginary representation with Mayenne shown presiding under a portrait of the Spanish Infanta, allegorical sketches of humiliation and suffering to the sides.

The Revocation of the Edict of Nantes, 18 October 1685

Demolition of the Temple at Charenton, 29 October 1685

Cartoon: The New Missionaries (the Dragonnades)

The duc de Sully

Marie de Médicis, Queen-Regent of France (from the
author's collection)

The Cardinal de Richelieu

Louis XIII de Bourbon, King of France (from the author's collection)

The duc de Lesdiguières

Philippe du Plessis-Mornay

The Duke of Buckingham

Anne of Austria, Queen-Regent of France

The Cardinal Mazarin

Mme. de Maintenon (about 1687)

NRY DVC DE RO ... HAN Pair de France f.
s anciens Rois de Bretagne ... Prince du Sang de Navarr.
Ecoße, General des Armées ... Roy, Fils de Rene Vicomte de Roh.
e Caterine de Partenay, porta les arm ... es de l'age de 16 ans au Siege d'Amien
eut vn chual tue fous luy et vn l'av ... acha l'echarpe a vn des principaux e
les Ennemis qu'il prefenta au Roy. xv ... vyagea en Allemagne, Holande, A
rre, et Ecoße, ou comme premier Pr ... ince du Sang il fut choisi pour par-
n de Charles Stuart de pius Roy d'A ... ngleterre, on traita de fon mariage
la Sœur de Gustaue Adolph Roy de ... Suede, mais le Roy Henry IIII. voulu

The duc de Rohan

Louis XIV de Bourbon, King of France (about 1691)

Michel LeTellier, Marquis de Louvois

Sebastien Le Prestre de Vauban, Marshal of France

Henry IV de Bourbon, King of France and Navarre,
shortly before his death (from the author's collection)

The Murder of Henry IV, 14 May 1610

proscription of heretics from some trades and professions—with the implication that the list might grow longer, while at the same time they were offered monetary advantages for becoming Catholics. Such great numbers converted that the tax exemptions thus gained eventually posed some serious fiscal problems. In fact, so successful was the program that in 1681 Madame de Maintenon, at first the governess of the king's natural children, then his mistress, and eventually his second wife, estimated that if God preserved the king for another twenty years, the Huguenots would simply cease to exist. At least some modern historians concur with her judgment, with perhaps a slight reservation for the small underground church, fanatically dedicated but numerically insignificant, which might have survived as the Waldensians had done in remote parts of the country.

One can, of course, query the sincerity of such conversions, obtained by threats and blatant bribery. Seventeenth-century people were not so naïve as to take them all at face value. But it was a serious legal matter to accept conversion, take the king's money, and then relapse into heresy—grounds for fines, prison sentences and even the loss of custody of one's children. In any case, efficacy seems to have been considered more important than sincerity. Conversions so achieved, even if not very heartfelt, could have considerable results: the demise of a congregation so that a church could be closed for lack of members, the elimination of a school, and at the very least the education of a new generation as Catholics. A number of prominent people expressed skepticism about the credibility of the conversions that were being obtained under pressure but consoled themselves with the thought that it meant the salvation of the children.

INEVITABLY, THE HISTORIAN of the Huguenots must confront the multi-faceted question why patience and persuasion were abandoned when they appeared to be working well. Why was a policy of violence and terror adopted with all that it meant by way of martyrs, atrocity stories and adverse foreign reactions? Why, in 1685, did Louis XIV revoke his grandfather's "unrevokable" edict? Over the course of nearly three centuries a great many speculative explanations have been advanced. Some are based upon the political situation of the early and middle 1680s; others are rooted in assumptions about the king's character; and still others seek scapegoats among the members of the king's entourage. As is common in human affairs, the simplistic single-factor analyses are unpersuasive, while most of the proposed explanations contribute something to understanding the king's decision.

Certainly, several political developments, both international and domestic, affected the situation of the Huguenots adversely. One of the most recent historians of the revocation of the Edict of Nantes sees these as the crucial factors. Louis and the team of very able and very aggressive bureaucrats that he had put together were seriously dedicated to building a modern state and were instinctively resentful of any competing authority and hostile to any claims to exemptions or immunities from the government's commands. This general outlook partly explains the escalating pressure for conformity put upon the Reformed church, of course; but it also involved the king in another quarrel, which put the Huguenots into the role of sacrificial victims.

French churchmen were very sensitive to the question of Gallican "liberties," very attached to their long tradition of relative autonomy, and fully convinced that papal power in the French Church should remain limited. Consequently, Louis XIV was able to depend upon the support of most of his bishops when what had begun as a minor disagreement with the pope escalated into a major quarrel. The specific question was control of appointments and money in some bishoprics added to the French Crown since these matters had been regulated generally by Francis I's Concordat of Bologna, but the underlying issue was once again the conflict of interest between the national ambitions of a monarch and the supra-national policies of the papacy. Both King Louis XIV and Pope Innocent XI were stubborn, uncompromising men, each convinced of the rectitude of his position and of the importance of the principle that he was defending. In consequence, the confrontation that began about 1678 grew steadily more serious. It did not really ease until after Innocent's death in 1689 and the election of a less aggressive pope.

Aggravating the situation in the 1680s, Innocent XI's consuming passion was the old papal ideal of another crusade against the Muslim world, while Louis XIV was quite happy to see the Holy Roman Emperor distracted by the threat of the Ottoman Turks in the middle Danube Valley, Muslims though they were. The Turks were very active at this period, even besieging Vienna in 1683, and the pope was infuriated that His Most Christian Majesty of France refused to take any action. The fact that the emperor—with the aid of papal money, Venetian fleets and the King of Poland's troops—won a stunning victory, saved Vienna, and began a counterattack, made things worse rather than better. So king and pope were at odds on at least two important matters. But neither really wanted an open break, for they had too many mutual interests despite these disagreements. Consequently, Innocent XI refrained from using serious spiritual weapons against Louis for a decade; and it can be argued credibly, though there is little direct evidence, that Louis XIV sought to improve his Catholic reputation in Europe generally and in Rome particularly through the final abolition of heresy in his kingdom.

It is also relevant, and a matter that Louis referred to himself, that the restoration of peace in 1684 made it possible for him to give greater attention to domestic affairs. Louis had been at war most of his life—against Spain in the 1650s and 1660s, against the Dutch in the 1670s, and against a league of German princes in the early 1680s. The period following each war had largely been spent in planning the next. However, Louis had acquired most of the territory that he had been fighting for, had observed a stiffening resistance to his aggressions, and was, in any case, becoming more distracted by family and dynastic considerations. Consequently, he hoped that the twenty-years' truce signed in 1684 could be converted into a durable peace. As it happened, he was to be disappointed, for the war resumed, and on a larger scale, in 1688. But for a brief time he felt free to turn from international affairs, which had always occupied his chief attention as a ruler, to the domestic scene, where many problems clamored for attention, among them the religious situation.

This was also the period of a marked increase in the king's personal religious observances. He attended Communion more frequently. He discussed religion at length with Madame de

Maintenon, with Bossuet, and with his Jesuit confessor. Only a few months after the queen's death in mid-1683 he secretly married Maintenon, thus regularizing his personal life. And the next year he observed Lent strictly, criticizing courtiers who did not. Some authors have tried to make much of this new piety, have written of a personal "conversion" and have imputed far-reaching effects. It is true that there were no more royal mistresses and that the king's family life seems to have settled into an unprecedented tranquility; but there simply is no evidence that his apparent deepening religious interests had any particular effect upon policy, such as his action toward the Huguenots.

Some consideration ought to be given to the people around the king and the influence that they might have had upon his decision. Again the results are disappointing. There are no grounds at all for the widely repeated story that Madame de Maintenon played a major role in bringing about the revocation. Her memory has suffered from the harsh remarks of the snobbish memoirist, the duc de Saint-Simon, whose poisonous pen destroyed many a reputation. In fact, she seems to have been a kind and rather gentle person. Her piety was indisputable, and she converted some of her relatives. Far from urging Louis to harsh measures against Protestants, she maintained a discreet silence about the revocation even after it was enacted, when most people at the Court were praising the king's action loudly, and she protected her own Huguenot domestics.

Churchmen, of course, had a special interest, and the many great clergy at the Court constantly urged upon the king the idea that the final obliteration of heresy in the realm would be a glorious achievement. In addition to such general admonitions, they also could draw his attention to something more specific, the problem of new Catholics who relapsed. There seems to have been a rather widespread experience of missionary preachers enjoying considerable success, with or without the assistance of "conversion funds," but of less eloquent local priests being unable to hold the new converts after the missionary's departure. Rightly or wrongly, the clergy and the government attributed this backsliding to the efforts of the Huguenot pastors, who worked tirelessly to preserve their congregations. Since revocation certainly would close all "temples," expel most pastors, and drive underground the handful who might risk their lives to defy the law, Louis' counsellors continually advised him that such a course would make it far easier for the priests to hold converts to their new commitments.

Finally, some notice should be taken of the ministers of the Crown, the great public servants who carried out the king's will and on whose advice he had to rely heavily as his affairs grew more complex year by year. Dominating this ever larger administration were the two great bureaucratic families of the Colberts and the Le Telliers. Jean-Baptiste Colbert was controller-general of finances and many other things. In effect he controlled taxation, royal budgeting, trade, colonies, the navy, programs of economic stimulation, and the king's buildings. Michel Le Tellier was chancellor of the realm, and his son, the marquis de Louvois (1641–1691), was secretary of state for war and later also took over from Colbert the responsibility for the king's buildings. Both families had dozens of relatives, in-laws, allies, and hangers-on webbed all through the government. Colbert often is portrayed as the moderate, Louvois as the extremist. In fact both men could be equally ruthless in pursuing personal and family interests, though both served the king faithfully and well.

Possibly, as sometimes is alleged, Colbert gave some protection to the Huguenots through the repressions of the 1670s and the early 1680s. His unwavering goals were economic growth and fiscal reform; and many Huguenots were important in French industry and commerce, especially in such export-oriented products as cloth and tapestries, in west coast shipping and in banking all over the country. In opposing some of Louis' more bellicose foreign ambitions for fiscal reasons, Colbert had shown that he was not afraid to offer unwelcome advice on occasion. In any case, he died in 1683, and the Le Telliers were left dominant in the king's inner circle for awhile.

The question to what extent Louvois shaped the king's policy toward the Huguenots and to what extent he simply carried it out can never be answered. That he was a harsh, violent man is undeniable, though his correspondence reveals occasional attempts at a rather heavy-handed humor. Generally, he was impatient, demanding and unforgiving of both obstructionism and inefficiency. To such a mind, uniformity and neat organization were virtues, almost ends in themselves. Certainly, if the king desired conformity, subjects had an obligation of obedience. In sum, while he gave the king his total loyalty and served him with a bull dog-like tenacity, he was quite intolerant and thoroughly unlikable. He has received rather bad press from historians despite the respect that his work with the army commands. As this was the man who stood foremost in the king's councils in the last years before the revocation, it probably was inevitable that many would believe him to have been the instigator of it. But again, no evidence proves it so. However, he certainly was the director of the last stages of the repression before the revocation, and he cannot escape responsibility for the brutality of those programs.

As the king frequently expressed his pleasure concerning the growing numbers of conversions, in the early 1680s Louvois developed new techniques to increase the pressure on the Huguenots—the dragonnades. This involved the quartering of troops upon Protestant households. Seventeenth-century soldiers were recruited largely from the dregs of society. The best of them were peasant boys displaced from their homes by famine or the ravages of war. Many were vagabonds and beggars pressed into the king's service, often actual criminals hiding from the law or accepting military service as an alternative to prison. They were governed by force and fear, taught to march and fight by the use of brutal discipline. As their pay usually was far in arrears, they looted and stole constantly and deserted in droves at every opportunity.

These soldiers were rough and violent. Supposedly "friendly" troops often proved as dangerous to local populations as a hostile army—even when their officers tried to control them, which they often did not do. There was not much to choose from one unit to another, except for a few elite formations, but the dragoons—very heavily armed and therefore necessarily large men, capable of fighting on foot or mounted—enjoyed a particularly evil reputation, probably because originally they often were German mercenaries. When these troops were quartered in civilian homes, the householder supposedly had limited obligations to provide a bed, salt, a place at the fire, etc. In fact, the soldiers usually took what they wanted.

There were many precedents, both in France and elsewhere, for using the quartering of troops as punishment in areas that were behind with their taxes or seethed with frequent revolt. Louvois adapted the policy to the problem of conversion, especially after the truce of 1684 freed many of his troops from active service. He quartered upon Protestant households soldiers who were told to make themselves as unpleasant as possible. Judged purely in terms of results, the policy was very successful. To escape the dragonnades, masses of Huguenots converted—initially in the south, in the regions of Nîmes, Montauban, Montpellier and Bordeaux, and then also in the west. The tales of violence and terror that this policy occasioned were carefully censored from the reports of mass conversions that reached the king's desk. But it is difficult to believe that Louis XIV had no suspicion of the horrors being perpetrated upon his subjects in his name, as many historians, even some unfriendly to him, have maintained.

Slowly events moved toward a climax. The tax exemptions granted to new converts had created serious disparities since the conversions had risen into the hundreds of thousands. Revocation would end the granting of these exemptions. Amid quarrels with the papacy and notable inaction in the matter of the Turkish siege of Vienna, the king's religious reputation was somewhat tarnished. Revocation might brighten his Catholic image. Despite growing numbers of conversions, there were relapses, and false converts secretly continued as Reformed believers. Revocation would eliminate the pastors and the shadow churches which kept these problems alive. Finally, in the light of massive conversions, it was alleged that, besides pastors, only a handful of recalcitrant heretics survived anyway. Thus the Edict of Nantes had become needless and useless, an unnecessary stain upon the religious fabric of France, serving no purpose.

At the beginning of October 1685, the question of revoking the Edict of Nantes was discussed by the king's inner council. The dauphin, Louis' son and heir to the throne, expressed some concern that revocation might cause revolts and perhaps mass emigration ruinous to commerce. The king himself replied that in such matters he would rely upon his troops, and, in any case, that he thought these were unworthy considerations. Finally it was decided. The

Edict of Nantes would be revoked. By 8 October most of the details had been worked out. Two days later, the Venetian ambassador, well informed as always, wrote to his government about the decision that had been taken. Louis signed the edict of revocation at Fontainebleau on 18 October, and on 22 October it was registered by the Parlement of Paris.

The Edict of Fontainebleau stated that until 1685 war had made it impossible for the king to do anything about resolving the matter of religion, "as he had always intended." However, now that peace was restored and "the best and largest part of our subjects of the so-called reformed religion have embraced Catholicism," it was the king's pleasure to wipe out the memory of the troubles and evils caused in the kingdom through false religion by revoking its whole basis. The edict went on to declare that all pastors were to leave the country, and all temples were to be destroyed. All Huguenot schools were to be closed, all children were to be sent to mass regularly, and everyone born into the false religion was to be rebaptized by priests. Nonetheless, so long as there was absolutely no practice of religion outside the Roman Catholic Church, adults might continue to enjoy freedom of conscience. Finally, emigration by laymen was forbidden. Confiscation of property and condemnation to the galleys were threatened as punishment for attempts at illegal flight. The era of toleration in France had ended.

# Epilogue

THE TURMOIL AND confusion of the years immediately following the revocation have been described many times with varying degrees of pathos. No more than ten per cent of the Huguenot population fled abroad. The rest stayed and tried to cope with the new situation. Many of them appear to have hoped that this, too, would pass away, as had the sixteenth-century persecutions; but this time they confronted determined royal policy backed by a much improved governmental apparatus. Some accepted the freedom of conscience left them and lived quietly, without the consolation of their churches. Some recent converts, when they learned that people would be left their private beliefs, relapsed; but many of these soon learned that while private recalcitrance was barely tolerable, conversion and relapse was punishable. Some held clandestine services, as had their sixteenth-century predecessors, in darkened houses and woodland glades. And some few carried on as before, ignoring the law.

All of these people posed a problem for the government, and a stream of declarations and administrative ordinances continued for years in an attempt to "complete" the work. Willing hands were found to destroy temples and schools. With known Huguenots, zealous officials and churchmen maintained the pressure and even the dragonnades, despite the promise of free conscience. Even the final indignity was often visited upon those who died refusing the

175

sacraments, as they were denied decent burial and their bodies were simply tossed upon refuse heaps. Probably the greatest recurring tragedy was the tearing of children from their families so they could be sent to Catholic schools were they would be safe from corruption by heretical parents.

Those who tried to carry on despite the law were a more straightforward problem. Manhunts dug out pastors who tried to hide rather than leave, and generally they were hanged with little ceremony. Secret congregations were uncovered, and when they were found troops were ordered to fire into the unarmed crowd. Six hundred were slaughtered in one instance. Surviving males were sent to the living hell of the king's galleys, women to the prisons—only a little less terrible, and children to Catholic orphanages. The details that had to be arranged were endless. In Paris special action was needed to stop numbers of people from visiting Protestant embassies on Sundays, obviously to attend worship service. The property of those who were arrested for illicit worship, like that of those who emigrated illegally, was confiscated, of course; and that posed the problem of its distribution. Most often it appears to have been given to Catholic relatives of the former owners. If such could not be found, sometimes it was taken by the king. Usually it went to someone he wished to favor or to a Catholic charity, for there were always many petitioners. Finally, regulation of the book trade became a more serious affair, for there was extensive smuggling of illicit works, both criticisms of Louis and his policy and unauthorized devotional works for secret Calvinists.

For the most part, resistance to the new law was crushed quickly and ruthlessly, but one group stubbornly refused to submit and eventually rose in armed rebellion. The Cévennes region north of Nîmes comprises wild uplands which rise eventually to the central mountains. This was old Waldensian country and one of the few areas where the Huguenots counted many adherents among the peasantry. There, through the late 1680s and the 1690s, recalcitrants clung to their Calvinist confession and held their services despite the efforts of government officials and Catholic clergy, whose attempts at repression sometimes included bloody raids. As the contest wore on, mystics and *illuminati* began to appear among the Protestants—preaching in a trance, claiming the gift of tongues, or falling into fits in the middle of prayer.

Finally, in 1702, with no apparent premeditation or planning, armed rebels—called *camisards* because of the long shirts that they pulled over their outer clothes for recognition—began freeing prisoners and burning Catholic churches. Though the rebels probably never numbered more than about five thousand, they knew the country intimately and had a great deal of local support and sympathy. They quickly became a serious embarrassment for the government, which—like later governments confronted by popular guerrilla wars—found that it had to commit several times their numbers of troops. In 1704 the foremost rebel leader surrendered, in exchange for amnesty and a commission in the royal army, so the worst of the fighting ended; but the rebellion spluttered on until about 1710. Clearly, the Protestant problem in France had not been ended in 1685.

In an excess of optimism, early in 1715 Louis XIV announced that he had finally put an end to all Protestant worship in France. But less than half a year later, while the king lay dying at Versailles, at the gates of the great southern city of Nîmes a worship service and protest meeting, called the "First Synod of the Desert," was held by dissident Huguenots, who there began the reorganization of the Protestant Church.

In the eighteenth century the Reformed faith spread again, as the spirit of the Enlightenment pervaded government circles, encouraging tolerance—or, more accurately, indifference—so that the anti-heretical laws remained unenforced despite the rantings of some clergy. On the eve of the French Revolution Louis XVI (1774–1792), who probably fancied himself an "enlightened despot," in the spirit of his times, eased the position of the religious dissenters by recognizing their marriages before the law and thus protecting their testaments and their children. Early in the French Revolution religious freedom was proclaimed, opening the way for the development of modern French Protestantism. But this is a different story, set in a very different society. For all practical purposes, the history of the Huguenots as a significant minority group in France—self-aware, related to the tremendously dynamic international Calvinist movement, and stimulated by the intellectual vitality

of the religious debates that ran all through western and central
Europe—extends from the early sixteenth century into Louis XIV's
reign.

Despite the prohibitions against laymen emigrating, and the
dire penalties threatened, many did flee. Often they were helped by
sympathetic Catholic neighbors—who thus risked sharing their
punishment of condemnation to the rowing benches of the king's
galleys if caught. Escape routes were organized "underground
railways" they would be called in a different age, with guides and
"safe houses" for refuge. Mule trains picked their way through
Alpine passes, and fleets of small boats sailed down the western
rivers to rendezvous with Dutch ships offshore.

There are, of course, no reliable figures for the numbers of
refugees, only approximations. French provincial officials had an
interest in minimizing reports of their failures to halt the exodus.
Refugee diaries and memoirs are suspect of the opposite bias, of
exaggerating the initiative and courage of the Huguenots and their
willingness to abandon everything for the preservation of their
faith. Records of the arrival of fleeing immigrants in places where
they took refuge—Switzerland, the Netherlands, Brandenburg,
Denmark, England, even Russia and South Africa—offer firmer
data, for of course they were supposed to register and take oaths of
loyalty to local governments; but such reports are incomplete, and
many were lost in subsequent fires and wars. In consequence,
greatly varying estimates of the numbers of those who fled have
been offered from time to time, ranging from a hundred thousand
to nearly half a million. Most modern scholars agree on a figure
around two hundred thousand, perhaps one per cent of the population of Louis XIV's France.

FRENCH REACTIONS TO Louis XIV's decision to revoke the Edict
of Nantes were almost invariably favorable. Congratulations
poured in, though one should reflect upon the judgment of La
Bruyère, a contemporary writer contemptuous of the showy
Catholic devotion of many courtiers. He remarked that theirs was
the sort of piety that under an atheistic king would make them all
atheists. Nonetheless, it is indisputable that the revocation was
extremely popular, even if courtly sycophants are discounted. All

over the country pamphlets, poems, and special prayers paid tribute to the king. Louis' best biographer has pointed out the irony that while this was the decision that subsequent historians have most condemned, when the king died three decades after the revocation this was the one action of his life that was invariably praised in the funeral orations composed to commemorate his reign.

Within France there were few dissenters, or at least few who voiced their dissent. Perhaps the most forceful criticism came from the brilliant and often outspoken royal engineer, Vauban (1633–1707), one of the key figures in Louis' military "team" and a man who already had a reputation for both humanitarianism and bluntness. The king was quite intelligent enough to value honest and informed opinion even if he did not always like it. He had once encouraged Vauban to "write to me personally" about anything. In the matter of the revocation, Vauban accepted the invitation. In October of 1687 he attached a plea in favor of the Huguenots to some plans for fortifications that he sent Louvois; but the minister refused to forward the memo and returned it to the author ordering that he suppress it. However, Vauban was not a man to be discouraged easily.

After several Protestant officers had emigrated, including one of his own promising junior engineers, Vauban became more concerned. In 1689 he sent another memorandum, *A Memoir in Favor of the Recall of the Huguenots*. This was a fully developed treatise including the bold statement: "Kings are indeed masters of the lives and goods of their subjects, but never of their opinions, for God alone can direct those as he pleases." These were strong words for a man who held the king's commission, and are often quoted to his honor. His analysis of the adverse impact of the revocation is also well known. He estimated that the king had lost eighty to one hundred thousand subjects through flight and that they took a lot of hard cash with them; that many artisans had fled, damaging French commerce; and that some manufacturing techniques previously a French monopoly were known abroad, to the detriment of French exports. He noted that the military forces of France had suffered, the navy losing eight to nine thousand sailors and the army ten to twelve thousand soldiers, with five or six hundred officers. And he claimed that the unfavorable propaganda generated abroad was a greater danger to French interests, especially among the king's Protestant allies. Consequently, he argued that the Edict of Fontainebleau should be withdrawn and the Huguenots should be invited to return, with proper guarantees for their security.

In January of 1690 the war minister acknowledged receipt of this treatise and promised, with unusual cordiality, that he would pass it on. But before anything further could happen, he died. It appears that Vauban then tried to pass the *Memoir* and another on the same subject which he wrote in 1693 through Madame de Maintenon, whom he knew. She replied that this was not a matter that the king was willing to reconsider. Hence, it is likely that Louis never saw these memoranda nor, probably, any other serious criticisms from people whose opinions he was accustomed to listen to.

Foreign reactions to the revocation were predictable. Catholic princes congratulated Louis, but none changed their policy toward him. The pope gave only a lukewarm approval, while deploring the use of violence. In the perspective of his on-going quarrel with the king, he probably saw the action as a further affirmation of royal authority over the Gallican Church. Not surprisingly, the reaction of Protestant Europe was bitterly hostile.

Just a week after the revocation, the Great Elector of Brandenburg, an old ally of France, issued the Edict of Potsdam, which invited the Huguenots to settle in his lands. More practically, he offered to pay their transport, and he established refugee collection centers in Hamburg and Frankfurt. Brandenburg had been badly war-torn, and its economy had never been very fully developed in any case, so he valued new settlers, especially those with middle-class skills. To tempt them, he promised that in devastated areas they would be given empty houses, six years of tax exemptions, and free entry into local craft and mercantile associations. Other German princes soon followed his example, though none so elaborately.

Many Protestant states accepted the refugees and helped them. The city of Amsterdam offered them full citizenship, while the provinces of Holland and Friesland respectively promised twelve years free of taxes and full rights equal to native born residents. The government of the United Netherlands also offered to subsidize the travel of those who wished to re-emigrate to the Cape Colony in southern Africa. Comparably, in England a royal proclamation promised free exercise of trades and handicrafts, without interference from local associations, an important privilege in the heavily regulated economy of the seventeenth century. And so they scattered across Europe and beyond.

Where the Huguenots settled in large numbers, the printing presses were soon busy, and from them poured masses of books and pamphlets attacking the revocation, recounting the persecution and the atrocities that accompanied it, and describing the king as an ogre and a tyrant. Whatever else may be said about the revocation and the emigrations that followed, this vast literature doubtless helped to reinforce the great coalitions that eventually were formed against Louis. When illicitly distributed in France it probably stiffened courage and stimulated resistance on the part of the Huguenots who stayed.

William III of Orange, the greatest statesman opposing Louis, appears to have made good use of the many refugees in the Netherlands. So numerous were they that shortly after the revocation there were sixty-two French churches in Holland. He employed some, subsidized the publications of others. Among the most noteworthy was Pierre Jurieu (1637–1713), formerly a pastor near Orléans, then professor of Hebrew at the University of Sédan until that institution was closed in 1681, and finally a pastor again in Rotterdam. A prolific writer, he authored several bitter works such as his *Pastoral Letters Addressed to the Faithful in France* and *The Sigh of Enslaved France*. Important, too, was Elie Benoist (1640–1728), a former pastor from Alençon, who ministered to a congregation in Delft. Contacting hundreds of refugees for copies of letters, edicts, pamphlets, and personal papers from their private collections, he wrote a massive (five folio volumes) *History of the Edict of Nantes*, which is still invaluable as it reproduces many documents no longer available in the original. And the efforts of Jurieu and Benoist were supplemented by the work of many others who studied, spoke, maintained illicit correspondence with co-religionists still in France, and wrote and wrote. Thus, there was built in the Netherlands a massive propaganda machine, probably supplemented by a fairly well developed espionage organization.

NOT ONLY DID the revocation evoke conflicting opinions among contemporaries, but even for historians it has been difficult to evaluate its significance. No one, of course, can ever estimate the quantity or quality of intellectual and artistic talent smothered by religious persecution or exiled by the revocation. Nor can anyone ever measure the moral price to a nation of teaching several generations of youth to measure their neighbors by single-factor and simplistic standards of conscience and faith rather than by talent, initiative, and sense of community. Some writers, eager to make history handmaiden to moral philosophy, have attempted to link the setbacks and disappointments of Louis' later reign to his treatment of the Huguenots. They blame his repressive religious policy for everything from the renewal of war in 1688 to the increasing economic difficulties that the kingdom faced. These exaggerated arguments will not bear close scrutiny.

The military conflict that opened in 1688, called the War of the League of Augsburg, did not break out by accident, still less because of some sort of Protestant crusade against Louis XIV's France. It began when Louis, not without some misgivings, decided to break the peace. Because he saw the emergent balance of power in Europe tipping against France, with both Spain and the Dutch hostile and the Holy Roman Emperor enjoying ever-greater successes over the Turks, he ordered his armies to take offensive action in the Rhineland.

The results were not what Louis had hoped. The emperor was willing to temporize with the Turks, so as to contest the French threat on his western flank. Because the commitment on the middle Rhine so reduced the threat of a French thrust northward, the Netherlands government was persuaded to allow William of Orange to use Dutch troops to support a revolution in England. Quick success gave him the English crown and control of England's resources, which he quickly cast into the balance against France. Thus, there emerged in 1690 a coalition of most of Europe's great powers, allied against France, and the war dragged on for nine years. Resentment of Louis' religious policies, and the mass of propaganda churned out by and about Huguenot refugees, may have played some role in heightened emotional commitment and in rallying popular support for the war in Protestant states. But tell-

gion certainly was not a significant causative factor in a war in which the Catholic powers of the Holy Roman Empire and Spain were allied with the Protestant powers of England and the Netherlands against Catholic France, the latter's only support coming from a vague association with the Muslim Turks.

In the same manner, one cannot attribute France's later economic difficulties to the revocation. This problem was first posed by Vauban, who was very interested in economics and was one of the first to attempt to compile and analyze statistics. The impact of the revocation upon French industry and commerce has continued to intrigue historians since. The nineteenth century witnessed a considerable increase of interest in economic questions in general and an attempt to explain the marked disparity between British and French growth in particular. It came to be widely believed that the revocation was an important factor. Some serious exploratory work in early modern economic history was undertaken in an attempt to substantiate the hypothesis. But given the inadequacy of the data and the gaps in the historical record, all that could be proved was the coincidence of timing.

In the middle of the twentieth century Professor Warren C. Scoville undertook a full re-examination of the problem. Probably no one can hope to get much beyond his patient analysis except insofar as further research clarifies details or fills in regional gaps. Scoville first points out the various ways in which the revocation might have harmed the French economy—emigration of crucial individuals, diffusion of French industrial secrets, capital export. He then examines each possibility, setting the whole study in the perspective of the total French experience in the second half of Louis XIV's reign. And he concludes that the revocation had no demonstrable economic significance.

If one accepts the figure of about two hundred thousand emigrants as a reasonable estimate, against a population of approximately twenty million, Louis lost about one per cent of his subjects. It is quite possible that a loss even in such small proportions could have a serious economic impact, but only if it involved key personnel, pivotal people upon whom great sectors of the economy depended. In an economy still well over ninety per cent agricultural, not even the most generous description of the Huguenots

could so define them. Even in the very small but important industrial and commercial sector of the economy, it must be remembered that the revocation came only after two decades of mounting
repression, one aspect of which was a definite religious bias in
political appointments and promotions. By 1685 there could be
very few Protestants in top positions either in direct governmental
service, as there had once been a Huguenot minister of finance
under Mazarin, or in the great protected enterprises which Colbert
had so carefully nurtured to promote economic expansion. Despite
their middle-class concentration, it cannot be shown that the
Huguenots occupied a crucial role in the French economy.

Comparably, while many refugees did not flee penniless,
neither do they appear to have removed great amounts of capital
from France. Escape was difficult, as passports were needed to cross
the frontiers. Recent Catholic converts were not allowed aboard
ships or over borders without obtaining special licenses and posting
bond for their return. While some specie certainly was smuggled
out, there is simply no evidence that it was of amounts big enough
to be significant in drastically reducing available investment capital.
And it just was not feasible to remove capital equipment in any
quantity.

All of this is not to say that the Huguenot refugees were not
economically significant to the areas where they settled. It already
has been noted that many governments were eager to have them
and offered generous settlement agreements and tax advantages to
tempt them. The Huguenots had the reputation of being industri-
ous and frugal, and their middle-class roots meant that many had
experience in economic areas that several early modern governments were trying to expand. They brought new techniques in the
manufacture of paper and cloth, especially luxury fabric such as
silk, to England. They doubled the size of Berlin, restored war-
devastated Magdeburg, and brought such fine manufactures as ribbons and laces to Germany. They even played a major role in
establishing the still important wine production of the great Paarl
Valley in South Africa.

Ironically, some evidence suggests that the emigrations also
may have improved the French export position. Only about one
tenth of the Huguenot population left France, the rest choosing to
remain and accept at least an outward conformity to Catholicism.

Thus, everyone who went abroad left behind innumerable relatives, friends, and business associates. In many instances the contacts were maintained, the emigrants becoming foreign representatives for French producers. This resulted for instance in some protests to the government that old Catholic firms found themselves forced into a non-competitive position in the Netherlands because of the enormously superior market information and distribution facilities of the new Catholics. The data remain too scanty to allow generalization, but certainly they do not support any assertion of export disaster and even offer some contrary evidence.

Perhaps most significant is the broader picture of the French economy from the early 1680s onward to 1715 or a bit after, in which it can be demonstrated that France was reeling under the impact of developments far more serious than Huguenot emigration. In recent years much light has been shed upon the early modern economy by a whole series of detailed regional studies focused upon such sources as parish records of births and deaths and local market records of sales and prices. By and large these studies reinforce Scoville's conclusion that economic problems in Louis XIV's later reign were broadly based. There is a random pattern of frequent poor harvests and occasional widespread crop failures, and a general contraction of population far greater than explicable simply by Huguenot emigration. And always there is the war, and again the war.

From 1688, when the War of the League of Augsburg was begun, until Louis' death in 1715, France knew only four or five years of peace. Eventually the king had nearly half a million men under arms, and the strain dislocated the French economy in many ways. Simply paying the troops and military suppliers was an almost intolerable burden. At one point the king and the Court nobility gathered up their gold and silver ornaments, vases, and tableware and sent them all to the mint to be coined, so as to be able to meet current obligations. This largely accounts for the relative scarcity of such items, bemoaned by lovers of antiques to this day. The squeeze for tax revenues, not Huguenot exports, drained off capital. Expedients such as monopolies and sale of offices multiplied bureaucratic and unproductive obstructions to commercial and industrial development. A few industries profited from military orders, of course, but most suffered. During the greater part of this period

Dutch and English ships commanded the high seas, virtually eliminating French seaborne commerce except in the Mediterranean. The resultant misery and even starvation had nothing to do with Louis' religious policy.

In the matter of government finance a somewhat stronger case can be made for the revocation playing some role, though a minor one, in a worsening fiscal crisis. Though the Huguenots were not key personnel, neither did they represent a cross section of the population. Most were middle class, which is to say they belonged to that part of the population that dealt in money more than in crops, livestock, and country estates—and money was the essential commodity for a king involved in as much military activity as Louis XIV. The emigration of Huguenot bankers, traders, and artisans, with such captial as they could smuggle out, doubtless hurt tax collection a bit at a time when the king's armies needed every penny that could be found. But even in this more limited context, the significance of the Huguenot role ought not to be exaggerated. Primarily, it was a primitive structure of government finance that made money so hard to get. So inefficient was it that a century later the government of Europe's most prosperous nation was to be pushed to the brink of bankruptcy through its inability to tap the wealth of the kingdom. When Louis XIV's reign ended, the debts of England and the Dutch Netherlands—both much smaller and far less populous than Louis' kingdom—were larger, on a per capita basis much larger; but their situations remained healthy because they had developed mechanisms that made debt the nation's obligation while France staggered from one fiscal crisis to another because the debt was the king's alone.

ULTIMATELY, ONE MUST attempt to define a context in which the Huguenot experience becomes comprehensible, a focus in which, stripped of adulatory myth and legend, the movement has some meaning for early modern history. Moral and philosophical reflections are not very helpful, for in a situation of such complexity they allow the experience to be interpreted to mean whatever each individual student of the problem may want it to mean—the transcendant value of courage and commitment or the ultimate futility of resistance to authority, the immeasurable inspiration of superhuman values or the capacity of humanity to compromise and denigrate the highest ideals.

Nor does an attempt at economic analysis produce very satisfactory results. Because they were largely middle class, the Huguenots can command an important position in early modern French economic studies, much of it still barely explored. But despite the inadequacy of the data and the gaps in the record, it seems to be a safe generalization that theirs was a participatory rather than a formative role in the economic crisis of late seventeenth-century France. Finally, then, the student of the Huguenots is forced back to such basic problems as trying to define their place in the religious history of western Europe and their part in the socio-political evolution of modern society.

The Huguenots were part of a long tradition of Christian spiritual and intellectual revitalization. For a brief time they were themselves important contributors to that revitalization. The Church of the early medieval period was challenged by an enormous number of social changes from about the twelfth century onward, to which it responded only slowly. Towns, universities, nascent middle classes, study of Arabic science, and restudy of classical authors all contributed to undermining the adequacy with which a rather austerely formal Church, based on order-power relationships, could satisfy the spiritual and intellectual needs of the society in which it existed. One consequence of the resultant tensions was, of course, the stimulation of tremendous vitality within the Church. This resulted in scholastic theology, the Gothic style, the enormous growth and sophistication of papal government, and the foundation of new orders, especially the mendicants. Another consequence was the emergence of dissident movements for which none of these developments was adequate to subsume the hunger for personal spiritual experience and the urge to bear witness personally without the intermediary roles of clergy and complex ritual.

From the thirteenth through the sixteenth centuries these movements abounded in much of Europe. Many of them could find no place for themselves within the religious establishment. The list of those that left, or were forced out of, the Church is long—the Waldensians, the Albigensians, the Spiritual Franciscans, the Lollards, the Hussites, the Lutherans, the Zwinglians, the Anabaptists, the Calvinists, and some others less prominent. To understand the Huguenots it is important to remember that they stood at the end, not the beginning, of a long protest movement.

By the middle of the sixteenth century the chief outlines of the Evangelical faith—Scripturalism, discipline, personal piety—were well established, and Calvin's followers in France were an important part of it. Famous writers who published voluminously and obscure pastors who preached endlessly all participated in the continuing expansion of Evangelical theology, moral philosophy, and the Christian conscience generally. The Huguenots made contributions equal to those of the great Swiss, German, Dutch, and Scottish writers and preachers. However, in the second half of the seventeenth century, under repression, their initiative and contribution to the international movement tapered off, although after the revocation they once again wielded their pens vigorously from exile. For the most part, under Louis XIV the problem was to endure. Forbidden to proselytize, forbidden to study abroad, forbidden to criticize the established Church, forbidden to conduct their daily lives as freely as their neighbors, and finally forbidden even to exist, their simple survival to recreate a vigorous Protestant community in modern France was no mean achievement.

Perhaps most of all, the Huguenots offer the opportunity to study the role of a large and very visible minority in a nascent modern national society. Whatever the debates concerning the proper definition and characterization of nationalism, few historians would contest the propostion that in western Europe the bases for it were laid in the late medieval and early modern periods. The Hundred Years War, which pitted Frenchmen and Englishmen against each other from the second quarter of the fourteenth century until the middle of the fifteenth century greatly heightened the sense of nationality in France. This new awareness was increased by the accelerating independence of the Gallican Church after the Pragmatic Sanction of Bourges of 1438 and by the emergence of the less feudal, more institutionalized government known as the "new monarchy" after the war.

The French sense of national identity was stimulated enormously by the pride of conquest in Italy in the early sixteenth century and by the fear of Spanish domination later in the century. And the Renaissance monarchy, with its growing authoritarianism based on Roman law and its growing depersonalization based upon the increased use of professional administrators, provided some institutional framework for growing national identity. This process came to fruition in the seventeenth century with the development of most of the essential elements of the bureaucratized modern state under Louis XIV. This national consciousness was not yet wholly state-centered, not yet detached from identification with the king or with a vague cultural heritage; but it was an aggressive, commanding force in French life, the basis on which modern nationalism as an abstract political ideology was to grow a century or so later.

This rising consciousness of national identity, pride, and purpose had no tolerance of opposition or exception. Noblemen who resisted the growth of the royal authority were crushed. Those who survived became servants of the Crown or ornaments of the Court. The international or supranational interests of the papacy found little sympathy; the Gallican Church was national. In such a context, minorities if very visible were just as unwelcome, were equally an obstruction to the vigorous assertion of national monarchy.

It was the Huguenots' misfortune, perhaps, that they were so readily identifiable. They were not just Frenchmen who attended a different church. Their discipline prescribed a sobriety of manner and of dress that set them apart. They did not observe saints' days and other Catholic festivals. They were concentrated in the middle class, which great segments of the society regarded as exploitative and parasitical in any case. And the ethics of their cult demanded frugality and hard work to an extent that often produced envied business success. Sometimes they did themselves a disservice, as when they allowed their strength to be used by and identified with noble elements of feudal resistance to the two Médicis queen mothers, or when they allied themselves with the king's foreign enemies, as did La Rochelle and the duc de Rohan in the 1620s.

In retrospect, one is forced to the conclusion that the real "crime" for which the Huguenots were so often and finally so severely persecuted was neither their religious practice nor their occasionally treasonable political activity. It was, rather, their resistance to a national consciousness, emerging not just in France but across much of western Europe, that demanded conformity and submission. The liberal notion that individuals might have rights and not just obligations *vis à vis* authority was barely conceived in the seventeenth century. Even after its clear enunciation in the Enlightenment of the next century and its vigorous assertion in the French Revolution, it was by no means universally accepted. Ultimately, the Huguenot experience may simply demonstrate that the modern national state has no love for dissident minorities.

# Bibliographical Essay

The mass of material, both old and modern, relevant to the Huguenots, poses serious problems for any endeavor to suggest further studies. A standard academic bibliography frequently is ponderous and largely undifferentiated in terms of quality, significance and availability of the materials cited. The brief list of "Suggestions for Further Reading," common in many recent books, often seems both excessively abbreviated and too concerned with easy availability. Therefore, for this book I determined upon a bibliographical essay, as it allows some grouping by subject matter, brief comments concerning the nature and quality of the most important works cited, and some attention to particularly significant materials, even if they are a bit difficult of access. Unavoidably, many of the works indicated are in French, but English materials have been cited whenever possible.

## I. Histories of France in the Sixteenth and Seventeenth Centuries, including collections of documents and memoirs relevant to the period.

Good modern books exist in English for the history of France in both of the centuries under consideration. Recently an excellent work filled a long recognized need: Salmon, John H. M., *Society in Crisis: France in the Sixteenth Century* (London, 1975). For the subsequent period there are two good summaries: Treasure, Geoffrey R. R., *Seventeenth Century France* (London, 1966); and the somewhat more culturally oriented Lough, John, *An Introduction to Seventeenth Century France* (London, 1954). For those who read French, there is a work that continues to be indispensable, though outdated in interpretations: Lavisse, Ernest, gen. ed., *Histoire de France depuis les origines jusqu'à la révolution*, 9 vols. (Paris, 1900–1911); relevant to present concerns are vols. V through VII, each in two parts, and vol. VIII, pt. 1. Some works that deal with only part of the period under consideration nonetheless are of sufficient general significance to deserve attention. Prominent among these

191

are: Romier, Lucien, *Le Royaume de Catherine de Médicis*, 2 vols. (2nd ed., Paris, 1922–1925); Burckhardt, Carl J., *Richelieu. His Rise to Power* (New York, 1940, reissued 1964); and *Richelieu and His Age*, 2 vols. (London, 1967); Tapié, Victor-Lucien, *France in the Age of Louis XIII and Richelieu* (New York, 1975); and Wolf, John B., *Louis XIV* (New York, 1968), by definition a biography but actually of far broader relevance and significance.

Also widely useful are two biographical aids, unfortunately available only in French: Hoefer, Jean C. F., *Nouvelle biographie générale*, 46 vols. (Paris, 1853–1866); and Michaud, Joseph F., *Biographie universelle*, 45 vols. (Paris, 1845–1865; reprinted Graz, Austria, 1966). Comparably broad in application is a great collection of royal legislation: Isambert, François, *et al.* eds., *Recueil général des anciennes lois françaises*, 29 vols. (Paris, 1822–1833).

Several collections of documents make contemporary materials relatively accessible. In English are the comments of official English observers of French events, unfortunately very limited after about 1590. See: Great Britain, Public Record Office, *Calendar of State Papers:* the relevant series are *Foreign, for the Reign of Elizabeth*, and the much smaller *Roman, Spanish* and *Venetian* sets. An enormously rich source is the French government's publication, the *Collection de documents inédits sur l'histoire de France*. Most notable among the major collections relevant to Huguenot problems are: *Relations des ambassadeurs Vénitiens sur les affaires de France au XVIᵉ siecle; Négotiations, lettres et pièces diverses relatives au règne de François II; Lettres de Catherine de Médicis*, 11 vols.; *Recueil de lettres missives de Henri IV*, 9 vols.; *Procès-verbaux des Etats-Généraux de 1593; Negotiations, lettres et pièces relatives à la conférence de Loudon;* and *Lettres du cardinal Mazarin*, 9 vols. Please note that to these should be added the collection by Cimber, M. L. and F. Danjou, eds., *Archives Curieuses de l'histoire de France depuis Louis XI jusqu'à Louis XVIII*, 27 vols. (Paris, 1834–1840); and François, Michel, ed., *Lettres de Henri III* (Paris, 1959).

Two great collections of memoirs exist, comprising literally hundreds of contemporary records: Petitot, Claude B., ed., *Collection des mémoires relatifs à l'histoire de France*, 131 vols. (Paris, 1819–1829); and the rather better edited Michaud, Joseph F., and Jean F. Poujoulat, eds., *Nouvelle collection des mémoires relatifs à l'histoire de France*, 34 vols. (New ed., Paris, 1854). Separately published memoirs also worthy of note are: Condé, Louis Iᵉʳ, prince de, *Mémoires du prince de Condé*, 5 vols. (Paris, 1743); and Marguerite de Valois, *Mémoires* (Paris, 1858).

Two keen observers also left useful papers. Pierre de L'Estoile wrote extensive *mémoires-journaux;* unfortunately only a few excerpts are available in English: Roelker, Nancy L., ed. *The Paris of Henry of Navarre* (Cambridge, Mass., 1958). Modern editions do exist in French; Lefèvre, Louis-Raymond, ed., *Journal de l'Estoile pour le règne de Henri III* (Paris, 1943), and with Martin, André, eds., *Journal de l'Estoile pour le règne de Henri IV*, 2 vols. (Paris, 1958). Etienne Pasquier also was a careful recorder of events; see: *Lettres historiques pour les années 1556–1594*, ed. D. Thickett (Geneva, 1966), the most accessible collection of his papers. Two notable, though partisan, historians also left accounts of the turbulent sixteenth-century events to which they were contemporary or near-contemporary: Aubigné, Agrippa d', *Histoire universelle*, 9 vols. (Paris, 1886–1897); and Thou, Jacques-Auguste de, *Histoire universelle*, 11 vols. (The Hague, 1740).

Finally, two collections of papers shed light upon the years immediately before and after the revocation of the Edict of Nantes: Clément, Pierre, ed., *Lettres, instructions et Mémoires de Colbert*, 7 vols. in 9 (Paris, 1861–1873); and Depping, Georg B., ed., *Correspondence administrative sous le règne de Louis XIV*, 4 vols. in 6 (Paris, 1850–1855).

## II. Calvin, Calvinism, and Geneva.

No attempt to evaluate broad histories of the Reformation and of Protestantism can be made here, but a good recent work, equipped with an excellent bibliography, is Léonard, Emile G., *A History of Protestantism*, 2 vols. (London, 1965–1967; French original, 1961).

Most biographies of Calvin range from uncritical to adulatory, but concise and reasonably objective is Hunt, R. N. Carew, *Calvin* (London, 1933). The earliest account of Calvin's life was written by one of his great disciples: Bèze, Théodore de, *A Discourse Written by M. Theodore de Beza, containing the life and death of M. Iohn Caluin* [sic] (London, 1578; French original, Geneva, 1564).

Of Calvin's own writings, there are several complete Latin editions, *opera omnia*, as well as a French *Oeuvres complètes* (Paris, 1936). His *Institutes* and collections of his letters, sermons and Biblical commentaries are numerous, including English editions.

Calvin has, of course, been the subject of many special studies. The following list is by no means exhaustive, but it may suggest the scope of modern investigations: Pannier, Jacques, *Recherches sur l'évolution réligieuse de Calvin jusqu'à sa conversion* (Paris, 1924); Boegner, Marc, *Les Catéchismes de Calvin* (Pamiers, 1905); Bois, Henri, *La Philosophie de Calvin* (Paris, 1919); Biéler, André, *La Pensée économique et sociale de Calvin* (Geneva, 1961); and Breen, Quirinus, *John Calvin, a Study in French Humanism* (2nd ed., New York, 1968).

Perspectives on Calvin are enriched by: Church, Frederic C., *The Italian Reformers, 1534–1564* (New York, 1932); Eels, Hastings, *Martin Bucer* (London, 1931); and Jourda, Pierre, *Marguérite d'Angoulême, duchesse d'Alençon, reine de Navarre, 1492–1549*, 2 vols. (Paris, 1930).

There are also extensive Latin and French collections of Theodore de Beza's letters, sermons, theological discourses and Biblical tracts, as well as some fragmentary English materials.

Geneva requires special attention. Useful books, fairly representative of an extensive literature are: Foster, Herbert D., *Geneva Before Calvin, 1387–1536* (New York, 1903), a short work but insightful; Dunant, Emile, *Les Relations politiques de Genève avec Berne et les Suisses* (Geneva, 1894); Roget, Amedée, *Histoire du peuple de Genève depuis la Réforme jusqu'à l'Escalade*, 3 vols. (Geneva, 1870–1883); Choisy, Eugène, *La Théocratie à Genève au temps de Calvin* (Geneva, 1897), and *L'Etat Chrétien Calviniste à Genève au temps de Théodore de Bèze* (Geneva, 1902); and Borgeaud, Charles, et al., *Histoire de l'Université de Genève*, 4 vols. in 6 (Geneva, 1900–1959). For Geneva's influence in France, consult: Bourchenin, Pierre D., *Etudes sur les académies protestantes en France au XVI^{me} et au XVII^{me} siècles* (Paris, 1882); Naef, Henri, *La Conjuration d'Amboise et Genève* (Geneva, 1922); and Kingdom, Robert M., *Geneva and the Coming of the Wars of Religion in France, 1555–1563*

(Geneva, 1956), and *Geneva and the Consolidation of the French Protestant Movement, 1564–1572* (Geneva, 1967).

## III. The Huguenots, general histories.

Several older works recount the Huguenot experience. Standard in English are: Grant, Arthur J., *The Huguenots* (London, 1934, reissued 1969), a sympathetic survey; and Will, Joseph, *Protestantism in France,* 2 vols. (New York, 1921). Modern French works are: Viénot, John, *Histoire de la Réforme français,* 2 vols. (Paris, 1926–1934); Mours, Samuel, *Le Protestantisme en France au XVI<sup>e</sup> siècle* (Paris, 1959), based upon many provincial studies; and Boegner, Marc, *et al.*, *Protestantisme français* (Paris, 1945). Of a more limited nature are Autin, Albert, *L'Echec de la Réforme en France* (Paris, 1918); and Hauser, Henri, *Etudes sur la Réforme française* (Paris, 1909). Brief but evocative is Richard, Michel, *La Vie quotidienne des Protestants sous l'ancien régime* (Paris, 1966).

The history of the early years of the Huguenot movement was written by Beza himself: *Histoire Ecclesiastique des Eglises Reformées au Royaume de France,* 2 vols. (Geneva, 1580; new ed. Toulouse, 1882). The whole history of the Huguenots was surveyed by a pastor who lived through the revocation and the expulsion, a partisan work but one distinguished by the inclusion of careful documentation: Benoist, Elie, *The History of the Famous Edict of Nantes,* 2 vols. (London, 1694; French original, 5 vols., Delft, 1693–1695). Two other highly sympathetic works also deserve notice: Jean Crespin's martyrology, first published in Geneva in the third quarter of the sixteenth century, subsequently appeared in many multi-volume editions and in translations, including English; and Haag, Eugène, *La France Protestante,* 10 vols. (Paris and Geneva, 1846–1859; reprinted Geneva, 1966).

## IV. The Huguenots, special studies and sources

Books about limited periods or areas or aspects of Huguenot history are so numerous that even selective listing is difficult. The citations that follow simply reflect their enormous variety.

Though terribly dated, the works of Henry M. Baird cannot be ignored: *The Huguenots and the Revocation of the Edict of Nantes,* 2 vols. (New York, 1895); *The History of the Rise of the Huguenots of France,* 2 vols. (New York, 1900; reissued, 1970); and *The Huguenots and Henry of Navarre,* 2 vols. (New York, 1903). Somewhat fresher is Bailly, Auguste, *La Réforme en France jusqu'à l'Edit de Nantes* (Paris, 1960). Evocative are Herminjard, Aimé L., ed., *Correspondance des réformateurs dans les pays de la langue française, 1512–1544,* 9 vols. (2nd ed., Paris and Geneva, 1864–1897); and Viénot, John, *Promenades à travers le Paris des Martyrs, 1523–1559* (2nd ed., Paris, 1914), the latter an illustrated stroll through Paris that sets ghosts whispering.

Useful special studies are: Dieterlen, Henri, *Le Synode général de Paris, 1559* (Montauban, 1873); Romier, Lucien, *Catholiques et Huguenots à la cour de Charles IX* (2nd ed., Paris, 1924); Serr, Gaston, *Une Eglise Protestante au XVI<sup>e</sup> siècle, Montauban* (Aix-en-Provence, 1958); and Viénot, John, *Histoire de la Réforme dans le pays de Montbéliard,* 2 vols. (Montbéliard, 1900). There are dozens more of the same sort, limited in scope but each adding something to the whole picture.

The civil wars have attracted a great deal of attention. One of the earliest histories was Davila, Enrico C., *The History of the Civil Wars of France* (London, 1678; Italian original, Venice, 1630). Another interesting early history is Mainbourg, Louis, *The History of the League* (London, 1684; French original, Paris, 1683). Other standard works are: Anquetil, Louis-Pierre, *L'Esprit de la Ligue,* 4 vols. (Paris, 1771); Chalambert, Victor de, *Histoire de la Ligue sous les règnes de Henri III et Henri IV,* 2 vols. (Paris, 1854); Goulart, Simon, ed., *Mémoires de la Ligue, 1576–1598,* 6 vols. (Amsterdam, 1758). Finally, there is a survey in English: Wilkinson, Maurice, *A History of the League or Sainte Union, 1576–1595* (Glasgow, 1929).

Works of a narrower perspective are: Thompson, James Westfall, *The Wars of Religion in France, 1559–1576* (2nd ed., New York, 1957); Armstrong, Edward, *The French Wars of Religion, Their Political Aspects* (Oxford, 1904); and Romier, Lucien, *Les Origines politiques des guerres de réligion,* 2 vols. (Paris, 1913–1914, reprinted Geneva, 1974). Interesting source material may be found in Coudy, Julien, ed., *The Huguenot Wars* (Philadelphia, 1969; French original, 1962); and Louchitzky, Jean, ed., *Documents inédits pour servir à l'histoire de la Réforme et de la Ligue* (Paris, 1875). Also useful is a small book that tries to make sense of the arguments concerning motivations: Salmon, John H. M., ed., *The French Wars of Religion: How important were religious factors?* (Boston, 1967).

A contemporary account of the period of the wars is Mornay, Philippe de, sieur du Plessis-Marly, called Duplessis-Mornay, *Mémoires et correspondance,* 12 vols. (Paris, 1824–1825). Related to this is Mornay, Charlotte de, Mme du Plessis-Marly, *Mémoires sur la vie de Duplessis-Mornay,* done by his wife. There are several nineteenth-century French editions and one modern translation: Crump, Lucy, ed. and trans., *A Huguenot Family in the Sixteenth Century. The Memoirs of Philippe de Mornay . . . Written By His Wife* (London, 1926).

There are innumerable biographies of Henry of Navarre, none of them very impressive. A recent French example is Estailleur-Chanteraine, Philippe de, *Henri IV, roi de France et de Navarre* (Paris, 1954). In English are Pearson, Hesketh, *Henry of Navarre, the King Who Dared* (New York, 1963, reprinted Westport, Conn., 1976); and Russell, Edward F. L., Baron, *Henry of Navarre; Henry IV of France* (New York, 1970). Biographies also exist for a number of other prominent Huguenots: Whitehead, Arthur W., *Gaspard de Coligny, Admiral of France* (London, 1904); Dufayard, Charles, *Le Connétable de Lesdiguières* (Paris, 1892); and Clarke, J. A., *Huguenot Warrior: the Life and Times of Henri de Rohan, 1578–1638* (The Hague, 1968).

One of the most notable specialized studies in recent years is Sutherland, Nicola M., *The Massacre of St. Bartholomew and the European Conflict, 1559–1572* (London, 1973). This is a work of far greater importance than the modest title suggests, as it brings to focus the internationalization of the Protestant challenge to Catholic Europe. Older but also of considerable assistance are: Anquez, Léonce, *Histoire des assemblées politiques des reformés de France, 1573–1622* (Paris, 1859); Pannier, Jacques, *L'Eglise reformée de Paris sous Henri IV* (Paris, 1911), and *L'Eglise reformée de Paris sous Louis XIII, 1621–1629,* 2 vols. (Paris, 1931–1932); Mervault, Pierre, *Le Journal des choses les plus memorables qui se sont passées au dernier Siège de La Rochelle* (Rouen, 1671); and Villemain, Pierre, *Journal des assiègés de la Rochelle* (Paris,

1958). For the end of the period of toleration, see: Orcibal, Jean, *Louis XIV et les protestants* (Paris, 1951), a study by a scholar noted in the religious history of this reign; and Depping, Guillaume, *Un Banquier protestant en France au XVII<sup>e</sup> siècle* (Paris, 1879). Michel, Adolphe F., *Louvois et les protestants* (Paris, 1870) is a hostile account nonetheless useful for the government's repressive measures in the last years before the revocation.

Finally, some note should be taken of studies relevant to the Huguenots after the debacle of 1685. Bosc, Henri, *La Guerre des Cévennes, 1705–1710* (Lille, 1974); Dodge, Guy H., *The Political Theory of the Huguenots of the Dispersion* (New York, 1947); Israels Perry, Elizabeth, *From Theology to History: French Religious Controversy and the Revocation of the Edict of Nantes* (The Hague, 1973); Janzé, Charles A., baron de, *Les Huguenots: cent ans de persécution, 1685–1789* (Paris, 1886); O'Brien, Louis, *Innocent XI and the Revocation of the Edict of Nantes* (Berkeley, 1930); Scoville, Warren C., *The Persecution of the Huguenots and French Economic Development, 1680–1720* (Berkeley, 1960); Smiles, Samuel, *The Huguenots in France After the Revocation of the Edict of Nantes* (London, 1875); and Weiss, Charles, *The History of the Protestant Refugees of France,* 2 vols. (London, 1854; French original, 1853). In addition, there are numerous publications sponsored by the Huguenot Society of America, the English Huguenot Society and the many regional societies, as well as the *Société de l'histoire du protestantisme français.*

## Other Sources

In addition to the works listed above, there are literally hundreds of books contributory to a further understanding of the Huguenots—family biographies, military histories, administrative studies, analyses of emergent absolutism, etc. One also should consult the lists of unpublished doctoral dissertations available through University Microfilms, Ann Arbor, Michigan, a source of much careful research that has not yet found its way into print. Finally, there are the journals, several in both French and English. In the first category, by far the most massive collection of material is to be found in the *Bulletin de la société de l'histoire du protestantisme français,* which began in 1852 and is still publishing, though many interesting articles also appear in the historical reviews. In English, the most useful journals are *The Journal of Modern History, The Canadian Journal of History, Past and Present, Church History, History,* and—above all—*French Historical Studies.*

# Index

197

## About the author

George A. Rothrock is professor of history at the University of Alberta in Edmonton. He was educated at the Universities of Delaware and Grenoble, France, and received his Ph.D. from the University of Minnesota in 1958. He has taught at the Universities of Omaha, Michigan, and Saskatchewan. His other books include *Europe, A Brief History, (1971),* Second edition with T. B. Jones *(1975),* and a translation of Sebastien Le Prestre de Vauban's *A Manual of Siege-craft and Fortification (1968).* He has been widely published in various scholarly journals, among them *The Historian, Church History, French Historical Studies, History Today,* and *The Canadian Journal of History.* He is a member of the Society for Studies in French History.